S0-BOD-770

NEW ORLEANS

...LIKE A LOCAL

Horse and a carriage in the French Quarter. © Jean-Pierre De Mann/age fotostock

NEW ORLEANS...LIKE A LOCAL

Chief Contributing Editor	Peter Greenberg
Editorial Director	Cynthia Clayton Ochterbeck
Editorial Manager	Jonathan P. Gilbert
Editor	Rachel Mills
Principal Writer	Anne-Marie Scott
Production Manager	Natasha G. George
Cartography	John Dear
Photo Editor	Yoshimi Kanazawa
Photo Researcher	Chris Bell
Proofreader	Liz Jones
Interior Design	Chris Bell
Layout	Michelin Travel and Lifestyle North America, Rachel Mills, Natasha G. George
Cover Design	Chris Bell
Cover Layout	Michelin Travel and Lifestyle North America
Peter Greenberg Editorial Team	Sarika Chawla, Lily J. Kosner, Alyssa Caverley, Adriana Padilla
Contact Us	Michelin Travel and Lifestyle North America One Parkway South Greenville, SC 29615 USA travel.lifestyle@us.michelin.com www.michelintravel.com
	Michelin Travel Partner Hannay House 39 Clarendon Road Watford, Herts WD17 1JA, UK ✆ 01923 205240 travelpubsales@uk.michelin.com www.ViaMichelin.com
Special Sales	For information regarding bulk sales, customized editions and premium sales, please contact us at: Travel.Lifestyle@us.michelin.com www.michelintravel.com

Note to the reader Addresses, phone numbers, opening hours and prices published in this guide are accurate at the time of press. We welcome corrections and suggestions that may assist us in preparing the next edition. While every effort is made to ensure that all information printed in this guide is correct and up-to-date, Michelin North America, Inc. accepts no liability for any direct, indirect or consequential losses howsoever caused so far as such can be excluded by law.

HOW TO USE THIS GUIDE

INTRODUCTION
The Introduction section at the front of the guide explores the city today, architecture, art and culture, and nature. It includes a section of full-color photographs representative of the city's neighborhoods, architecture, culture, festivals, nightlife, cuisine and excursions.

PLANNING YOUR TRIP
The Planning Your Trip section gives you ideas for your trip and practical information to help you organize it. You'll find tours, practical information, a host of outdoor activities, a calendar of events, information on shopping, sightseeing, kids' activities and more.

DISCOVERING
The Discovering section presents Principal Sights by neighborhood, featuring the most interesting local Sights, Walking Tours, and nearby Excursions. Admission prices shown are normally for a single adult.

ADDRESSES
We've selected the best hotels, restaurants, cafes, shops, nightlife and entertainment to fit all budgets. See the Legend on the cover flap for an explanation of the price categories.

STAR RATINGS★★★
Michelin has given star ratings for more than 100 years. If you're pressed for time, we recommend you visit the ★★★, or ★★ sights first:
★★★ Highly recommended
★★ Recommended
★ Interesting

MAPS
All maps in this guide are oriented north, unless otherwise indicated by a directional arrow. A complete list of the maps found in the guide appears at the back of this book.

LIKE A LOCAL... FEATURES
Full page features give you the low-down on the best little things that make each neighborhood of New Orleans special.

ASK PETER...
One-on-one Q&A sessions with Peter answer your worries so that you can enjoy your visit.

Travel Tips:
Peter's Travel Tips give you the inside track on local deals, tricks and techniques that you might otherwise miss.

SIDEBARS
Throughout this guide you will find short sidebars with lively anecdotes, detailed history and background information.

CONTENTS

YOUR STAY IN NEW ORLEANS

Background: Map of North and South America (1746) by Unknown Artist © The British Library / age fotostock

NEIGHBORHOODS

Like New Orleans' population and culture, the city's neighborhoods cultivate differences and distinctions, celebrate uniqueness and avoid homogeneity at all costs. The French, Creoles, Italians, Irish, Anglo-Americans and African-Americans who created communities in various sectors of the city all left their distinctive stamp, making for endlessly interesting variations in scenery and atmosphere from neighborhood to neighborhood.

Explore any or all: the mansions on the leafy streets of the Garden District, the slightly-seedy-and-proud-of-it Lower Garden District, the bohemian Marigny and Bywater, the residential Mid-City and its City Park, the artsy Warehouse District or the festive lanes of the French Quarter.

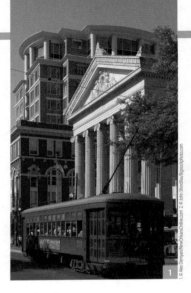

1 The St. Charles Avenue streetcar trundling past Gallier Hall. A rolling slice of history, the streetcars shuttle delighted riders on a slow, scenic trek past neighborhoods from the French Quarter to Uptown. *See Garden District p124.*

2 Tombs in Lafayette Cemetery. Intriguing and beautiful above-ground tombs with dates reaching back to the early 18C grace a New Orleans historic "City of the Dead." *See Garden District p126.*

3 Decorative corbels and windows of a French Quarter Creole townhouse. Festooned with Mardi Gras garlands and decorations. *See French Quarter p80.*

4 Palms, Spanish moss and oak trees. Reflected in the waters of a City Park lagoon as a yellow-crowned night heron feeds (lower right). The park is a haven of nature in the city. *See Mid-City p147.*

5 Colorful façades are a hallmark of homes in the bohemian Faubourg Marigny. Coffeeshops, nightspots and art galleries dot the residential streets of the funky, gentrified neighborhood. *See Faubourg Marigny p141.*

1 St. Louis Cathedral and Jackson Square. A symbol of New Orleans, the beautiful cathedral occupies the same spot as the first church built when New Orleans was just a Colonial outpost. *See p82.*

2 Cornstalk fence detail at Colonel Robert Short's house, Garden District. Cast-iron detailing such as this, ornament fences and balconies throughout the city. *See p126.*

3 Lafitte's Blacksmith Shop. Legend surrounds this historic structure, one of the oldest in New Orleans. Now a popular watering hole, it's a good example of the way Creole cottages were built in the late 18C. *See p103.*

1. © Cosmo Condina/age fotostock 2 & 3 © Pat Garin/New Orleans Convention and Tourist Bureau

ARCHITECTURAL GEMS

4 Longue Vue House and Gardens. The elegant Metairie home of wealthy businessman and philanthropist Edgar Bloom Stern typifies the Greek Revival style. *See p151.*

New Orleans' buildings come in a wonderful variety of styles. Some structural types were developed specifically for the city's singular environment and climate, and are rarely found anywhere else but here, giving New Orleans a look all its own. Modest Creole cottages and shotgun houses can be found in almost every neighborhood, while Mid-City, Esplanade Ridge and the French Quarter boast much more elaborate Creole townhouses. The renowned Garden District, neighborhood of choice for wealthy Anglo-American settlers in the 19C, features beautiful and elaborate mansions in the Greek Revival, Italianate and other styles.

5 Cast-iron balconies of the LaBranche Buildings, French Quarter. Intricately whorled designs in ornamental cast iron are a hallmark of New Orleans architecture, gracing many Creole and Italianate town-houses in the French Quarter. *See p100.*

CRESCENT CITY CULTURE

New Orleans' vibrant cultural life encompasses everything from the classical traditions in the visual and performing arts to street-corner bands, jazz funerals, sidewalk performers and a cutting-edge contemporary arts scene. Diverse population streams during the city's early days infused New Orleans culture with influences from around the globe and created unique traditions like second-line parades, jazz brunches and Mardi Gras Indian tribes, to name a few. It's possible to browse a Fine Art gallery, get caught up in a parade, take in a classical ballet performance and end the night in a cozy jazz bar, all in a single day in the Big Easy.

1 **New Orleans Museum of Art, City Park.** The handsome Greek-Revival museum houses a trove of outstanding works of fine art, and an excellent sculpture garden. *See p148.*

1. © Andre Jenny/Alamy 2. Courtesy of The National World War II Museum

2 **The Stage Door Canteen at The National World War II Museum.** The concert hall and its tribute performing groups replicate the historic New York venue where A-list celebrities entertained servicemen about to ship out to the front. *See p184.*

3 Maple Street Bookshop.
The charming independent bookshop and the adjacent children's bookstore stock a wealth of works by local authors and leading lights of New Orleans' literary scene. *See p132.*

4 Royal Street Art Gallery.
High-end art and antiques galleries line the blocks of Royal Street, rubbing shoulders with funky folk-art shops and galleries for contemporary photography and design. *See p192.*

5 Second-line Parade.
Held in neighborhoods throughout New Orleans, sometimes for no particular reason, second-line jazz parades are a quintessential way to celebrate life in the Big Easy. *See p60.*

3 ©Veronica Brooks-Sigler/Maple St Books

4 © Jean-Paul Guilloteau/NewOrleansOnline.com; 5 © NewOrleansOnline.com

MARDI GRAS AND OTHER FESTIVALS

New Orleans' mild climate, thriving cultural scene and local penchant for parading and partying at every opportunity make for a full calendar of festivals and events, many of them world-renowned. During the Carnival season, which culminates on Mardi Gras day, visitors from all over flock here to eat, drink, take in parades and celebrate New Orleans-style. The New Orleans Jazz & Heritage Festival, the French Quarter Festival, the Tennessee Williams Literary Festival and a host of other celebrations speak to New Orleanans' delight in throwing a party and letting the good times roll.

1 The Leviathan Float, Orpheus parade. Super-floats like the Leviathan hold hundreds of bead-throwing riders and brighten Mardi Gras parades with fiber-optic light effects to the delight of cheering throngs. *See p22, 64 & 76.*

2 Krewe of Rex. The King of Mardi Gras is drawn each year from the ranks of the Krewe of Rex, one of the most venerable parading organizations in the city. Most float riders wear elaborate costumes with masks. *See p22, 64 & 76.*

3 French Market collage of masks.
Masking is a Carnival tradition, both for masquerade balls and for Mardi Gras day, when elaborately costumed partiers take to the streets. *See p92 & 193.*

4 French Quarter Festival. Live music, delicious food, and fine spring weather combine to make the free, outdoor French Quarter Festival one of New Orleans' most popular annual events. *See p64.*

5 New Orleans Jazz & Heritage Festival. The ten-day cultural and music festival welcomes thousands to multiple stages, craft booths and food stands spread throughout the New Orleans Fairgrounds. *See p64 & 65.*

3. © Michael Marry/iStockphoto.com 4 & 5 © Alex Demyan/NewOrleansOnline.com

1 Bourbon Street at dusk. Visitors well know that Bourbon Street is a nonstop party, but the energy and the crowds increase as the evening rolls along. *See p101.*

2 Interior of Napoleon House Bar and Cafe. Storied as a prospective haven for the deposed French emperor, Napoleon House is a charming, historic and popular spot for dinner or cocktails. *See p96.*

3 Preservation Hall. Bare-bones and time-burnished, Preservation Hall mounts nightly sets of the finest traditional New Orleans jazz performed by experienced artists. *See p102 & 185.*

New Orleans really wakes up when the sun goes down. The Big Easy's endless and varied nightlife offerings are a huge draw for visitors in search of great music, excellent food, and a bit of bawdiness. Live bands, many of them home-grown, take to the stages of nightclubs, particularly in the French Quarter and the Marigny, to perform rock, folk, blues and especially jazz. Bars, drinks-to-go stands and strip joints flash their endless neon invitations up and down Bourbon Street, where indulgence in all forms is tolerated and even encouraged.

4 Jackson Square by night. Backdropped by St. Louis cathedral, a mule-drawn carriage awaits passengers for a romantic tour of the French Quarter by night. *See p58 & 82.*

5 The stage at Tipitina's. The stage at this perennially popular uptown music venue welcomes both well-known and up-and-coming music talent. It's one of New Orleans' best-known spots for live music. *See p187.*

A TASTE OF NEW ORLEANS

With a seemingly endless number of fine restaurants and a long repertoire of dishes that just don't taste the same anywhere else, New Orleans is a foodie's dream come true. The list of iconic specialties is long and mouthwatering, leading many visitors to plan entire vacations around mealtimes. Guided culinary tours (by bike or on foot), food shopping, and the excellent Southern Food and Beverage Museum enhance the foodie experience.

1 Arnaud's, Bienville Street, French Quarter. Fine Creole cuisine headlines the menu at this historic restaurant, along with live jazz music and broad windows overlooking Bourbon street. *See p105 & 176.*

2 Galatoire's, Bourbon Street, French Quarter. Lunch spot of choice for New Orleans high society, Galatoire's serves up longstanding New Orleans traditions along with excellent Creole specialties. *See p176.*

1. © Jeff Greenberg/Alamy 2. © Gala Images/Alamy

3 Antoine's, St. Louis Street, French Quarter. Antoine's has been delighting diners since 1840 with original Creole cuisine, elegantly served in its historic dining rooms. *See p99 & 177.*

4 Crawfish étouffée. One of the signature dishes of Creole cuisine, étouffée is a delectable stew of seafood and vegetables smothered in sauce and served over rice. *See p26.*

5 Absinthe Gallery, Southern Food and Beverage Museum. Celebrating the food and drink of the South with permanent and changing exhibitions. *La Galerie d'Absinthe* showcases an extensive absinthe-related collection. *See p118.*

6 Beignets and coffee. The hot, square doughnuts known as beignets, showered with powdered sugar and served with aromatic chicory coffee, sweeten countless coffee breaks in New Orleans. *See p26.*

1 Men's Parlor, Houmas House, Darrow. Exceptionally beautiful Houmas House lies at the heart of lovingly restored grounds and gardens that were part of a 19C plantation. The elegant Greek Revival house dates from the early 19C. See p158.

2 Chalmette Battlefield, Chalmette. Just a few miles east of New Orleans, the area was the site of the 1915 Battle of New Orleans, in which troops led by Gen. Andrew Jackson prevailed over attacking British troops. See p156.

3 Cajun culture, Lafayette. Locals and regulars swirl and stomp nightly at Randol's Restaurant and Dance Hall in Lafayette, a famed outpost for traditional Cajun music and dancing. See p165.

EXCURSIONS

Within an easy day's drive of New Orleans lie numerous stately plantation homes, the Louisiana capital city of Baton Rouge, and the Cajun Country, home to descendants of Louisiana's original Acadian settlers. For an adventure that feels far removed from New Orleans take the short trip to Lafayette, in the heart of the Cajun Country, with numerous sights related to Acadian history. Small towns in the vicinity are well worth exploring for their homey restaurants, dance halls and other hallmarks of the vibrant and distinctive Cajun culture.

4 Louisiana State Capitol Building, Baton Rouge. Commissioned by controversial governor Huey P. Long in 1930, the 34-story spire is the tallest state capitol building in the US. *See p161.*

5 Laura Plantation, Vacherie. The carefully restored plantation house was home to a modestly wealthy family of Creole sugarcane planters in the mid-19C. *See p159.*

6 Acadian Village, Lafayette. A charming collection of residential and village structures, all original and moved to this spot, show the gentler side of life in late 19C and early 20C Acadiana. *See p164.*

WELCOME TO
NEW ORLEANS

Mardi Gras float
Photo: © Mitchel Osborne/NewOrleansOnline.com

New Orleans Today

In its topography, architecture, people and culture, New Orleans resembles no other American city. Lying an average of 5ft below sea level, its lands are naturally swampy, made livable by an extensive system of levees, pumping stations and drainage canals.

The city's long succession of inhabitants—encompassing the Native American indigenous population, French and Spanish colonists, West Indian and African slaves, and settlers from Europe and the eastern US—has created a rich mix of peoples and cultures. Creativity, romance, drama and fun are always encouraged here, enticing residents and visitors alike to drop their cares by the wayside, relax, raise a glass and *"Laissez les bons temps rouler!"* (**"Let the good times roll!"**). Its colorful cultural ambience, excellent restaurants and nowhere-else-but-here traditions make New Orleans one of the most popular tourist destinations in the US.

People and Society

There is no better example of the American "melting pot" metaphor than New Orleans. The city's early French and Spanish colonists were joined by immigrants from all over the world be-

SOUTHERN BELLES AND BEAUS

Mardi Gras is generally known to visitors of New Orleans as parades, parties and drinking, but the celebration actually has a very long tradition and association with the debutant season. January 6 is Epiphany or Twelfth Night in religious terms, but it's also the kick off for Mardi Gras season in the society world. Parading organizations or *krewes* are historical societies that in the mid-19C were formed by groups of high society men who, after taking part in Mardi Gras parades, would attend a formal ball in order to meet eligible debutantes. Traditional and lavish balls were exclusive invitation-only events for the great and good of New Orleans society (as some are still today). After the opening tableaus of the ball (a depiction of the ball's theme presented by silent and motionless costumed participants), young society ladies would be "called out" for dances with krewe members. Not all parading krewes host a ball, but invitations to those that do can be wonderful and elaborate works of art considered by many as collector's items.

CREOLE IDENTITY

The term **Creole** is often used to describe the people and culture of New Orleans, but its exact definition and meaning are complex and sometimes controversial. In its broadest sense the term refers to anyone born in Louisiana of non-indigenous ancestry, but in the late 18C Creole described white people of French or Spanish ancestry who were born in New Orleans (as opposed to having arrived from elsewhere). In the 19C the term also applied to light-skinned black people who spoke French, many of them descendants of mixed-race marriages and who regarded themselves as quite distinct from both whites and darker-skinned blacks. Today those who consider themselves Creole, by whatever definition, may bristle when the term is claimed by others. To further complicate matters, Creole also denotes the French-speaking black people of rural southwestern Louisiana, distinguishing them from their white neighbors, the Cajuns.

ginning in the late 1700s. Some were brought here unwillingly; others were fleeing strife in their homelands. All have left their mark on the city's present racial and ethnic makeup.

Since the 18C when huge numbers of slaves were brought here from West Africa and the city supported a large community of free people of color, African-Americans have formed a significant slice of New Orleans' total population, occupying every class and social stratum and leaving an indelible stamp on the city's culture. Recent census figures put the number of African-Americans living here at less than 60 percent, down from almost 67 percent prior to Hurricane Katrina; the storm decimated underprivileged black neighborhoods whose residents lacked the means to quickly return and rebuild.

Many families of New Orleans' wealthy white upper classes have resided here for generations, descended from settlers who took advantage of business opportunities in shipping, banking, warehousing, and brokering after the Louisiana Purchase in 1803. German farmers arrived soon after the first European settlers, producing food for the new settlement. The city's Irish population originated largely with immigrants who came in the first half of the 19C, establishing traditions that thrive today like the annual St. Patrick's Day celebration. New Orleans' vibrant Italian community is descended from a late-19C wave of immigrants from Sicily who brought culinary and cultural influences that are inextricably linked to New Orleans. A large number of Vietnamese immigrants in the mid-1970s established a sizeable enclave in eastern New Orleans, creating a market-garden landscape that reflected their agrarian heritage, and large numbers of immigrants from Latin America today live in communities on the West Bank and in the western suburbs.

Against the rich backdrop of New Orleans' turbulent history, the city's diverse and passionate people are its greatest asset. Thrown together in this isolated corner of the New World, newcomers absorbed each others' languages, customs and culinary and musical traditions. Melded from these abundant and extremely varied origins, New Orleans culture—eccentric, iconoclastic, and proud of it—thrives today and resists homogenization like no other American city. Though it suffers from its share of prejudice and racial and ethnic conflict, New Orleans is equally noteworthy for its tolerance and the ease and frequency of contact between people of differing backgrounds. Far less rigidly segregated than other cities, New Orleans' various racial groups often live close together, sharing many customs, speech patterns, music, and food preferences.

Government and Economy

New Orleans' economy has always been closely tied to the Mississippi River. Shipping, trade, and transportation were all early economic underpinnings as agricultural and later, manufactured goods from the heart of the US found their way to buyers at home and abroad by way of New Orleans. Oceangoing vessels continually ply the river in both directions, and the Port of New Orleans together with other port facilities in south Louisiana today handles more cargo traffic by volume than any

CITY/PARISH GOVERNMENT

The city of New Orleans and some of its suburbs occupy Orleans Parish, the smallest of Louisiana's 64 parishes (as counties are called here). The city's mayor looms large in the city's political life, although the mayoral administration's powers are limited by the seven-member city council elected to represent five districts (plus two at-large members). New Orleans' large and powerful black community elected the city's first mayor of African-American descent, Ernest "Dutch" Morial in 1977. The current mayor, Mitch Landrieu, is a member of a Louisiana family with strong political ties: Landrieu's father Maurice "Moon" Landrieu, an ardent advocate of civil rights, served as mayor prior to Morial, and oversaw the desegregation of city government and public facilities during his term from 1970-78.

other US port. The early-20C discovery of oil and natural gas in Louisiana and in the Gulf of Mexico spawned a huge industry related to petroleum exploration and drilling, along with a host of related service and manufacturing industries such as petrochemical production, engineering, shipbuilding and marine construction. Drilling platforms took root in the gulf and refineries and chemical plants rose on both banks of the river. Numerous domestic and international petroleum firms made their headquarters here in the 20C; a still-significant number remain today although several have decamped for Houston in recent years.

The city is a preeminent US rail hub, with lines bringing all kinds of freight from the north, east and west. A long-established food processing industry handles Louisiana's agricultural bounty including sugar, sweet potatoes, rice and especially seafood. And the city has benefited enormously from federal government offices, installations and contracts ranging from shipbuilding facilities to naval and coast guard stations.

The Mercedes-Benz Superdome and the enormous, kilometer-long Ernest N. Morial Convention Center, along with a proliferation of hotels, have brought New Orleans to the forefront of the US convention and tourism industry. Convention attendees and their dollars fuel dozens of service industries and boost the quality and quantity of restaurants, which in turn attracts more visitors and supports nationally renowned events such as the Tennessee Williams Literary Festival and Jazz Fest. And Mardi Gras is an industry unto itself, financed almost entirely by local dollars but serving as another engine of tourism.

In recent years state initiatives have attracted a growing number of film shoots to New Orleans, and efforts are ongoing to develop infrastructure and a labor force that would make the state a destination for all phases of film production and digital media development. There have been efforts to build on New Orleans' renowned music performance scene by establishing a music business industry here similar to that of Nashville and Los Angeles. And the recent groundbreaking inception of the Nucor steel plant in neighboring St. James Parish brings the possibility of a new industry sector in steel production.

Media

New Orleans' main daily print **newspaper** is the *Times-Picayune*. Established in 1837 as *The Picayune* (available at a price of a Spanish picayune coin worth one-sixteenth of a US dollar), the newspaper in 1914 merged with its rival, the *Times-Democrat*. The *Times-Picayune* has won several Pulitzer prizes in past years, most recently for its coverage of Hurricane Katrina and its aftermath. *Gambit*, a free alternative weekly paper, began publication in 1981 and has attracted the talents of numerous local authors and activists to its reporting ranks. *The Lens*, a nonprofit journalism organization founded in 2009, concentrates on investigative reporting about New Orleans and Gulf Coast issues, publishing its work electronically. Local business news and the economy are the focus of *New Orleans CityBusiness*, published weekly. The monthly publication *The New Orleans Levee* produces critical, largely irreverent writing about New Orleans issues, government and hurricane recovery. All major US **television** broadcast networks maintain New Orleans affiliates providing local news, commentary, community information and educational programming, including ABC (WGNO, channel 26), CBS (WWL, channel 4), FOX (WVUE, channel 8), NBC (WDSU, channel 6), and PBS (WYES, channel 12 and WLAE, channel 32).

The **radio** airwaves teem with dozens of local news, music and talk radio stations, some of which stream programming to the Internet. WWOZ (90.7FM) is known as the jazz and heritage station for its quality programming of local music and live Jazz Fest broadcasts. WWL (870AM and 105.3FM) features New Orleans Saints coverage, and KBON (101.1FM) broadcasts Cajun, swamp pop, zydeco and other local music.

Food and Drink

New Orleans is one of the world's great food destinations. Rooted in traditions more than two centuries old, New Orleans cuisine reveals the divergent influences of the varied cultures that populated the city. The French, the Spanish, the Italians, slaves from Africa and the West Indies, even the native Americans who preceded everyone here all left their mark on the dishes cooked and served today in home kitchens and restaurants throughout the city. Dependent as they are on the use of fresh local ingredients, many specialties are difficult to duplicate outside the region, making eating out, for some visitors, the *raison d'être* of a visit to the Big Easy.

EAT ON THE STREET

Not all New Orleans' specialties can be found on restaurant menus. Stands, takout counters, and even a mule-drawn cart are the only places you'll find these typical treats. Don't pass by without picking up a taste.

Snowballs are a cooling summertime treat made of finely shaved ice topped with sweet flavored syrup; try your hand (and your tastebuds) at combining flavors. The red and white **Roman Candy** wagon plies streets all over New Orleans, selling gourmet taffy in three flavors. Corner stores often sell **pralines** handmade by the owners; the sweet round disks are made of brown sugar, cream, and pecans, cooked and cooled to an almost fudgelike consistency. And **daiquiri** stands appear all over the city, purveying tall, icy rum drinks in various flavors, like snowballs for grownups.

The origins of **Cajun** cooking lie in the simple foodways of agrarian France, adapted in Canada by Acadian settlers, transferred to Louisiana when those settlers were exiled here, and further adapted with local ingredients. Dishes were prepared simply with whatever ingredients were readily available—corn, garden vegetables, potatoes, orchard fruits, wild fruits, and game. Simple Cajun-style dishes like *gâteau sirop*, (syrup cake), round steak with rice and gravy, *tarte à la Bouillie* (sweet-dough pies) and glazed sweet potatoes are still cooked and enjoyed with relish in homes around New Orleans and Acadiana, but seldom appear on restaurant menus.

The Cajun style of cooking was widely commercialized around the 1980s after Paul Prudhomme, a native of Opelousas who trained in the kitchen at Commander's Palace, opened K-Paul's Louisiana Kitchen in the French Quarter. Prudhomme's technique of flash-frying or "blackening" highly spiced fish and meat over extremely high heat caught the public's attention and the restaurant's popularity spread Cajun cooking (and many less-than-authentic varieties of it) around the US and even abroad.

Considered more complex, **Creole** cuisine began in New Orleans and was influenced by the culinary traditions of the city's French, Spanish, African, West Indian, German and Native American populations. The cuisine incorporated chili peppers and spices from Spain and Haiti; bay laurel, corn and sassafras from Native Americans; elegant soup and sauce techniques from France; sausages and charcuterie from Germany; okra, kidney beans and the practice of slow-cooking from Africa; and the tradition of multiple courses from the European aristocracy. Complex combinations of herbs and spices spike many Creole dishes, creating a succession of flavors that builds slowly in the mouth, heady but not overpowering.

Today you'll find many of the same dishes on both Cajun and Creole menus, reflecting the culinary cross-pollination that has always been a hallmark of New Orleans cuisine. In both types of cooking you'll find many dishes based on roux, a mixture of flour and fat cooked until dark brown and often seasoned with New Orleans' "holy trinity" of onions, celery and bell peppers chopped fine. Gumbo, a rich stew, starts with a roux, then incorporates stock and some combination of *andouille* (a spicy smoked sausage), chicken and seafood; the mix is then typically thickened with okra or *filé* (powdered sassafras leaves) and served over rice, with a side of potato salad (Cajun style).

ASK PETER...

Q: Are cabs safe to take in New Orleans?
A: Yes, and as a bonus, just about every taxi driver is a pretty good storyteller, and the ride is always entertaining. Your best bet is to hire United Cabs Inc., (*℡ 504-522-9771, www.unitedcabs.com*) which in my experience is quite reliable. The drivers know a lot of the alternate routes and back alleys, which is always helpful when the city is crowded.

Jambalaya is another dish now common to both styles in which vegetables, meats or seafood, spices and sometimes tomato (Creole style) are simmered together with rice. *Étouffée* is another roux-based dish in which meat or seafood is "smothered" in a rich, spicy, vegetable-laden sauce, also often served with rice. Turtle soup, made with beef or seafood stock and turtle meat enlivened with sherry, is a local treat found on menus in New Orleans fine-dining restaurants.

Fish and seafood drawn from Louisiana rivers, lakes, brackish coastal wetlands, and the Gulf of Mexico headline many a menu. Shrimp, oysters, and crawfish (a freshwater shellfish resembling a miniature lobster) appear in countless forms: *étoufée*, chilled and dressed with piquant *rémoulade* sauce; or dusted with cornmeal then fried and heaped on French bread in a po-boy sandwich. Amberjack, redfish, pompano and speckled trout are all fished locally and served up fried or sautéed with almonds and napped with *meunière* sauce or broiled and topped with sweet lump crabmeat.

Airy French bread with a crackly crust accompanies most restaurant meals, and New Orleaneans rarely finish a meal without coffee and a sweet. Bananas Foster originated at Brennan's restaurant in the French Quarter and is popular on menus throughout the Big Easy; the decadent preparation is a sauté of bananas in butter and brown sugar, flamed with rum and served over ice cream. Bread pudding is another New Orleans favorite, a custardy combination of eggs, milk and bread, flavored with sweet spices or chocolate, then baked and topped with rum or whiskey sauce.

New Orleaneans love to eat, and city residents talk about food and restaurants with seriousness and enthusiasm. Life in the city is marked by food traditions, such as the custom of eating red beans and rice on Mondays, king cakes during the Carnival season and gumbo at the first snap of fall. Spring brings the arrival of the crawfish season, when neighbors and families gather at crawfish boils to feast on pounds of spicy shellfish boiled in seasoned water along with chunks of corn and potatoes.

TRAVEL ...LIKE A LOCAL

What's the definition of a tourist? Someone who only eats at the hotel, takes the tour bus, and shops for souvenirs at the airport. Why would you do that when you can travel like a local? That means getting a real feel for a destination and not looking for the same cookie-cutter experience you would find in any brochure. Believe me, when you travel like a local, you're truly traveling. **Here are my top five tips on how to really immerse yourself in the experience:**

Tip One: Get off the computer

I've said it before and it's worth repeating. Don't do all your research online. You learn so much more by talking to a human being. In New Orleans you can find some of the best Cajun and Creole foods by just walking the streets. Want to know who's playing that night? Don't look in the newspaper. Just ask in the music stores.

Tip Two: Eat like a local

Most hotels have their own restaurant, but you won't find many locals there. Whether it's street food or fine dining, eat somewhere different every day. Check out Palm Court Jazz Café (1204 Decatur Street) where you can experience traditional New Orleans food and great jazz music.

Tip Three: Visit residential neighborhoods

The Garden District in New Orleans is one of the more upscale neighborhoods in the city. Here, you will find a collection of beautiful antebellum-era mansions and gardens. Although you can wander on your own, ask about an finding expert guide who can explain the history and architecture of these homes.

Tip Four: Make your own excursions

You'll find tour operators waiting to put you on a bus or boat to Cajun Country. If it's the weekend, please don't go. It will be crowded with tourists. Mid-week is your answer to mingle with the locals.

Tip Five: Visit local hot spots

Many concierges will recommend the House of Blues in the French Quarter, but that won't be the local experience. Check out **The Bombay Club** *(830 Conti Street)* for authentic jazz music in an elegant spot. A jazz quartet plays on weekends and a pianist fills the place with music every night of the week. The restaurant bar boasts a menu with 110 different martinis.

History

Native American tribes, among them the Tangipahoa, Chitimacha, Houma and Choctaw, lived in present-day Louisiana for thousands of years before European explorers set their sights on the New World. Explorers from Hernando de Soto's Spanish expedition floated past the future site of New Orleans in 1543, but didn't attempt to establish a settlement. In 1682 the French explorer Robert de La Salle, on a canoe expedition of the Mississippi River, claimed all the lands drained by the river in the name of French king Louis XIV, calling it "Louisiane." The French established a few settlements in the territory, most notably at Ocean Springs, Natchez and Mobile. But it wasn't until about 1716, under the administration of Scotsman John Law, France's finance minister, that the French government began to invest in developing Louisiana.

A French and Spanish Colony

Law knew that France needed to solidify its claims in the New World. He also grasped the economic importance of the Mississippi River as a gateway to the rich resources of the Louisiana Territory, and saw colonization there as a way to fill the coffers of the French Crown. When the territory's governor Jean-Baptiste Le Moyne, sieur de Bienville, requested permission to build Louisiana's capital near the mouth of the Mississippi, Law and his administration approved. The site Bienville selected sat atop a naturally raised embankment with access to both the river and to Lake Pontchartrain, which offered a safer, more direct water route to the Gulf of Mexico. In 1718 Bienville arrived there with a flotilla of ships carrying craftsmen and convict laborers, and officially founded **La Nouvelle Orléans**, naming it for the Duke of Orléans.

By 1721 French engineer Adrien de Pauger had laid out a town grid with streets radiating out from a central plaza (today's Jackson Square). But the location presented challenges. Tropical storm winds blew down the first structures, and early colonists battled floods, alligators and diseases as they struggled to maintain the trappings of French society in the muddy outpost. The French Colonial government developed a reputation for corruption and graft but still, the settlement grew as a center for trade between Europe, the Caribbean and mainland settlements in the New World. The population swelled steadily, bolstered by more settlers and also slaves brought in bondage from West Africa to work on cotton and sugarcane plantations.

In 1762, in a secret agreement, France ceded New Orleans and the Louisiana Territory lands west of the Mississippi to Spain, its ally in the Seven Years War with England. Although the French community in New Orleans rebelled, Spanish sovereignty was eventually established, and lasted more than three decades. Throughout, the resident French Creole population refused to assimilate Spanish culture; French language, customs and culture persisted. In terms of growth and prosperity, the Spanish government was a great success: burgeoning agriculture boosted the region's economy and the port of New Orleans thrived. In 1788 and 1794 devastating fires swept the town, but the Spanish government and private investors quickly rebuilt.

The Louisiana Purchase

In 1800, another secret agreement returned the Louisiana Territory to French rule. Measuring 828,000sq mi, the territory encompassed New Orleans plus lands west of the Mississippi River to the Rocky Mountains and as far north as the Canadian Border. US president Thomas Jefferson, aware of the territory's strategic and economic value and concerned about the colonial government's ability to block and impose duties on trade along the Mississippi River, approached French Emperor Napoleon Bonaparte with an offer to buy New Orleans for $2 million.Napoleon, short of funds and focused on maintaining his empire in Europe, offered instead to sell the entire the Louisiana Territory for $15 million. The land transfer, known as the **Louisiana Purchase**, was signed at the Cabildo in New Orleans on April 30, 1803.

The US government was forced to defend its new lands against invasion by the British in one of the final battles of the War of 1812. Despite the fact that a peace agreement had ended the conflict in December 1814, word of the treaty did not reach Louisiana, and British troops fired on American boats in Lake Borgne on December 14. American general Andrew Jackson, arriving in the city barely ahead of the British, raised a fighting force of locals to supplement his troops and, though outnumbered, decisively beat the British in the **Battle of New Orleans** on January 8, 1815.

The Louisiana Purchase doubled the size of the United States and settlers flooded west to occupy the new American territory. The stable government, the development of shallow-draft steamboats to ply the inland rivers, and New Orleans' continuing growth as a port brought an influx of profit-minded Anglo-Americans to the city. The newcomers were shunned by the long-established Creole families, but gradually came to dominate New Orleans' business and political life. Americans built

homes and established banks, warehouses and other businesses in newly settled suburbs upriver of Canal Street. But cultural antagonism persisted and for a time New Orleans was divided into three separate municipalities, with Canal Street forming the border, or "neutral ground," between the Creole-dominated Vieux Carré and the American Faubourg St. Mary upriver (the Faubourg Marigny was the third).

The early 1800s also brought substantial numbers of free blacks to the city, many of them refugees from the Haitian Revolution; these French-speaking free people of color were welcomed by the Creoles as a way of cementing New Orleans' French culture.

Civil War, Reconstruction and the 20C

As a major southern US port, New Orleans was a center for the slave trade, and Louisiana became the sixth state to secede from the United States of America after Abraham Lincoln was elected US President. Louisiana existed as an independent republic for two weeks before joining the Confederate States of America. When the **Civil War** erupted in 1861, Union forces set their sights on capturing New Orleans, and the poorly defended city surrendered to Federal naval forces in May 1862. Military rule was immediately established, and although the war ended in 1865, Federal troops and repressive, corrupt carpetbag regimes governed New Orleans until **Reconstruction** ended in 1877.

Throughout the 19C and even into the 20C the city's humid climate and poor sanitation contributed to terrible epidemics of yellow fever, Asiatic cholera and bubonic plague that killed thousands of New Orleans residents. Not until the early 20C, when measures were implemented to clean up the city and control rats and mosquitoes, did disease outbreaks abate.

Despite New Orleans' long history as home to a sizeable population of free and educated people of color, racial tensions were sharpened during and after Reconstruction. A challenge to racial segregation laws of the day by Tremé resident Homer Plessy went all the way to the United States Supreme Court in 1896; in **Plessy v. Ferguson** the Court ruled in favor of "separate but equal" facilities for whites and blacks, setting a national precedent that prevailed until the Court reversed its decision in 1954. Nor were blacks the only victims of discrimination; resentment toward the city's burgeoning Southern Italian community climaxed in a bloody riot and lynchings in 1891.

The early 20C saw the city taking on its present form. New Orleans had annexed the upriver suburbs of Faubourg St. Mary, Lafayette and Carrollton (now the Central Business District, the Garden District and the Riverbend) in the latter half of the 19C. Tall buildings rose in the Central Business District, and the port of New Orleans was enhanced by the opening of the Industrial Canal connecting Lake Pontchartrain with the Mississippi River. The discovery and exploitation of oil resources beneath the Gulf of Mexico further expanded New Orleans' economy.

Development spread away from the natural high ground near the river and eventually came to occupy all the land between the river and Lake Pontchar-

Medjet keeps me in the game.

Medical emergencies
don't play games.

So whether I am on the Tour or vacationing with my
family I make sure Medjet is there with me. It's priceless
peace of mind.

If you become hospitalized 150 miles or more from home, Medjet will arrange medical
transfer to the hospital of your choice. All you pay is your membership fee.

Best of all, with Medjet memberships starting at $99 you don't have to be a PGA Tour
winner to travel like one.

Jim Furyk: 16-Time PGA Tour Winner & Medjet Member

 MedjetAssist. | Medjet.com | 800.527.7478

Travel, Dine and Explore with Confidence

TRAVEL ADVICE

mustsees MICHELIN
Charleston
Savannah and the
South Carolina Coast

- Must Read Information
- Must See Sites
- Must-Do Activities
- Must-Know Practicalities

mustsees MICHELIN
Cancun & the Yucatan

- Must Read Information
- Must See Sites
- Must-Do Activities
- Must-Know Practicalities

MICHELIN
Road Atlas
USA CANADA MEXICO

NORTH AMERICA

The Michelin Man is a registered trademark of Michelin North America, Inc. Copyright © 2012 Michelin North America, Inc. All rights reserved.

Michelin, experts in travel guides and maps for more than 100 years. Available wherever books are sold.

www.michelintravel.com

MICHELIN
A better way forward

train. Much of this area, which lies in a bowl of land below sea level, was an unlivable cypress swamp at the time New Orleans was founded, but was made habitable when levees were built to hold back water from Lake Pontchartrain to the north and the Gulf of Mexico waterways to the east and south. A network of canals and pumping systems was established to drain water into Lake Pontchartrain, enabling development of present-day Lakeview, Gentilly and east New Orleans.

The years after World War II found New Orleans grappling with the social turmoil of the Civil Rights era, and trying to hold its own as a center of American commerce. Plans to build a highway through the heart of the historic French Quarter were defeated as city leaders began to appreciate the value of New Orleans' unique architectural and historic character as a means of attracting visitors to the city.

The planning and building of the Superdome in the 1970s, the Ernest N. Morial Convention Center in the 1980s and many new hotels bolstered tourism as one of the mainstays of the city's economy by the turn of the 21C.

Hurricane Katrina

In August 2005, Hurricane Katrina formed in the Atlantic Ocean, crossed the tip of Florida and continued toward southeast Louisiana through the Gulf of Mexico. On August 29, the massive storm made landfall at the town of Buras, 60mi southeast of New Orleans, and continued north, passing just east of the city limits before going ashore in Mississippi. A category 5 hurricane while out in the Gulf of Mexico, Katrina had weakened just before it passed New Orleans and the city was spared catastrophic wind damage. But the storm drove a huge surge of water up to hurricane protection levees, into Lake Pontchartrain and backward into the city's drainage canals. Unable to withstand the surge, the levees and canal walls collapsed or were overtopped in more than 50 places, allowing water to enter New Orleans and neighboring St. Bernard Parish. Eighty percent of the city was inundated.

Complying with a mandatory evacuation order, most residents had left New Orleans in the days prior to the storm but many thousands remained. In the areas closest to the levee breaks, people were forced by fast-rising water to scramble to attics and rooftops to await help. Others made their way to the convention center, languishing there without supplies for several days before transportation was organized to evacuate them from

ASK PETER...

Q: Is it safe to travel to the lower Ninth Ward?

A: Post-Katrina, New Orleans' lower Ninth is haunted by the empty, decaying homes still standing. Many buildings are up buildings are marked with "For Sale" signs and local businesses like corner stores continue to suffer. Redevelopment has slowly been improving the neighborhood, but crime rates here are still twice the national average. I've never had any trouble here, but go with a local guide who knows the neighborhood well.

NATIONAL GUARD

FEMA (Federal Emergency Management Agency) responded to Hurricane Katrina by deploying more than three times the number of National Guard troops it ever has for a single national disaster. The National Guard rescued more than 17,000 people and evacuated 70,000.

One visible scar left behind after Katrina were those made by troops during their post-Katrina search. In the days immediately following the hurricane, the National Guard searched every home and building. Each structure was marked with an X. In the left quadrant marked the search team's identity code. On the top quadrant, the date and time the rescue team left the building. In the right quadrant, a notation of any hazardous substance and in the bottom quadrant, markings made for the number of live people and dead bodies found.

the flooded city. The failure of the federal levee system made Katrina the costliest natural and engineering disaster in the history of the US.

More than 1,500 people perished in the flood or because of the evacuation and many thousands were permanently displaced. Recovery efforts began immediately and continue today; though the city bears scars, the levees are now strengthened, neighborhoods are rebuilding and tourism is rebounding *(see p142–143)*.

In April 2010, the Deepwater Horizon oil-drilling platform exploded in the Gulf of Mexico; the resulting oil spill brought new challenges to southeast Louisiana's ecology and economy. But recovery continues on all fronts as both resident and non-resident devotees of New Orleans honor the city's economic and cultural importance and work to preserve it.

Architecture

New Orleans is a city that looks like no other. Like its food and its music, its distinctive architecture results from the diverse influences of other places, carried here and adapted to the swampy terrain and subtropical climate. Colonists from Europe, slaves from Africa and the West Indies, free people of color from Haiti and settlers from the northeastern US all brought their design and engineering tastes, techniques and experience to bear on New Orleans' built environment. And this is a city that treasures its past; a high regard for the value of historic structures has resulted in far-reaching measures designed to preserve New Orleans' unique architectural character, particularly in the French Quarter.

Early French Colonial buildings were designed with climate and terrain in mind, and many of their features and techniques were carried on into later styles. Thanks to New Orleans' low elevation and high water table, below-ground basement foundations were all but impossible. In fact, early settlers quickly learned the necessity of building their homes atop piers to raise them above the muddy ground, keep them safe from floods and enhance ventilation. To further combat the hot, humid Gulf Coast climate, buildings were topped with tall, steeply pitched roofs; dormers drew warm air up and away from the living areas, while opposing doors and windows provided cooling cross-ventilation. Broad galleries and balconies shaded by deep overhanging roofs essentially functioned as outdoor living spaces as well as exterior hallways; later buildings had louvered shutters that could be opened to welcome breezes but closed against sun and rain. Walls were thick, which also helped keep the interior cool, and were framed with cypress posts filled in by a combination of mud, lime and moss *(columbage)* or bricks *(briqueté-entre-poteaux)*, and coated with plaster to shield against rain.

Devastating fires in 1788 and 1794 leveled much of the early French Quarter (the Old Ursulines Convent on Chartres Street is the only surviving French Colonial building), but many early building techniques persisted through the Spanish period and on into the 19C, even as Spanish influences began to predominate. To prevent further conflagrations, Spanish Colonial government instituted building codes mandating tile roofs and brick or adobe walls for all buildings taller than two stories. As the city continued to develop, established Creole families

LOUISIANA'S RIVER ROAD PLANTATIONS

Beginning in the mid-18C, Louisiana's French Colonial government encouraged agricultural development of the area by granting plots of land to individuals who established plantations *(see Excursions p156–159)*. Cotton, indigo, rice and especially sugar-cane all thrived in the rich soil of the Mississippi River floodplain, providing planters with the means to live extravagantly. Large homes built by slave labor formed the heart of most plantations; houses were placed close to the river, with the principal entryway facing river traffic; fields and outbuildings stretched inland along the narrow plots. After 1803, Greek Revival became the popular style, and many Creole-style homes were updated with Classical ornamentation. **Madewood** (1846) in Napoleonville *(see map p159)*, designed by Louisiana architect Henry Howard, is considered among the area's finest examples of Greek Revival architecture.

made wealthy through shipping, brokering and agriculture hired architects to design elaborate multistory townhouses in the French Quarter and Esplanade Ridge, while Anglo-American businessmen brought Victorian-era trends such as the Italianate and Greek-Revival styles to their comfortable homes and ornate mansions in the Garden District and Uptown. More modest homes, including shotgun houses and simpler townhouses designed and decorated as their owners could afford rose in working-class neighborhoods like Tremé, the Marigny, the Lower Garden District and the Irish Channel.

A number of prominent architects were active in New Orleans in the antebellum period, leaving their characteristic stamp on the city's neighborhoods. Responding to their clients' demands for fashionable architectural details, some worked from pattern books to incorporate Greek Revival, Neoclassical and Italianate elements into their designs; these trends were copied throughout the 19C city, resulting in a less indigenous look than that of the French Quarter's older buildings. **James Gallier Sr.**, an Irish immigrant who got his start in England, created distinctive treasures like the Pontalba Buildings in the French Quarter and Gallier Hall, the former city hall on St. Charles Avenue. Gallier's elaborately designed cast-iron railings for the Pontalba Buildings inspired a flourishing of ever more elaborate ironwork festooning buildings in the French Quarter and the Garden District. His son, **James Gallier Jr.** designed several homes in the Garden District as well as Italianate-style Gallier House, his own residence in the French Quarter. **Henry Howard** was one of the

most prolific Garden District architects, creating over two dozen opulent homes for wealthy clients. The following architectural styles all contribute to New Orleans' distinctive appearance.

Creole Cottage

Early Creole cottages were constructed from the late 18C through the mid-19C, and can be seen today mostly in the French Quarter, Tremé and the Marigny. The diminutive, one-story buildings are topped with tall, steeply-pitched roofs that run parallel to the façade and are sometimes pierced with dormers. The stucco or wood façade usually has four openings, some combination of doors and windows, and extends right up to the property line or sidewalk. Creole cottages sit either at ground level or slightly raised on piers.

Creole Townhouse

The hallmark of wealthy Creoles, townhouses were built mainly in the French Quarter, along Esplanade Avenue and in the Marigny during the first half of the 19C. The grand, two- to four-story residences are constructed around a central courtyard, with arched carriageways allowing access to the street. Exterior stairs in the courtyard lead to the upper floors; kitchens and other service areas were located on the lower floor. As with Creole cottages, some townhouses are slightly raised, and façades are flush with the street, which creates a solid front wall all along some blocks in the French Quarter. Elaborately whorled cast-iron balconies or galleries adorn the upper levels; in the French Quarter these are sometimes contiguous from house to house and are separated by a fearsome-looking iron baffle, called a *garde-de-frise*.

Centerhall Cottage

Though the word "cottage" tends to evoke images of a small, cozy dwelling, centerhall cottages in New Orleans are spacious and often grand homes, single-story but raised above ground level and fronted by broad, columned galleries. The front door in the middle of the façade leads to a central hall extending to the back of the house, with rooms opening onto it. Most have wooden exteriors, and feature side-gabled roofs with dormers. Centerhall cottages were built up until the latter part of the 19C in the Garden District, Lower Garden District, Uptown and Esplanade Ridge neighborhoods.

American Townhouse

Tall and relatively narrow with three openings in the façade, sidehall townhouses appeared during the decades before the

Civil War in the areas upriver from Canal Street, today the Ware-house District and the Lower Garden District. Most were faced in brick, and sported an upper level gallery.

Shotgun House
Affordable one-story shotgun houses proliferated in working-class neighborhoods such as the Irish Channel, the Marigny and Uptown. Long and relatively narrow, most are set right at the property line but some are fronted with a small porch or stoop. Rooms lead from one to the other all the way to the back of the house.

Raised Plantation House
Wide galleries, a double-pitched roof and a main level raised over a ground-level basement characterize this type of house, influenced by plantation homes in the West Indies. Walls were thick, usually of brick coated in stucco, and there were no hall-ways; rooms led from one to the other, with openings on to the exterior galleries and an outside stairway leading up to the main level.

Double Gallery House
Uptown, the Lower Garden District, the Garden District and Mid-City all boast fine examples of double gallery houses, which evolved during the antebellum period. The two-story houses feature broad galleries with piers or columns across the main façade. A roof covers the upper gallery, and the house is usually set back from the property line to allow a yard or garden in front.

Art and Culture

New Orleans is certainly well known for its bawdy nightlife, but the city's burgeoning cultural scene also attracts its share of visitors. Performing arts traditions here date from centuries ago, and the city's climate, scenery and crazy-quilt cultural mix have nurtured generations of writers and artists.

Art
During the 19C American artists discovered that New Orleans was a welcoming place to spend the fall and winter months. It was easy to find visual inspiration here, in the architecture of the developing city, in the colorful social customs and in the lush

natural environment produced by the tropical climate. A steady stream of noteworthy artists such as portraitist **John Wesley Jarvis** spent time in New Orleans in the early part of the century, finding employment painting portraits and miniatures for wealthy Creole and American residents.

Following a failed business venture and a bankruptcy, American naturalist illustrator **John James Audubon** lived in New Orleans and the surrounding area intermittently throughout the 1820s, completing an ambitious catalog of painted illustrations of American birds. Published in four volumes between 1827 and 1888, Audubon's *Birds of America* is still considered one of the finest ornithological works ever completed.

Perhaps the most important artistic event of 19C New Orleans was the 5-month sojourn of painter **Edgar Degas**, the only significant French Impressionist painter to travel and paint in the US. The artist's mother was a Creole woman, born in New Orleans but educated in Paris; her brother Michel Musson had established himself here as a successful cotton and insurance broker. At a crossroads in his painting career, Degas traveled to the city in 1872 to visit his relatives, staying in their mansion on Esplanade Avenue. The artist's paintings of his family and their daily lives, friends and business associates were telling portraits of fading Creole society in the postbellum period.

The turn of the 20C brought the establishment of the **Newcomb Pottery** at Tulane University's Newcomb College for women. A means of vocational training as well as education for its students, the pottery operated for 50 years and was one of the most acclaimed American art potteries of the early 20C.

New Orleans native **Walter Anderson**, born in 1903, worked at his brother's Shearwater Pottery and on mural projects for the Works Progress Administration in the 1930s before retiring to the Mississippi coast and a solitary life of drawing and painting. Etchings, prints and paintings of French Quarter architecture and flora were a focus for **Morris Henry Hobbs**, who came to New Orleans in 1938 intending a short stay and remained permanently. Born and raised in New Orleans, **Ida Kohlmeyer** graduated from Newcomb College before training with Hans Hoffman and Mark Rothko; Abstract Expressionism was the focus of her early works before she shifted to figuration, Synthesis paintings, and later, sculpture.

The Carnival season and its traditions have spawned a memorable only-in-New-Orleans art form. Designer **Henri Schindler** has made his name as the city's preeminent creator of jewelry, invitations, sets, costumes, posters and floats for some of New Orleans' old-line krewes. Jazz Fest has given rise to another indigenous art form; every year a noted artist is commissioned

to design a limited-edition **Jazz Fest poster** commemorating the event. Posters, which usually feature a stylized image of a famed New Orleans musician, sell out quickly and past editions are collectors' items.

Today New Orleans nurtures an active visual arts scene centered in the Warehouse District and along Royal Street. Acclaimed painters **George Rodrigue** and **James Michalopoulos** both maintain studios and galleries here; Rodrigue's iconic image of the haunting and ubiquitous Blue Dog rocketed him into the stratosphere of commercially successful artists. An experimental, hip arts movement is growing in the new St. Claude Arts District edging the Marigny, and the city has in recent years welcomed various new art installations and shows such as Art in Public Places and Prospect.2, a citywide biennial international art show.

Music and Dance
Classical Music and Dance

New Orleans has had a long history as a capital of **opera** in the southern US. Multiple theaters and opera houses in the early 19C, as well as a cultural rivalry between the directors of the Théâtre d'Orleans in the French Quarter and the St. Charles Theater in the American sector ensured plenty of entertainment for New Orleans audiences as each side tried to outdo the other in the quality of their programming and performances.

A box at the opera was a must-have for Creole and American society of the day. Itinerant opera companies frequently performed here, and in the 1840s twelve operas by Italian composer Gaetano Donizetti had their American premieres in New Orleans, including *Lucia di Lammermoor* and *Don Pasquale*.

The Civil War and Reconstruction put a damper on live opera in the city, but performances were regularly staged by a permanent company at the elegant French Opera House on Bourbon Street from the 1870s until the building burned down in 1919.

Since its founding in 1943, the **New Orleans Opera** has maintained regular performance seasons, and today stages its productions at the Mahalia Jackson Theater. The opening night performance in the fall traditionally inaugurates New Orleans' social season.

Although chamber music concerts and solo performances have been popular here for generations, New Orleans did not have a resident **symphony orchestra** until 1936. In the 1970s the New Orleans Symphony Orchestra was ranked among the ten best in the US; Leonard Slatkin was a former director (1977-80), and the orchestra attracted guest soloists such as Itzhak Perlman, Van Cliburn and Jean-Pierre Rampal through

FAMOUS NAMES OF NEW ORLEANS JAZZ

Whether you're browsing a music store or perusing a nightclub calendar, look for the following names, all great luminaries of New Orleans jazz past and present.

Past:	Present:
Louis Armstrong	Pete Fountain
Jelly Roll Morton	Irvin Mayfield
Sidney Bechet	Nicholas Payton
George Lewis	Ellis Marsalis and sons Wynton,
Kid Ory	Branford and Delfeayo
Al Hirt	Kermit Ruffins
Louis Prima	Preservation Hall Jazz Band
King Oliver's Creole Jazz Band	Rebirth Brass Band
The Original Dixeland	Olympia Brass Band
Brass Band	Donald Harrison

the 1980s. The organization went bankrupt and disbanded in 1991 but quickly regrouped to form the **Louisiana Philharmonic Orchestra**, owned by its musician members. Hurricane Katrina flooded the LPO's home hall, the Orpheum Theater; today, the orchestra performs at the Mahalia Jackson Theater and various other venues around the city.

Like opera, theater and classical music, **dance** has a long tradition in New Orleans. Dancers formed part of the company for operas and plays through the 19C, and burlesque was a popular live-performance tradition. Today the **New Orleans Ballet Association**, founded in 1969, welcomes internationally acclaimed dance companies to its productions at the Mahalia Jackson Theater.

Seasoned dancers Marjorie Hardwick Schramel and Greg Schramel, a New Orleans native, founded the New Orleans Ballet Theater in 2002, with a resident company performing modern and contemporary ballet. And the Metairie-based **Delta Festival Ballet**, the state's largest resident professional company, operates the New Orleans Youth Ballet and mounts a popular annual production of *The Nutcracker*.

Jazz

New Orleans is widely accepted as the **birthplace of jazz**. Its earliest influences might have been the music performed on rude drums and stringed instruments during slave dances held in Congo Square, but the style took form in the 1890s when syncopated ragtime rhythms, traditional negro spirituals and expressive strains of the blues coalesced in the ears and instruments of black and Creole musicians in the neighborhoods of New Orleans. Home-grown brass bands perfected the sound for their neighbors while polished combos honed it further on riverboats, in social clubs and on stages in Storyville, a red-light district of dance halls, saloons and brothels created by city ordinance around Basin Street outside the French Quarter. Jazz clubs also sprang up in the blocks around South Rampart and Perdido streets, known as Back O'Town.

Jazz was a radical departure from typical musical forms of the day, and improvisation was its hallmark; the melody of a piece served as a mere starting point around which the players would create spontaneous solos, flying off into their own musical territory and bringing it home at the end. Small ensembles of cornets (for the melody), clarinets (for counterpoint), and trombones, tubas and percussion (for rhythm) played standard and improvised melodies backed by lively, mixed rhythms.

As the style evolved, colorful **Dixieland** music added banjo, piano and a wild mix of instrumental solos played at once in a magical blend.

New Orleans pianist **Jelly Roll Morton**, cornetists **Joe "King" Oliver** and **Charles "Buddy" Bolden** and clarinet player **Sidney Bechet** were some of the greatest influences on early jazz. The most famous New Orleans jazzman of all, trumpet player **Louis Armstrong**, grew up in New Orleans but left in 1922 to join Oliver, his mentor, in Chicago. Armstrong returned to his native city throughout his life however, playing to packed houses. Trumpeter **Al Hirt** and clarinetist **Pete Fountain** were more recent practitioners of the Dixieland style.

The traditional New Orleans style of jazz reached the ears of the rest of the US when the Original Dixieland Jazz Band, a quintet of white musicians, recorded *Livery Stable Blues* in New York in 1917. Traditional jazz music continued to flourish in New Orleans even as new evolutions of the style began forming in Chicago, Memphis and other US cities. By the mid-20C, the swing era and other jazz styles like bebop, cool jazz, model jazz and avant-garde jazz bypassed the Dixieland style in terms of popularity but the sound enjoyed a later resurgence, and it has never been out of fashion in the Big Easy.

When the Saints Go Marching In, *Basin Street Blues* and *Royal Garden Blues* are among some of the best-known traditional standards; today they're expertly performed at Preservation Hall in the French Quarter, a nightclub dedicated to preserving traditional New Orleans jazz. Newer groups such as the **Rebirth Brass Band** and **Kermit Ruffins' Barbecue Swingers** meld traditional sounds with funk, soul and hip-hop. A long list of artists born and bred in New Orleans have made their names at home and abroad specializing in various jazz styles, including **Irvin Mayfield**, **Donald Harrison**, **Nicholas Payton** and the **Marsalis Family** (dad Ellis and sons Wynton, Bradford and Delfeayo). And vibrant programs like the New Orleans Jazz National Park's weekly *Music for all Ages* and the Jazz Studies program at the New Orleans Center for Creative Arts ensure that the city's indigenous musical tradition will thrive into the next generation.

Rock & Roll, Rhythm & Blues

By the 1930s and 1940s, radio was bringing funk, rock & roll, soul and R&B influences to Louisiana from places like New York, Memphis and Nashville.

New Orleans musicians like **Clarence Gatemouth Brown**, **Allen Toussaint** and later, Pontchatoula native soul singer **Irma Thomas** and **Dr. John** blended the new styles with jazz to create their own brand of R&B. **Professor Longhair** and Lower Ninth Ward resident **Fats Domino** both popularized new sounds with their own piano blends; Domino quickly gained fame with rollicking hits like *Walkin' To New Orleans* and the slower-paced *Blueberry Hill*.

New Orleans' vibrant nightlife scene continues to nurture performing artists and groups of many genres, and both homegrown and traveling bands take stages at the annual Jazz Fest. The **Neville Brothers** have risen to fame from their music-steeped beginnings in New Orleans, and traditionally perform their characteristic repertoire of funk-influenced R&B hits at the festival's packed closing set.

Music on the Bayou

In Cajun Country, the fun begins when the day's work is done, and for many Cajuns fun means heading to local stages or dance halls to step, swing and stomp to the pulse-quickening sounds of Cajun and zydeco music. Typical Cajun bands incorporate accordions, fiddles and guitars along with bass and percussion (including washboards and tambourines), all accompanying a lead singer warbling in French about ill-fated love, family relationships and the joys of eating, drinking, dancing and living life to the fullest.

In the course of its evolution from its roots in Acadian folk music, Cajun music has been much influenced by African, country and bluegrass musical traditions. In recent decades it has enjoyed something of a boom thanks to star performers such as **Michael Doucet** and his band **BeauSoleil**. Well-beloved locally but less widely known are accordionist **Bruce Daigrepont**, and singer/songwriter **D.L. Menard**.

GHOSTLY SIGHTINGS

Voodoo queens, tarot card readers, séances… New Orleans has long been linked to the paranormal, so it's no surprise that so many of its landmarks are thought to be haunted. From hotels to historic mansions, eerie cemeteries and even a haunted golf course, ghostly sightings are practically *de riguer* in New Orleans.

Why is New Orleans so full of restless spirits? Paranormal experts point to the tragedies that have plagued the city over the years: the devastating fires of 1788 and 1794; a long history of slavery and the horrors of the Civil War; an outbreak of yellow fever that ravaged the city in 1853; not to mention its legacy of voodoo and vampire lore.

One of the best places to start your experience is to learn about the historic events that shaped the city's spookiest spots. Haunted History Tours *(see p57)* takes curious spectators to some of the most haunted places in the French Quarter, like the legendary LaLaurie House and Lafitte's Blacksmith Shop (now a bar), and tells the real stories behind the ghost tales, drawn from police reports and historical documents.

The cemeteries of New Orleans are an integral part of the city's mystique. Take a stroll through St. Louis Cemetery No 1, where dramatic above-ground vaults hold the remains of the city's most notable figures, including Voodoo Queen Marie Laveau. And that's not all… even the City Park Golf Course is believe to be haunted, with the ghost of an older, white-haired gentleman lingering around the 18th hole.

Once you've gotten a taste of the city's spooktacular history, you'll want to sleep with one eye open by spending a night in a haunted hotel. The Hotel Monteleone *(see p171)* is one of the oldest and the ghostliest, which according to members of the International Society of Paranormal Research, has at least a dozen spirits floating around. One favorite spot is on the 14th floor, where numerous guests have discovered the ghosts of children; the hotel bar has also been the site of some chilling encounters. Also in the French Quarter, Hotel Provincial *(1024 Chartes Street)* has a long and interesting history as a former Civil War military hospital, and to this day, countless guests have spotted apparitions of injured Confederate soldiers.

Of course, New Orleans isn't all about doom and gloom. Come Halloween, this city comes to life like no other. Locals celebrate all week long, culminating in a parade through the French Quarter that's nearly as wild and elaborate as Mardi Gras.

Also accordion-based, zydeco music developed in the mid-20C on the prairies of southeastern Louisiana at the hands of such pioneers as **Clifton Chenier** and **Boozoo Chavis**, who applied rhythm-and-blues elements to traditional Creole music forms. Soul, disco and reggae music continue to exert an influence on zydeco, and a profusion of zydeco dance halls attests to its growing popularity, boosted by talented musicians like **Buckwheat Zydeco** and accordionist **Geno Delafose**.

Theater

Professional stage drama came to New Orleans around the 1790s with the arrival of an itinerant troupe of French-speaking actors from St. Domingue, and a few theaters were quickly built to accommodate productions in French.

After the Louisiana Purchase, a group of American settlers invited impresario James Caldwell to establish an English-language theater company as an answer to the cultural advantages enjoyed by the Creoles. After 1835 Caldwell's operation moved to the grand St. Charles Theater, considered the most luxurious and important theater in the southeast; Caldwell's illustrious stock company and active touring troupe ushered in a golden age of theater in New Orleans.

The early 20C brought construction of the Orpheum Theater and the Saenger Theater, both presenting silent movies, plays and vaudeville. A still-active community theater organization, **Le Petit Théâtre du Vieux Carré**, began productions in its home at the corner of St. Peter and Chartres in 1923.

Today New Orleanians enjoy a wide range of live-performance theater options ranging from contemporary American and British comedy and drama to Broadway musicals presented by organizations like Le Petit Théâtre, Southern Repertory Theater and the Jefferson Performing Arts Society. The theater and drama departments at Tulane and Loyola universities, the University of New Orleans and the New Orleans Center for Creative Arts provide further alternatives, as do for-profit and nonprofit groups like Cripple Creek Theater and Shadowbox Theater. The Contemporary Arts Center also maintains a full calendar of experimental theater works and performance art.

Cinema

The city of New Orleans is like a ready-made movie set. Live-oak trees swagged in Spanish moss, steam rising from ponds and bayous, ships plying the broad Mississippi River, ornate aboveground cemeteries and annual happenings like Mardi Gras and Jazz Fest all make an endlessly atmospheric showing. New Orleans' colorful people and their culture, not to mention

the corruption and graft that shadow the history of city and state government, create stories that beg to be told onscreen. Movie producers have long been aware of this, and for decades have brought Hollywood to the Big Easy in order to bring New Orleans to the moviegoing public.

Some of the best-known films set and shot in New Orleans include the Oscar-winning adaptation of the Tennessee Williams play *A Streetcar Named Desire* (1951), set in the French Quarter of the 1940s, and the Bette Davis film *Jezebel* (1938), about high society in antebellum Louisiana. Peter Fonda and Dennis Hopper's drug trip in a groundbreaking scene of the road-trip movie *Easy Rider* (1969) was shot in St. Louis Cemetery No 1; the movie also featured depictions of Mardi Gras as it was celebrated in the 1960s.

The Big Easy (1987), set entirely in New Orleans, explored corruption in the city's police force, complete with river and voodoo scenes. The 1989 film *Blaze* featured French Quarter strip joints and other locations in its fictionalized retelling of the later years of Governor Earl K. Long. The rise and regime of Long's older brother Huey Long, the flamboyant and corrupt governor of Louisiana from 1928 to 1932 has been featured in several films, and was the subject of a documentary by filmmaker Ken Burns in 1985. Several noteworthy filmmakers covered Hurricane Katrina and its aftermath in documentaries such as *When the Levees Broke* (2006) and *Trouble the Water* (2008).

Literature

New Orleans' romantic beauty, air of tropical mystery and intriguing mix of people has made the city a magnet for journalists, novelists, poets and playwrights who find endless material for their work here.

In 1845, a group of Creole writers calling themselves **Les Cenelles** ("the hollyberries") published a collection of French Romantic poetry, the first anthology of Creole literary work in the US. Staunch social reformer **George Washington Cable**, a resident of the Lower Garden District, wrote fiction about Creole society of the late 19C; his short-story collection *Old Creole Days* (1883) and the novel *Les Grandissimes* (1880) were among his best-known works. Journalist, poet and artist **Lafcadio Hearn** lived for a decade in New Orleans, working at newspapers and writing *Chita*, a novella about the devastating Last Island hurricane in 1856; his other works included an obituary of Marie Laveau. In 1840 **Francis Parkinson Keyes**, who lived in the French Quarter, penned *Dinner at Antoine's*, a loving tribute to a meal at New Orleans' oldest restaurant that included delectable descriptions of dishes like Oysters Rockefeller. Born into an

WHAT TO WATCH

New Orleans' made-to-order scenery makes the whole city seem like a movie set. If you can, prep for your visit with one or more of the following films "starring" New Orleans.

Jezebel (1938)
This classic movie pits a headstrong Southern belle (Bette Davis) against the restrictive mores of antebellum New Orleans, through characteristic situations such as a society ball, a duel and a yellow-fever epidemic.

Birth of the Blues (1941)
Dixieland jazz is the true star of this music vehicle about a feckless band of musicians led by a carefree clarinet player (Bing Crosby); it's a stitched-together series of hot musical numbers and great jam sessions in the swinging New Orleans of the 1920s.

A Streetcar Named Desire (1951)
The classic movie version of Tennessee Williams' hard-hitting stage drama centering on a mentally disturbed woman (Vivien Leigh) visiting her sister and brutish brother-in-law (Marlon Brando) in their apartment in the sleazy, steamy French Quarter.

King Creole (1958)
Elvis Presley as a young musician faced with working as a singer or hooking up with gangsters to support his impoverished family in the French Quarter; lots of classic nightclub scenes.

The Big Easy (1987)
This steamy crime drama weaves voodoo, nightclubs, courtrooms and a Cajun fais-do-do into a story about corruption in the New Orleans police department.

**When the Levees Broke:
A Requiem in Four Acts** (2006)
Director Spike Lee's documentary showcases the suffering and the spirit of New Orleans residents struggling to rebuild their lives in the aftermath of Hurricane Katrina and the federal levee failures.

**The Curious Case of
Benjamin Button** (2008)
This modern fantasy film set in New Orleans tells the tale of a man (Brad Pitt) who is elderly when born, and grows progressively younger throughout his life.

Tremé (2010)
The storyline of this popular dramatic television series set in present-day Tremé brings numerous aspects of New Orleans culture to light as it follows several characters in the aftermath of Hurricane Katrina.

aristocratic New Orleans family whose fortunes were reversed during and after the Civil War, **Grace King** was a leading literary figure around the turn of the 20C and in 1916 published *The Pleasant Ways of St. Medard*, a telling account of life in the city during Reconstruction.

In the early 20C, novelist **Sherwood Anderson** lived in the French Quarter and hosted Thornton Wilder, Thomas Wolfe, Sinclair Lewis, John Steinbeck and John Dos Passos during their passages through the city. In 1925, **William Faulkner** lived behind St. Louis Cathedral at 624 Pirates Alley, writing his novel *Soldier's Pay*. Faulkner House Books, a popular independent bookshop and center of an active New Orleans literary community occupies the building today. Mississippi native **Tennessee Williams** lived periodically in the French Quarter as a young man in the 1930s and 1940s and created unforgettable portraits of the neighborhood in his Pulitzer prizewinning play *A Streetcar Named Desire* (1947).

Novelist **Shirley Anne Grau** and playwright **Lillian Hellman** were both born in New Orleans and lived in neighborhoods upriver of Canal Street. Grau, who graduated from Newcomb College, is known for piercing portrayals of African-American life in the segregated South. Hellman, author of *The Little Foxes* and other theatrical works, peopled her social critiques with characters loosely modeled on her New Orleans friends and relatives. Author of the novel *The Moviegoer* (1961), **Walker Percy** mentored several local writers including **John Kennedy Toole**, whose posthumously published novel *A Confederacy of Dunces* (1980) about eccentrics in New Orleans won a Pulitzer Prize.

Contemporary literary lights include novelist **Anne Rice**, creator of the enormously popular *Vampire Chronicles* (1976-2003); Rice set several of her stories in and around her Garden District home, most notably *The Witching Hour*. **Ellen Gilchrist**, who resided for many years here, has written several novels depicting race and social relations in the city.

Popular children's author **Coleen Salley** published her first book in 2001 at the age of 72, winning young hearts and minds with her *Epossumondas* stories about a unique opossum. Financial journalist **Michael Lewis**, born and raised in Uptown, produces a steady stream of entertaining nonfiction investigating the financial underpinnings of aspects of modern culture, including sports; his books *Moneyball* (2003) and *The Blind Side* (2006) have been made into popular movies.

WHAT TO READ

Whether fiction or nonfiction, stories of New Orleans are rife with political intrigue, natural disasters, eccentric characters, bawdy parties and gumbo. Start your read-up on the city with the works below.

Fabulous New Orleans
Lyle Saxon (1928)
Saxon's witty renderings of New Orleans life and history were published early in the century, and remain a fun and accurate introduction to enduring traditions, legends and places in the city.

Gumbo Tales: Finding My Place at the New Orleans Table
Sarah Roahen (2008)
A witty, tender and mouthwatering romp through New Orleans' culinary traditions, culture and personalities.

New Orleans Mon Amour: Twenty Years of Writings from the City
Andrei Codrescu (2006)
Short essays by poet Andrei Codrescu illuminate the good, the bad, the beautiful and the rotten of life and death in New Orleans.

Breach of Faith: Hurricane Katrina and the Near Death of a Great American City
Jed Horne (2006)
The former metro editor of the New Orleans *Times-Picayune* weaves wrenching personal stories of storm victims through a narrative of the disaster and the federal, state and local response.

A Confederacy of Dunces
John Kennedy Toole (1980)
The Pulitzer prizewinning comic masterpiece about a memorably eccentric misfit in New Orleans has long been lauded for its accurate portrayal of the city.

Feast of All Saints
Anne Rice (1979)
The celebrated author of *The Vampire Chronicles* penned this novel exploring the lives of free people of color *(gens de couleur libre)* in early 19C New Orleans.

In the Land of Dreamy Dreams *Ellen Gilchrist (1981)*
Short stories by contemporary novelist and Penn award-winner Ellen Gilchrist explore the lives of upper-class women in Uptown New Orleans.

The Moviegoer
Walker Percy (1961)
Percy's award-winning novel about a young man who, discontented with his privileged life in postwar New Orleans, sets off on a search for meaning around the city, the Gulf Coast and Chicago.

Nature and Environment

New Orleans lies in the southeastern corner of Louisiana, about 30 miles from the Mississippi border. The city is situated about 100 miles northwest of the mouth of the Mississippi River, along a crescent-shaped bend that accounts for one of New Orleans' best-known nicknames. The Mississippi River essentially flows south, and the "Crescent City" is technically located on its east bank. But the river makes a sharp curve to the east and then flows due north as it passes the French Quarter before curving back and continuing southeast to the gulf. The opposite bank, the "West Bank," therefore lies due east of the city at this point. Outside of the French Quarter, New Orleans' street plan mostly accommodates the curve of the river, and for this reason, it's not much use to refer to the points of the compass when talking about directions here. Far better to do as the locals do and use Uptown, Downtown, river and lake (Pontchartrain) as your coordinates; it makes much more sense.

To the north of downtown lies Lake Pontchartrain, a 630sq mi coastal estuary of the Gulf of Mexico. Broad and shallow (its average depth is 12–14ft), the lake is traversed by the 24mi Lake Pontchartrain Causeway bridge, which accesses the "north shore" communities of Covington, Mandeville, Madisonville and Slidell. The low-lying ground south and east of New Orleans is a completely flat and largely aquatic terrain of marshes, swamps, coastal lakes and bayous. This coastal wetland nurtures diverse wildlife species including alligators, snakes, turtles, opossums, armadillos and nutria; deer wander the upland areas. It's also a bird-lover's paradise, home to snowy egrets, herons, pelicans and even bald eagles. Ducks and geese fly overhead on their twice-yearly migrations. Many species of fish thrive here naturally or are farmed in the warm waters, including oysters, shrimp, crawfish and finfish such as catfish, bass, redfish and speckled trout.

New Orleans' climate is subtropical, and many exotic species of flora thrive in the hot, humid environment. Bougainvillea, hibiscus and crape myrtles create explosions of color amid the lush green of palm and banana trees. Cypress and live oaks are very common here, often draped in Spanish moss; the deciduous oaks drop and regrow their shiny green leaves throughout the year, while cypress trees keep their needles long into the Fall.

THE MISSISSIPPI RIVER

New Orleans wouldn't exist without the Mississippi River. The city was established here to take advantage of the Mississippi's confluence with the Gulf of Mexico, and access to the riverine gateway to the continent's interior was so highly prized that it precipitated the Louisiana Purchase. Almost every facet of the city—its geography, its economy, its culture—depends on the river to some extent.

Originating some 2,530 miles north of New Orleans in western Minnesota, the Mississippi River and its tributaries drain 32 states and parts of Canada; its watershed encompasses almost 40 percent of the territory of the continental US. Estimates put the river's flow at between 2,000 and 7,000 cubic feet of water per second. The river is nicknamed "The Big Muddy" thanks to the runoff and sediment that cloud the water as it moves past New Orleans.

The Mississippi is extremely difficult to navigate. Though it flows generally north–south, a closer look reveals a meandering path of innumerable twists and turns, particularly as the river cuts east across Louisiana on its way to the gulf. In places the river nearly returns to itself; it makes one of its sharpest curves as it bends around Algiers Point opposite the French Quarter. If you happen to be on the Moonwalk when a giant freighter goes by, pay attention to the way the currents affect the vessel as it rounds the bend. Oceangoing ships approaching this particular stretch of the river are guided by special pilots who board temporarily just to navigate the sandbars, curves and treacherous currents.

Rivers seek the shortest route to the sea, and for decades the Mississippi has been attempting to straighten its meandering course, seeking a new main channel via the Atchafalaya River, a smaller but more direct tributary that flows due south to the Gulf of Mexico west of Baton Rouge. The US Army Corps of Engineers has spent billions of dollars constructing levees and diversions to keep the river on its present course, but re-routing is inevitable over time—and it could happen instantly in the event of an earthquake or a major flood. If so, New Orleans would sit beside an empty riverbed, drying up its port activity and other economic engines.

The river's geological instincts were emphasized in the summer of 2011, when snowmelt and rain in the Midwest funneled vast amounts of water downriver, causing the it rise precipitously and threaten to overtop levees in Louisiana. To prevent this, the A.C.O.E. (the US Army Corps of Engineers who are in charge of water resources management in the city) opened floodgates that diverted water into the Morganza and Bonnet Carre spillways upriver of New Orleans, keeping the water level within safe limits as it flowed past the city.

PLANNING YOUR TRIP TO
NEW ORLEANS

The streetcar in New Orleans
Photo: © J Royan/Blickwinkel/age fotostock

Travel Tip:
For LGBT travelers visiting the Crescent City, Cafe Lafitte in Exile *(corner of Bourbon and Dumaine St.)* is the oldest gay bar in the French Quarter and it is a a lively place at all hours—in fact, it's open 24/7 Tuesday through Sunday!

ASK PETER...

Q: What if I want to volunteer for a day during my stay in New Orleans?
A: You can help rebuild a home, shovel mud, or install a new floor for a day, week or month with St. Bernard Project in Chalmette, Louisiana. SBP works with those affected by the devastation caused by Hurricane Katrina. SPB has rebuilt 410 homes since its launch in 2006. Because it is a non-profit organization, housing, transportation and meals are not provided. However, some area hotels offer volunteers discounted rates as a thank you for their time and efforts.

When to Go

Unlike many other US destinations, New Orleans experiences an **"off season"** during the summer months, mostly thanks to the heat and extreme humidity. Daily highs reach into the 90s from June through the end of September and humidity tops a wilting 85 percent or higher. Most afternoons bring a brief thunderstorm. Because of this, many hotels discount their rates during the summer, and it can be easier to reserve a table at popular restaurants. You should consider that **hurricane season** extends from June through November, with most of the tropical activity occurring in August and September.

In **winter**, temperatures fluctuate anywhere from the 30s to the 70s; January tends to be the coldest and rainiest month. **Spring** (April–May) and **fall** (October–November) are the most pleasant times to visit, when temperatures stay moderate, humidity stays low and rain stays away; most outdoor events and music festivals are scheduled during these months. Mardi Gras and the Carnival weeks leading up to it, as well as the weekends of **Jazz Fest** (end of April–early May) and the days around the Sugar Bowl are the busiest seasons for tourism in New Orleans.

Where to Go

Weekend Break

On Friday evening, enjoy dinner out in the **French Quarter★★★**, then head over to **Preservation Hall★** for some live, traditional New Orleans jazz. If partying in the streets is your thing, take a turn up and down **Bourbon Street★** for some Friday night fun.

Begin Saturday morning with a stroll through the French Quarter, on your own or with a guided walking tour; Café du Monde is a good place to stop for a break. Wander down the **Moonwalk★** to visit the **Audubon Aquarium★★**, then grab lunch at Mother's and spend the afternoon in the **Warehouse Arts District★** visiting the **National World War II Museum★★** or wandering through art galleries.

Saturday evening take the **St. Charles Avenue streetcar★★** uptown to the Riverbend; have dinner here or head back to the **Marigny** to hear great live music along **Frenchmen Street**.

KING CAKE SEASON

Mark your calender for January 6th, which is the start of king cake season! Sweet cinnamon rolls are covered in icing, decorated in the traditional Mardi Gras colors and traditionally baked with a small plastic baby inside (to represent Jesus). **Haydel's Bakery** *(4037 Jefferson Highway)* makes some of the best king cakes in town—this family business has been baking for three generations. Also check out **Manny Randazzo King Cakes** *(3515 N.Hullen St., Metairie)*, which has been serving a family recipe since 1965.

Start Sunday morning with breakfast at Brennan's or brunch at Commander's Palace; walk it off with a stroll around the **Garden District★★★** to see the magnificent 19C homes.

Sunday afternoon head to **City Park★** to see the **New Orleans Museum of Art★** and **Sculpture Garden★**; wind up your weekend with dinner out in the French Quarter or the Warehouse Arts District.

One Week

Plan two full days to see the **French Quarter★★★** thoroughly, including house tours and museum visits. Commercial operators offer a variety of guided walking tours; this is the best (and safest) way to explore New Orleans cemeteries. If you can, try to visit the **Warehouse Arts District★** on a Saturday afternoon; it's a great time for a gallery crawl. Sights in the **Garden District and Uptown★★★** areas could easily fill two days, particularly if you plan to visit the **Audubon Zoo★★** and shop along **Magazine Street★**. It will take a day to see all the sights in **Mid-City**, and a half-day for a leisurely visit to **Tremé** and the **Faubourg Marigny**; from here head out along St. Claude Avenue to see the **Chalmette Battlefield★**.

If you want to see the **River Road plantations★★**, count on a day for the East Bank and a day for the West Bank. You can see most of the **Cajun Country★** in a day; plan to spend the night if you'd like to hit a dance hall or a fais-do-do. You can sample a good cross-section of New Orleans restaurants over a week; treat yourself to a splurge at one of the historic old-line restaurants like Antoine's or Commander's Palace, but don't forget to try gumbo, muffalettas, po-boys and other down-home fare at local neighborhood eateries.

Budget Travel

Gazing at beautiful architecture in the **French Quarter★★★** and the **Garden District★★★**, and strolling the **Moonwalk★** alongside Woldenberg Park are great no-cost ways to experience New Orleans. Street performers set up on **Royal Street★★** (donations are up to you), and several **Frenchmen Street** bars don't charge a cover. If you want to cross the river, the Canal Street ferry is free for pedestrians. A streetcar ride will set you back a buck and a quarter; take the **St. Charles Avenue streetcar★★** to **Audubon Park★** or the **Canal Street line** to **City Park★**, where you can explore the art museum's beautiful **Sculpture Garden★★** for nothing. The flea market section of the **French Market★** is a bargain-hunter's paradise, and the dealers expect haggling.

Check with the Preservation Resource Center and the **New Orleans Jazz National Park** for free walking tour brochures. Art galleries and antique shops charge high prices for their wares, but it doesn't cost anything to look. And remember, although hotel prices are at a premium during Mardi Gras, the parades (and the beads) are absolutely free.

Senior Travel

Take a narrated van tour to see New Orleans highlights without a lot of walking. Warehouse Arts District museums the **National World War II Museum★★**, the **Civil War Museum★** and the **Ogden Museum of Southern Art** all lie within steps of each other. By night, avoid the nonstop **Bourbon Street★** party in favor of a jazz set at Irvin Mayfield's or the Palm Court Café. If it's Friday night, check to see if New Orleans jazz patriarch Ellis Marsalis is doing his regular gig at Snug Harbor. Book a riverboat dinner cruise, and don't forget the **New Orleans Museum of Art★★**; you can get there on the **Canal Street streetcar**.

Solo Travel

Amtrak's train service to New Orleans is a wonderful, safe way for solo visitors to travel here. Before you arrive, check to see what's playing at the Southern Repertory Theater or at the **Contemporary Arts Center★**. Rub shoulders with the locals and ask what they're ordering at neighborhood eateries like the Camelia Grill, Domilise's and Casamento's. Guided walking tours are a great way to learn about the city and meet other travelers, and **Audubon Zoo★★** is wonderful for a stroll.

Romantic Travel

Opt for a quiet bed and breakfast inn **Uptown★★** or in the **Garden District★★★**, and travel to the **Warehouse Arts District★** and the **French Quarter★★★** on the **St. Charles Avenue streetcar★★**. Wander among the sculptures in the New Orleans Museum of Art's **Sculpture Garden★★**, and rent a paddleboat for two if you're feeling energetic. Reserve a table at Café Degas in **Mid-City** for an intimate dinner, or for a splurge, make reservations at Antoine's, Emeril's or Restaurant August. Enjoy smooth jazz at Snug Harbor or Irvin Mayfield's, take a carriage ride through the French Quarter or a dinner cruise on the *Steamboat Natchez* or the *Creole Queen*. Wind up your evening with a stroll along the **Moonwalk★** and recover the next day with a pampering package at a day spa.

What to See and Do

On foot, by bike, or aboard a bus, boat or streetcar, New Orleans offers endless variety in its sights and the ways in which you can see them. **Guided tours** listed below are reliably good ways to put yourself in the hands of an expert when it comes to such things as architecture, cemeteries and "haunted" sights. And a little exercise in the city's numerous parks, paths, courses and courts can be the perfect antidote to too much sightseeing and too many delicious meals (if there is such a thing).

Sightseeing
Guided Walking Tours
Faubourg Tremé – *2hr. Sat 10:30am. Depart from the New Orleans African American Museum, 1418 Governor Nicholls St.* ℘ *504-566-1136. http://noaam.org. $23.* By the **New Orleans African American Museum**. History, architecture and culture of Tremé, the oldest African-American neighborhood in the US.

French Quarter – *2hr. Tue–Sun 10am & 1:30pm. Depart from the 1850 House, 523 St. Anne St.* ℘ *504-523-3939. www.friendsofthecabildo.org. $15.* By **Friends of the Cabildo**. Licensed and enthusiastic guides present the history, folklore and architecture of the French Quarter.

French Quarter Courtyards/Creole History – *2hr. Daily 10:30am. Depart from the Road Trip shop, 622 Royal St.* ℘ *504-232-8559. www.mondecreole.com. $22.* By **Le Monde Creole**.
Excellent, highly informative tours based on the memoirs of Laura Locoul *(see p158)* lead through carriageways to interior courtyards of the French Quarter while delving into the history and lifestyle of New Orleans' Creole population.

Cemeteries – *1hr. Fri–Sun 10am. Depart from Basin St. Station, 501 Basin St.* ℘ *504-525-3377. www.saveourcemeteries.org. $12.*
By **Save Our Cemeteries**. Excellent guided tours by knowledgeable guides offer an entertaining and safe exploration of historic St. Louis Cemetery No 1. Save Our Cemeteries also conducts tours of Lafayette Cemetery No. 1 in the Garden District *(1hr; Mon, Wed, Fri & Sat 10:30am; depart from cemetery main gate, 1400 block of Washington Ave.; $10).*

"Haunted" History – *2hr. Tours depart nightly from Rev. Zombie's Voodoo Shop, 723 St. Peter St.* ℘ *504-861-2727. www.hauntedhistorytours.com. $20.*
By **Haunted History Tours**. New Orleans is rife with ghost stories and legends of haunted places; this company leads Ghost Tours, Cemetery Tours, Vampire Tours and Voodoo Tours covering several French Quarter locations where stories abound. The same organization also conducts **Garden District walking tours** *(2hr; daily 11:30am; depart from Lafayette Cemetery main gate, 1400 block of Washington Ave.; $20).*

Culinary History – *3hr. Daily 2pm. French Quarter departure location varies.* ℘ *212-209-3370. www.noculinarytours.com. $46.* By **New Orleans Culinary**

History Tours. The walking and tasting tour visits several restaurants while discussing New Orleans history and the development of Cajun and Creole cuisine. Tasting of dishes like gumbo, muffalettas, pralines and other New Orleans treats is included.

New Orleans History – *2–3hr. Departure locations vary.* ℘*504-947-2120. www.tourneworleans.com. $20.* By **Historic New Orleans Tours**. This company runs a variety of themed walking tours in various neighborhoods including the French Quarter, the Garden District and St. Louis Cemetery No 1. They also offer a jazz/Music tour and nighttime tour of the haunted French Quarter.

Guided Bike Tours
Confederacy of Cruisers – *3hr. Depart from the Royal St. side of Washington Square Park (Marigny). Morning and afternoon tours by reservation.* ℘*504-400-5468. http://confederacyof cruisers.com.* Fun and friendly guides lead groups of bikers around the city on a variety of popular themed tours, including Creole New Orleans ($45), Culinary New Orleans *($85, including tastings)* and History of Drinking in New Orleans *($85, including libations)*. Bikes (fat-tire cruisers) and helmets are included, and tours can be customized.

Big Easy Bike Tours – *3hr. Depart from the French Quarter or your hotel (bicycles delivered). Daily 8am, 1:30pm & 5pm.* ℘*504-377-0973. www.bigeasy biketours.com. $49.* Knowledgeable guides begin with the French Quarter, then lead bikers on the Garden District/American Sector route or the Esplanade Avenue/Creole History route.

Carriage Rides
Horse-drawn and mule-drawn carriages are a fun and picturesque way to tour the French Quarter. Carriages line up at the foot of Jackson Square on Decatur Street (they're hard to miss). Expect prices to range from $75 to $100 for a half-hour tour, depending on the number of people. Carriages generally operate from 8:30am to midnight. To reserve in advance contact **Royal St. Carriages** (℘*504-943-8820; www.neworleanscarriages.com).*

Self-Guided Tours
Jazz History – *916 N. Peters St.* ℘*504-589-4841. www.nps.gov/jazz.* The New Orleans Jazz National Historical Park offers informative brochures directing walkers to significant jazz-related sites around the city. Tours include Tremé/Storyville, the CBD, Back O'Town, Decatur Street and the Central Vieux Carré.

Architectural History – *923 Tchoupitoulas St.* ℘*504-581-7032. www.prcno.org.* The Preservation Resource Center has self-guided tours of all of the city's historic districts. Pick up tour brochures at the PRC office, or download from their website.

Riverboat Cruises

Steamboat Natchez – *2hr. Daily 11:30am and 2:30pm. 504-586-8777. www.steamboatnatchez.com. $24.50. Depart from Toulouse Street Wharf behind Jax Brewery.* The historic three-deck paddlewheel steamboat departs daily for narrated harbor Jazz cruises up and down the Mississippi. Live jazz is performed on-deck; some cruise packages include a Creole lunch on board. Dinner cruises are also available.

Creole Queen – *2.5hr. Daily 2pm. 504-529-4567. www.creolequeen.com. $22.* Cruises on this handsome authentic paddlewheeler head downriver with a stop to visit the Chalmette Battlefield *(see Excursions p156)*. Dinner cruises are also available.

Bus/Van Tours

Gray Line – *Depart from Steamboat Natchez dock, Mississippi River at Toulouse St. 504-569-1401. www.graylineneworleans.com. $31–$38.* A variety of narrated motorcoach tours give a broad overview of New Orleans.

V.I.P. Tours – *504-329-2489. www.vipcitytours.com. $45.* Van tours cover the French Quarter, the Garden District, the lakefront, cemeteries and Hurricane Katrina recovery.

Swamp Tours

Honey Island Swamp Tours – *2hr. Daily 9am, 11:30am & 2pm. Crawford Landing, Slidell (40min from downtown New Orleans). 985-641-1769. www.honeyislandswamp.com. $23.* Small boat tours led by professional guides focus on the natural history, ecology and wildlife of the pristine cypress swamp.

Jean Lafitte Swamp Tours – *1hr 45min. Daily 10am & 2pm. 6601 Leo Kerner Pkwy, Marrerro (20min from downtown New Orleans). 504-587-1719. www.jeanlafitteswamptour.com. $25.* Guided boat tours cover local history and nature as they penetrate murky bayous overhung by moss-draped oaks teeming with wildlife. You can also book an Airboat Tour ($54) for an speedy, exciting trip through the Barataria swamps.

Travel Tip:

Movie tours in the city of New Orleans explore film locations and historical landmarks, districts and cemeteries. Featured films shot in the city include *Green Lantern*, *Red* and *Interview with a Vampire*, to name a few.

NONSTOP CELEBRATION: SECOND-LINE PARADES

In New Orleans, parading is more than a fun tradition—it's an art form, and a way of life. Although the massive, krewe-organized parades that roll during Carnival and Mardi Gras draw hundreds of thousands of visitors to the city, smaller, second-line parades march all year in the Big Easy, and elicit participation from everyone involved: the organizers, the bands, the marchers and best of all, the spectators.

A typical second-line parade is led by a brass brand tootling lively favorites like "Mardi Gras Mambo," "Jock-a-Mo" and "Second Line." The band and nattily dressed parade organizers form the "first line," followed by the "second line" of spectators who dance along behind, twirling parasols and waving handkerchiefs and fans. The second line tends to get bigger and bigger as spectators who can't resist the beat of the music jump in and take part.

Second-line parades happen for any number of reasons: to showcase the tradition for visitors during major annual events or conventions; to draw attention to protests or charitable causes; to celebrate anniversaries or to mark the passing of community leaders. Second-line parades are also a popular feature of wedding celebrations here, as the newly married couple, wedding party and guests parade from the church to the reception site, drawing plenty of attention and applause from spectators along the way.

New Orleans' social aid and pleasure clubs organize the majority of second-line parades. Originally founded to help members with funeral costs and medical emergencies, such clubs today serve to unify their communities with social events and charitable projects, and sport colorful names like the Treme Sidewalk Steppers, the Lady Buckjumpers, the Perfect Gentlemen, and the Black Men of Labor. Most weekends find a club-organized parade marching somewhere in New Orleans, usually in neighborhoods far from the typical tourist haunts but also in the French Quarter, Tremé and Mid-City.

New Orleanians don't miss a chance to throw a party or a parade; even the passing of a loved one occasions a celebration, usually begun by a **jazz funeral** in which a brass band leads the slow procession of mourners to the cemetery, playing sad hymns along the way. Following interment, the band switches to upbeat spirituals and lively jazz as the funeral morphs into a party celebrating the life of the deceased.

Sports and Recreation
Jogging, Walking and Biking
New Orleans' incomparable scenery can make for a memorable early morning run or evening walk. Some paths are marked with directions for both bikers and foot traffic; heed markings to avoid accidents.

Moonwalk★ – *French Quarter*. This boardwalked path along the Mississippi River and Woldenberg Riverfront Park is very popular with walkers and joggers at all times of the day; bikers may find it a bit crowded.

Audubon Park★★ – *Uptown*. The nearly 2mi path around Audubon Park may be one of the loveliest spots in New Orleans; the path winds around lagoons and around a picturesque golf course.

St. Charles Avenue★★ – *Uptown*. The streetcar track through the Garden District and Uptown makes a singularly beautiful path for a run or a walk (avenue traffic makes the route less welcoming for bikers). Take the left track, so you can see when to get out of the way of the oncoming streetcars, and be sure to check over your right shoulder at intersections.

City Park★ – *Mid-City*. Zemurray Trail winds for almost a mile around Big Lake, past placid lagoons, live oak trees and the sculpture garden of the New Orleans Museum of Art. The roadways of City Park are generally free of heavy traffic, making it a good spot for an extended bike ride.

Bayou St. John – *Mid-City*. A 1.7mi concrete path traces the eastern side of the pretty bayou, passing lovely homes along the way; footbridges lead from the path into the neighborhoods if you need a diversion.

Mississippi River Levee – A nicely paved path atop the levee extends 22mi from Audubon Park to the suburb of Kenner and beyond.

Bicycle Rentals
Most bike rental shops in the city provide maps and advice about the best ways to tour New Orleans by bike. Be sure to ask if a helmet is included in the price.

Joy Ride Bike Rentals – *City Park (Uptown)*. ✆ 504-982-1617. http://joyriderentals.com. *$30/day includes helmet, dropoff and pickup service.*

Bicycle Michael's – *622 Frenchmen St. (Marigny)*. ✆ 504-945-9505. www.bicyclemichaels.com. *$25/4hr, $35/day (10am–7pm).*

Travel Tip:
When stepping out of the realm of chain shops and restaurants while in New Orleans, be prepared to carry cash on you. Several eateries and stores around town are privately owned and accept cash only. Watch out for hefty bank fees in town and stick with indoor ATMs in well-lit areas.

Golf

New Orleans boasts two 18-hole public courses within the city limits. Reserve weekend tee times well in advance if possible.

Audubon Park Golf Course – *Uptown. ☏504-212-5290. www.audubon institute.org/visit/golf. Mon–Fri $30, Sat–Sun $40 (includes cart).* Live oaks, gentle hills and lagoons make for a scenic setting at this newly renovated par-62 course in the middle of Audubon Park.

North Course (City Park) – *Mid-City. ☏504-483-9410. www.citypark golf.com. $20 greens fee, $15 cart fee.* Four sets of tees at each hole make for a multi-level challenge at these lovely public links, newly rebuilt since Hurricane Katrina.

Tennis

Reservations for weekend court times are a must for New Orleans public tennis courts.

Audubon Park Tennis Courts – *6320 Tchoupitoulas St. ☏504-895-1042. www.auduboninstitute.org. 10 courts. $10/hr.*

City Park Tennis Center – *Marconi Blvd. between Harrison Ave. and I-610. ☏504-483-9383. www.neworleanscitypark.com/tennis. 19 courts. $10/hr hard court, $13/hr clay court.*

Atkinson-Stern Tennis Center – *4025 S. Saratoga St. ☏504-658-3060. 9 courts. $7/hr.*

Fishing

The Gulf of Mexico and its bayous, swamps and inland saltwater marshes offer some of the finest sportfishing in the US, all within an hour's drive of downtown New Orleans. Redfish, flounder, speckled trout, bass and catfish thrive here, making fishing an extremely popular pastime in these parts.

Visitors who want to try their luck in Gulf waters generally find it easiest to charter a fishing outing from a licensed guide who can provide boats and equipment, plus expert knowledge and experience. Along with boat and guide services, day packages generally include all necessary bait and tackle, snacks and soft drinks, plus cleaning and packaging of the catch. Prices vary seasonally; expect to pay about $250 per person per day.

Griffin Fishing Charters – *2629 Privateer Blvd., Barataria. ☏800-741-1340. www.neworleansfishintours.com.*

Jean Lafitte Charters – *4915 Joan Marie Dr., Barataria. ☏877-689-4120. www.jeanlafittecharters.com.*

Big Easy Fishing Charters – *1401 Ave. C, Marrero. ☏504-348-4830. www.bigeasyfishingcharters.com.*

Eccentric Fishing Charters – *5057 Kenal Rd., Lafitte. ☏504-382-2268. www.eccentriccharters.net.*

Activities for Kids

It's true that much of what draws visitors to New Orleans—fine food, historic architecture, raucous nightlife—will be less appealing to their children. But

that doesn't mean kids can't have a great time in the Big Easy. These kid-friendly sights and activities will make a visit to New Orleans a treat for the whole family.

Sights

Preservation Hall★ – *(French Quarter)*. Live shows at this family-friendly venue are a great way to introduce kids to traditional jazz; the first set starts at 8pm, and you can sit on the floor.

Louisiana Children's Museum★ – *(Warehouse District)*. This kid-centric museum is a wonder for youngsters; don't miss the "Proud to Call it Home" section about New Orleans architecture.

Audubon Insectarium★ – *(French Quarter)*. Bugs galore, and you're even allowed to eat them (if you dare).

Audubon Aquarium★★ – *(French Quarter)*. Play areas, touchpools and a walk-through tunnel complement the giant tanks where kids can get up close to the denizens of the deep. If little legs are tired, take in a movie at the IMAX theater.

Audubon Zoo★★ – *(Uptown)*. It's not just the animals; there's an extensive play area, a carousel, animal meet-and-greets, a climbing hill and a train tour.

Audubon Park★★ – *(Uptown)*. Toddlers and young kids love the playground near St. Charles Avenue. Or grab a kite and head for the Fly and its river breezes.

Café du Monde – *(French Quarter)*. Sweet *beignets* and juice or hot chocolate bring out the kid in everyone.

Blaine Kern's Mardi Gras World★ – *(Warehouse District)*. Gaily colored parade floats decorated with oversize figures of humans and animals make this warehouse look like a giant funhouse.

Storyland and Carousel Gardens – *(Mid-City)*. City Park's kid-oriented amusement parks are manageable in size, and a great way to treat the kids to some mild thrills.

Activities

Ride a riverboat – *(see p59)*. The *Steamboat Natchez* and the *Creole Queen* are a fun way to experience the Mississippi River. For a shorter journey, try the Canal Street ferry to Algiers *(see sidebar p112)*.

Ride a streetcar – Hop aboard the **St. Charles Avenue★★** *(Uptown)*, **Canal Street** *(CBD)* or **Riverfront★** *(French Quarter)* lines; it's like taking a ride on a giant toy.

Swamp Tours – *(see p59)*. Nature at its finest, and maybe an alligator or two.

Travel Tip:
Tap water in New Orleans meets all regulatory standards, according to the Environmental Protection Agency, but be aware that it has high levels of chlorine, which is used in excess to clean pollutants in the Mississippi River. Officials suggest running tap water until it runs cold, or you can simply stick to bottled water.

Travel Tip:
Want to hang out on
a float during Mardi
Gras? Most folks will
tell you it's easier
said then done. Each
float is organized
by a different
group, or krewe, so
the trick is finding
one that allows
open membership.
One krewe called
Orpheus invites
guest riders for a fee
of between $1,500 to
$2,500. That includes
your costume, a
position on the float,
invitations to other
events and parties…
and of course it
includes the beads!

Calendar of Events

Listed below is a selection of New Orleans' most popular annual events. Please note that dates may vary from year to year. For more detailed information, contact the numbers listed below or the New Orleans Convention & Visitors Bureau at ☏ *800-672-6124; www.neworleanscvb.com.*

January
Battle of New Orleans Re-enactment
Chalmette Battlefield. ☏ 504-281-0510. www.nps.gov/jela/battle-of-new-orleans-anniversary.htm.
Sugar Bowl
Mercedes-Benz Superdome. ☏ 504-525-8573. www.allstatesugarbowl.org.

February
Mardi Gras
Various locations and dates *(see Holidays p76)*.
☏ 504-566-5011. www.mardigrasneworlans.com.

March
Tennessee Williams New Orleans Literary Festival
French Quarter. ☏ 504-581-1144. www.tennesseewilliams.net.
Louisiana Crawfish Festival
Torres Park (Fred Sigur Civic Center), Chalmette. ☏ 504-2710537. www.louisianacrawfishfestival.com.
St. Joseph's Day Parade
French Quarter. ☏ 504-561-1006. www.iamcnola.org.
St. Patrick's Day Parade
Magazine St. ☏ 504-455-1255. www.irishchannelno.org.
Soul Fest
Audubon Park. ☏ 504-581-4629. www.auduboninstitute.org.

April
Crescent City Classic 10K Race
Starts at Jackson Square. ☏ 504-861-8686. www.ccc10k.com.
French Quarter Festival
French Quarter. ☏ 504-522-5730. www.frenchquarterfestivals.org.
New Orleans Jazz & Heritage Festival
New Orleans Fair Grounds. ☏ 504-410-4100. www.nojazzfest.com.

Insure Assist
For All Your Travel Insurance Needs

PASSPORT
TO CAREFREE TRAVEL

Insure Assist

TRIP CANCELLATION
TRIP MEDICAL
AD &D
EVACUATION

INSUREASSIST.COM
877.591.8739

Travel, Dine and Explore
with Confidence

Michelin, experts in travel guides and maps for more than 100 years. Available wherever books are sold.

www.michelintravel.com

The Michelin Man is a registered trademark of Michelin North America, Inc. Copyright © 2012 Michelin North America, Inc. All rights reserved.

Festival International de Louisiane
Lafayette. ✆337-232-8086. http://festivalinternational.com.
Ponchatoula Strawberry Festival
Ponchatoula. ✆800-917-7045. www.lastrawberryfestival.com.

May
Greek Festival
Greek Orthodox Cathedral of the Holy Trinity, Uptown. ✆504-282-0259.
www.greekfestnola.com.
New Orleans Wine and Food Experience
Various locations and dates. ✆504-529-9463. www.nowfe.com
Breaux Bridge Crawfish Festival
Breaux Bridge. ✆337-332-6655. www.bbcrawfest.com.
Mid-City Bayou Boogaloo
Bayou St. John. www.thebayouboogaloo.com.

June
Great French Market Creole Tomato Festival
French Market. ✆504-522-2621. www.frenchmarket.org.
Louisiana Seafood Festival
Old US Mint. ✆504-957-7241. http://louisianaseafoodfestival.org.

Jazz Fest: The New Orleans Jazz & Heritage Festival
The New Orleans Jazz & Heritage Festival was established in 1970 as an annual event celebrating New Orleans' vast and enduring musical heritage. The original concept called for a daytime festival centered around Congo Square with outdoor stages showcasing local music styles; counters selling indigenous foods; and booths for arts and crafts. Musical icons Pete Fountain, Al Hirt, Fats Domino, the Meters, Mahalia Jackson and Duke Ellington all performed during the first festival, which took place over five days in April 1970.
Jazz Fest, as it became known, quickly outgrew the space at Congo Square and by 1972 took up residence at the New Orleans Fairgrounds. Today the festival is held over two weekends in late April and early May, and it remains a wildly popular annual event, with attendance regularly topping 350,000. The list of performers who have played the fest is staggering, and includes many, many icons of rock and pop music as well as jazz, blues, R&B, zydeco, Cajun, bluegrass, world music and gospel. Unforgettable music blares forth from multiple outdoor stages and tents; you can wander from stage to stage, listening here, dancing there, and stopping when hungry to sample delicious cuisine such as fried oysters, *étouffées*, gumbos, sandwiches and pasta dishes, some of which appears only at the festival. Handmade craft items and artworks in the Craft Fair sections are among the best you'll find in New Orleans. Local sons the Neville Brothers traditionally close the festival on the last Sunday evening every year.

Travel Tip:
In New Orleans, Tours by Isabelle (*www.tours byisabelle.com*) offers a first-hand view of Katrina's destruction, taking visitors through the devastated regions of the city in order for them to understand the full impact of the hurricane. For $60, this half-day tour will take you through affected areas like the lower Ninth Ward.

July
Essence Music Festival
Mercedes-Benz Superdome.
www.essencemusicfestival.com.
Go 4th on the River
Riverfront. ✆504-566-5011. www.go4thontheriver.com.

August
Satchmo SummerFest
Old US Mint. ✆504-522-5730 or ✆800-673-5725.
www.fqfi.org/satchmosummerfest.
White Linen Night
Warehouse Arts District. ✆504-528-3800.
www.cacno.org.
Words & Music: A Literary Feast in New Orleans
Various locations. ✆504-586-1609.
www.wordsandmusic.org.

September
Southern Decadence (GLBT)
French Quarter. www.southerndecadence.org.

October
Art for Arts' Sake
Warehouse Arts District. ✆504-528-3805.
www.cacno.org.
Ghostly Galavant
Jackson Square. ✆504-523-3939.
www.friendsofthecabildo.org.
Louisiana Book Festival
Baton Rouge State Capitol Complex. ✆504-219-9503.
www.louisianabookfestival.org.
Crescent City Blues and BBQ Festival
Lafayette Square Park. ✆504-558-6100.
www.jazzandheritage.org/blues-fest.
Halloween
French Quarter. ✆504-566-5011.
www.neworleanscvb.com.
New Orleans Film & Video Festival
Various locations. ✆504-309-6633.
www.neworleansfilmsociety.org.
Swamp Festival
Audubon Zoo. ✆504-581-4629.
www.auduboninstitute.org/swamp-festival.
Voodoo Experience Music Festival
City Park. ✆504-208-4005. www.voodoomusicfest.com.

Festival Acadiens et Créoles
Lafayette. www.festivalacadiens.com.
Boo at the Zoo
Audubon Zoo. ☎504-581-4629. www.auduboninstitute.org.

November
Bayou Classic
Mercedes-Benz Superdome. ☎504-293-2619. www.mybayouclassic.com.
Opening Day Horse Races
Fair Grounds Race Course. ☎504-944-5515.
www.fairgroundsracecourse.com.
Po-Boy Festival
Oak Street. www.poboyfest.com.

December
Celebration in the Oaks
City Park. ☎504-483-9415. www.celebrationintheoaks.com.
Christmas New Orleans Style
Various locations and dates. ☎504-522-5730 or ☎800-673-572.
www.frenchquarterfestivals.org.

Mardi Gras Indians

Since the late 1800s, groups or "tribes" of African-American men have paraded the streets of certain neighborhoods on Mardi Gras dressed in elaborate Indian costumes. Why Indians? It's thought that the custom evolved as an homage to the Native Americans who formed bonds with African slaves during the days of gatherings in Congo Square *(see Louis Armstrong Park p136)*, often helping them to rebel or escape.

Tribes are dubbed with Indianesque names that sometimes incorporate the name of a street or ward, such as the Wild Tchoupitoulas or the Ninth Ward Hunters. The parade ritual is complex and filled with meaning, evoking tribal customs of yesteryear combined with elements of modern-day life. The actions and invectives of tribe members as they march may appear threatening; it's all a show for the most part, although in the past violence was common as marchers used the occasion to settle personal scores with each other. Parade routes are not publicized; the chief of each tribe determines the path his tribe will take. Parading Indians wear brilliantly designed costumes created entirely by hand of canvas, beads, feathers and ornaments. These costumes can take over a year to design and produce, can weigh as much as fifty pounds, sometimes cost as much as $10,000, and are worn just twice—on Mardi Gras and on Super Sunday, the Sunday preceding or following St. Joseph's Day (March 19), when tribes from all over the city congregate at Bayou St. John.

A DAY IN THE LIFE OF PETER GREENBERG

Instead of taking a taxi directly into the city from Louis Armstrong Airport, I always ask the driver to take the long way in—through the Ninth Ward and St. Bernard Parish. Although Hurricane Katrina was in 2005, it's still a haunting sight. The effects are not just visible; they are palpable. It's a sobering reminder that even when it's no longer considered front-page news, the story and rebuilding effort continues. There are great opportunities for all travelers to help, to give back, to participate.

Once I arrive in the French Quarter, and if I'm bringing a friend, then I must have the obligatory *beignet* and *cafe au lait* at Café du Monde *(800 Decatur St.)*. Yes it's a tourist experience, but a traveler's addiction (it really is that good!). That's when I ditch the cab. I can burn off the calories by walking less than two miles to the National World War II Museum where I indulge another addiction: military history. The museum boasts a treasure trove of artifacts, aircraft and great stories. You've heard the phrase "I could spend hours there?"... I do.

From there, it's a straight shot to **Mother's** *(see p178)*, where a debris *po-boy* and a side of homemade biscuits is a must. If I can get there early enough, the line for lunch isn't out the door (yet!).

Hopping on the St. Charles Avenue streetcar, I can take the scenic route up to the Garden District, including a walk across Audubon Park to get to the consistently outstanding Audubon Zoo. A nice touch? It's just about the only zoo where you can also get a beer.

Dinner at one of New Orleans' most celebrated restaurants is in order: drinks at **Emeril Lagasse's** flagship restaurant *(see p178)*, maybe even an appetizer, then dinner at John Besh's **Restaurant August** *(see p 178)*, complete with a great farm-to-table French menu. Remember, in New Orleans there are two times that matter: late and later. Eat late, then do jazz later. Preservation Hall in the French Quarter is the classic option, but for an even more local experience, I head to **Fritzel's European Jazz Pub** *(see p185)* for a really old-school scene. If there's time for a nightcap, it's off to the historic Roosevelt New Orleans for a sazarac in... the Sazarac Bar, of course!

Know Before You Go

New Orleans is a fun and interesting city to explore, be it your first visit, your tenth visit, your vacation or a business trip. It helps to do some homework however, particularly if you're attending a major event like Mardi Gras or Jazz Fest, when hotels book up and tourist attractions fill to capacity. Plan well ahead if you've got your heart set on eating in certain restaurants; reservations may be necessary months in advance for popular spots. The information below can help you make the most of your time in the Big Easy.

Useful Organizations
Contact the following organizations for information about sightseeing, packages, hotels, restaurant reservations, recreational opportunities and special events.

New Orleans Convention and Visitors Bureau
2020 St. Charles Ave., New Orleans, LA 70130.
☎504-566-5011 or ☎800-672-6124.
www.neworleanscvb.com.

Lafayette Convention & Visitors Commission
1400 NW Evangeline Thruway, Lafayette, LA 70501.
☎337-232-3737 or ☎800-346-1958.
www.lafayettetravel.com.

Useful Websites
www.neworleansonline.com
Published by the New Orleans Tourism Marketing Corporation, the city's official tourism website is loaded with helpful articles, links, seasonal happenings and current events.

www.neworleanscvb.com
Check here for travel tips, links and articles featuring the bureau's member organizations, including a hotel reservation system.

www.nola.com
This website features content from the *Times-Picayune*, New Orleans' Pulitzer prizewinning daily newspaper.

www.bestofneworleans.com
Here you'll find content from *Gambit*, the city's alternative weekly newspaper.

www.bigeasy.com
The site publishes a broad selection of helpful practical information from paid advertisers.

Travel Tip:
Believe it or not, the best place to be during Mardi Gras is not on Bourbon Street in the French Quarter, unless you like being in the middle of a stampede. You want to be above Boubon Street. To get a front-row seat, be willing to pay to get on a balcony or in a restaurant. Or, an even better tip is to get out of the French Quarter and onto the parade route on St. Charles Avenue, where you can join the party without being trampled!

LOCAL PUBLICATIONS

For the up-to-the-minute scoop on news, entertainment and issues affecting New Orleans:

The Times-Picayune (www.nola.com) New Orleans' daily newspaper publishes its excellent Lagniappe weekend section every Friday, with club, concert and entertainment listings. Check the website for restaurant reviews by local food writer Brett Anderson.

Gambit (www.bestofneworleans.com) Pick up a copy of this free alternative weekly publication for local news, politics, event listings and restaurant reviews.

Offbeat (www.offbeat.com) This glossy monthly magazine focuses on New Orleans' music and cultural scene with reviews, blogs and event listings.

The New Orleans Levee (http://nolevee.com) This free satirical monthly publication offers a fresh take on personalities and events in New Orleans.

Visitor Centers

French Quarter Welcome Center

529 St. Ann St., on Jackson Square. ℘504-568-5661. Open year-round daily 8:30am–5pm. Closed Mardi Gras & Christmas.

New Orleans Welcome Center

2020 St. Charles Ave. ℘504-566-5011. Open year-round Mon–Fri 8:30am–5pm. Closed Mardi Gras & Christmas.

International Visitors

Embassies and Consulates – Visitors from outside the US can obtain information from the New Orleans Convention & Visitors Bureau (above) or from the US embassy or consulate in their country of residence. For a complete list of US embassies and consulates, check the US State Department website at www.usembassy.gov. There are a number of foreign embassies and consulates located in New Orleans.

Entry Requirements – Travelers entering the United States under the **Visa Waiver Program** (VWP) must present a machine-readable passport to enter the US without a visa; otherwise a visa is required. Citizens of VWP countries are permitted to enter the US for general business or tourism for a maximum of 90 days without a visa provided they have obtained prior electronic authorization (ESTA). VWP requirements can be found on http://travel.state.gov. Citizens of non-participating countries must have a visitor's visa. Upon entry, nonresident foreign visitors must present a valid passport and a round-trip ticket. Travelers to and from Canada must present a passport or other secure, accepted document to enter or re-enter the US.

Customs Regulations – All articles brought into the US must be declared at the time of entry. **Exempt** from customs regulations: personal effects; one liter (33.8fl oz) of alcoholic beverages (providing traveler is at least 21 years old); either 200 cigarettes, 50 cigars or 2kg of smoking tobacco; and gifts that do not exceed $100 in value. **Prohibited items** include plant ma-

terial; firearms and ammunition (if not for sporting purpos-
es); and meat or poultry products. For updated information,
contact the **US Customs Service** (✆877-287-8667; www.
cbp.gov) or download their helpful brochure Know Before
You Go.

Accessibility

Federal law requires that existing businesses (including
hotels and restaurants) increase accessibility and provide
accommodations for the disabled. It also requires that
wheelchair access, devices for the hearing impaired and
designated parking spaces be available at hotels and restaurants constructed after 1992. For further information,
contact the Society for Accessible Travel and Hospitality
(347 Fifth Ave., Suite 610, New York NY 10016; ✆212-447-7284;
www.sath.org).

Streetcars on the Riverfront and Canal Street lines, as well
as all RTA **buses** are accessible to visitors with disabilities.
The RTA also offers a Paratransit service to riders with proof
of eligibility. Call the RTA (✆504-827-8345) for information.

National parks have facilities for the disabled, and
offer free or discounted passes. For details, contact the
National Park Service (Office of Public Inquiries, 1849 C Street
NW, Room 1013, Washington, DC 20240; ✆202-208-4747;
www.nps.gov). Passengers who will need assistance with
train or **bus** travel should give advance notice to Amtrak
(✆800-872-7245 or ✆800-523-6590/TDD; www.amtrak.com)
or Greyhound (✆800-752-4841 or ✆800-345-3109/TDD;
www.greyhound.com). Reservations for hand-controlled
rental cars should be made in advance with the rental
company. For further information, contact the following
organizations:

Advocacy Center for the Elderly and Disabled
8325 Oak St., New Orleans, LA 70118. ✆504-522-2337 or
✆800-960-7705 (voice or TDD). www.advocacyla.org.

Louisiana Commission for the Deaf
✆800-256-1523 or ✆800-543-2099/TDD.

Louisiana Relay Service
✆800-947-5277 or ✆800-846-5277/TDD.

Senior Citizens

Many hotels, attractions and restaurants offer discounts to
visitors age 62 or older (proof of age may be required).
American Association of Retired Persons (AARP) 601
E St. NW, Washington DC 20049. ✆202-424-3410.
www.aarp.com.

Travel Tip:
There is no logical
reason to drive your
car in the French
Quarter.
Meter cops win
Olympic sprint
races to ticket every
vehicle they can.
Park at the hotel, if
you can, or better
yet, skip driving in
the French Quarter
altogether.

Getting There and Getting Around

New Orleans is a big city, but the areas of interest to visitors are relatively compact. You'll find plenty of transportation options for getting around town during your stay. Some of them, like **streetcars** and **riverboats**, are attractions in their own right. Neighborhoods are very walkable, so once you park the car, exit the cab or hop off the bus or streetcar, you're good to go.

Getting There

By Air – New Orleans is serviced by **Louis Armstrong New Orleans International Airport** (MSY) located in the suburb of Kenner, about 11mi west of downtown New Orleans (*504-303-7500; http://flymsy.com).* A cab ride from the airport to the Central Business District costs about $33; airport shuttles cost $20 per person.

By Train – Service to **Union Station** *(1001 Loyola Ave.)* in New Orleans is provided by **Amtrak** (*800-872-7245; www.amtrak.com).* Lines include the **City of New Orleans** (from Chicago and Memphis); the **Crescent** (from New York and Atlanta) and the **Sunset Limited** (from Los Angeles and San Antonio).

By Bus – **Greyhound** provides service to and from Union Station in New Orleans *(1001 Loyola Ave.).* For schedules and fares, contact Greyhound (*800-231-2222; www.greyhound.com).*

By Car – I-10 runs through New Orleans from the east and west; head west to get to Baton Rouge and Lafayette. To get to New Orleans from the north, take I-55 south. US-61 (airline) offers an alternate route north to Baton Rouge.

Getting Around

By Car – New Orleans local police take the rules of the road very seriously, which includes mandatory use of seat belts and enforcement of speed limits, especially on the airport approach roads and in school zones. You'll notice that traffic lights blink after dark in some neighborhoods; this is a signal to slow down and check for other cars on the intersection before continuing on your way.

Driving Regulations – Visitors bearing a valid driver's license issued by their country of residence are not required to obtain an International Driv-

CAR RENTAL COMPANIES

Alamo	877-222-9075	www.alamo.com
Avis	800-331-1212	www.avis.com
Budget	800-527-0700	www.budget.com
Enterprise	800-261-7331	www.enterprise.com
Hertz	800-654-3131	www.hertz.com
National	800-227-7368	www.nationalcar.com
Thrifty	800-367-2277	www.thrifty.com

er's License. Drivers must carry vehicle registration and/or rental contract, and proof of automobile insurance at all times. Gasoline is sold by the gallon (1gal=3.8 liters). Vehicles in the US are driven on the right-hand side of the road.

Parking – Finding street parking in the French Quarter and the Central Business District is a challenge, and parking rules are strictly enforced. Be absolutely sure you are not blocking a driveway or pay close attention to posted signs or risk a tow. Parking meters accept cash or credit cards; you pay for the amount of time you need (up to two hours), print a receipt and leave it in view on the dashboard. New Orleans parking enforcement officers are known for being strict and will ticket you *($20)* for an expired meter at the slightest opportunity. You'll find many commercial parking lots and garages in the French Quarter and in the CBD; expect to pay between $10–$20 for the day (park before 9am for discounted Early Bird rates). Central Parking operates several garages in New Orleans; check their website *(www.parking.com)* for addresses. If you think your car has been towed, call the Claiborne Auto Pound *(400 N. Claiborne Ave. at Conti St.; ☏504-565-7450)*.

Taxis – United Cabs *(☏504-522-9771)*, Checker-Yellow Cabs *(☏504-943-2411)*, or White Fleet Cabs *(☏504-822-3800)* are the most common rides in town. Be sure the meter is turned on, and remember that a flat fare of $5 per passenger (or the regular meter rate, if it's greater) is in effect during special events, such as Mardi Gras and Jazz Fest, the Sugar Bowl and Saints home games. Questions or problems should be directed to the New Orleans Taxicab Bureau *(☏504-565-6272)*.

On Foot – New Orleans neighborhoods like the French Quarter, the Garden District, Magazine Street and the Warehouse District are very walkable, but traveling between them can be unsafe at night. Always move about in and stay in well-lit areas with plenty of pedestrian traffic. When in doubt, take a cab, particularly if you're heading out of the French Quarter at night.

By Public Transportation – *RideLine ☏504-827-7802; www.norta.com*. The New Orleans Regional Transit Authority (RTA) runs an extensive network of buses and streetcars throughout the metropolitan area. Maps, timetables, route planners and other tools are all available on the RTA's helpful website or you can call the 24-hr RideLine for route information. The fare for all buses and streetcars is $1.25, and exact change is required. If you're going to be riding more than a few times, consider buying a **Jazzy Pass card**,

ASK PETER...

Q: Do I need car insurance if I'm renting a car while in New Orleans?

A: It depends on what kind of coverage you already have. The most common way to insure your rental vehicle is either through a credit card or using personal auto insurance. Always check that your insurance is sufficient. If you're relying on your credit-card coverage, make sure it's primary, not secondary coverage, and pay for the rental with that card. Find out if you're covered for something called "loss of use." That's a fee levied by the car-rental company for the days a car is out of commission. Ask your auto insurance provider if you can add "non-ownership coverage" which would cover that loss-of-use fee, and may even lower your deductible if the car is damaged.

good for unlimited rides on all RTA lines. Jazzy Passes are available for 1 day *($3)*, 3 days *($12)*, 5 days *($20)* and 31 days *($55)*, and can be purchased on buses and streetcars (1-day pass only), at Walgreen's drugstores, at the New Orleans Convention & Visitors Bureau *(see p64)* and in some hotels.

There are 32 **bus** lines extending all over the city, many operating around the clock (with limited service from midnight–5am). Buses are all quite new, the entire fleet having been replaced after Hurricane Katrina. The 10 Tchoupitoulas, 11 Magazine and 15 Freret lines are handy for travel between the French Quarter and Uptown; the 5 Marigny-Bywater line traverses the Warehouse District, the French Quarter and the Marigny; the 25 Jackson-Esplanade is good for getting from the French Quarter to Mid-City.

There are three **streetcar** lines: the St Charles Avenue line *(see p124)*, the Canal Street line *(see p109)* and the Riverfront line *(see p88)*.

By Ferry – ✆ *504-250-9110; www.friendsoftheferry.org*. Canal Street Landing is located at the north end of Riverwalk Marketplace. Ferries service Algiers Point across the Mississippi daily except on Christmas Day. Ferries leave the Canal Street dock every half-hour beginning at 6:15am; the last ferry of the day departs at 12:15am. Pedestrians ride free; cars pay $1 for the return trip from Algiers.

Basic Information

Whether you're visiting New Orleans for business or pleasure, from nearby or abroad, the following general travel tips and phone numbers can help you plan appropriately, and may come in handy during your stay.

Communications

Area Codes: Greater New Orleans area: **504**; Lafayette: **337**; Baton Rouge/River Road: **225**.

The prevalence of cell phones and electronic communication have pretty much made pay telephones obsolete; you won't find many functioning public telephones in New Orleans. If you need to make a phone call and don't have a cell phone, your hotel is probably your best bet, but be aware that most hotels charge extra for phone calls from your room. Prepaid phone cards are the least expensive way to place long-distance calls; cards are available in most newsstands and drugstores.

Most hotels now offer wireless Internet (Wi-Fi) service to clients, sometimes for an additional fee; check with your hotel when booking. Coffee shops, restaurants and bookstores are good places to find free Wi-Fi for your laptop

or smartphone; websites such as www.wififreespot.com and www.openwifispots.com can give you an idea of free Wi-Fi hot spots around the city.

Electricity

Voltage in the US is 120 volts AC, 60 Hz. Foreign-made appliances may need AC adapters (available at specialty travel and electronics stores) and North American flat-blade plugs.

Emergencies and Personal Safety

No matter where you are in New Orleans, it's a good idea to be aware of your surroundings and let common sense be your guide. Don't carry a lot of cash or valuables, avoid moving about alone after dark, and avoid all parks, alleys, dark streets and cemeteries after the sun goes down. If you venture Uptown or to Mid-City after dark, take a cab unless your destination is right on the streetcar line. When in doubt, ask your hotel concierge.

Important Phone Numbers
Emergency 24hr (police/fire/ambulance): ☏ **911**
Police (non-emergency) ☏ 504-821-2222
Medical Emergencies
New Orleans Urgent Care
(Warehouse District) ☏ 504-552-2433
New Orleans Dental Association (referrals)
☏ 504-834-6449
24hr Pharmacies:
Walgreens (www.walgreens.com):
1801 St. Charles Ave.
(Lower Garden District) ☏ 504-561-8458
2418 S. Carrollton Ave. (Uptown) ☏ 504-861-5033
Poison Control ☏ 800-256-9822
Traveler's Aid Society ☏ 504-586-0010
Time and Weather ☏ 504-828-4000

Holidays

Most banks, post offices and government facilities are closed on the following Federal holidays:
New Year's Day (January 1)
Martin Luther King's Birthday (3rd Monday in January)
Presidents' Day (3rd Monday in February)
Memorial Day (last Monday in May)

Travel Tip:
Doing the most good in hurricane-stricken areas requires some careful planning—*before* you go. First off, relief organizations are primarily looking for people who can commit to 10 days or more of volunteer work—so if you can't, send a cash donation instead. If you can commit for this period of time, start by contacting your charity's local chapter to obtain the necessary training. Among the organizations seeking relief workers are Hands On USA and the Salvation Army, both of which provide volunteers with the opportunity to get their hands dirty by helping with the clean-up. The accommodations may be basic, but the experience is one-of-a-kind.

Independence Day (July 4)
Columbus Day (2nd Monday in October)
Veterans' Day (November 11)
Thanksgiving (4th Thursday in November)
Christmas (December 25)

Mardi Gras is the ultimate holiday in New Orleans. Businesses, retail stores, banks—essentially the entire city—shut down and take the day off so their employees can take to the streets and celebrate. Upcoming Mardi Gras dates are:

February 12, 2013
March 4, 2014
February 17, 2015
February 9, 2016
February 28, 2017
February 13, 2018

Liquor Laws/Gambling

The legal drinking age in New Orleans is 21, although it's legal to enter a bar without purchasing or consuming alcohol at age 18. In the city of New Orleans, it's legal to purchase and consume on the street any alcoholic beverage as long as it's in an open plastic container (no glass).

Bars can legally remain open 24hr, and many in the French Quarter stay open around the clock, although some close for a brief period around 5am. You must be 21 years old to gamble or to enter a casino in the state of Louisiana.

Mail/Post

New Orleans' main post office is located at 701 Loyola Ave. in the Central Business District *(open Mon–Fri 7am–7pm, Sat 8am–5pm; www.usps.com)*. Branch post offices are located near Lafayette Square in the Central Business District *(600 S. Maestri Pl.)* and Uptown *(2000 Louisiana Ave.)*. First-class rates within the US: letter 44 cents; postcard 29 cents. Overseas: letters and postcards 98 cents.

Money

Currency Exchange – Visitors can exchange currency at the Travelex America Business Center the International Airport. In the Central Business District you can exchange currency at Whitney National Bank *(228 St. Charles Ave.; ☎ 504-586-7456)*; there is also a Whitney Bank branch at the airport.

Banks are generally open Mon–Fri, 9am–3pm, although a few open on Saturday and some have later hours for drive-through service. Automated teller machines (ATMs) are located throughout the city.

For **cash transfers**, Western Union (☎ 800-325-6000; www.westernunion.com) has agents throughout the city (look for a Western Union sign in the window). Banks, stores, restaurants and hotels accept **travelers' checks** with picture identification. To report a lost or stolen **credit card**: American Express (☎ 800-297-8500); Diners Club (☎ 800-234-6377); MasterCard (☎ 800-627-8372); Visa (☎ 800-847-2911).

Smoking
Currently smoking is not allowed in public buildings in Louisiana. Smoking is banned in establishments licensed as restaurants (where more food than alcohol is sold), but is allowed in places licensed as bars (where the majority of sales are derived from alcohol), however, there is a gradual trend toward non-smoking in bars in nightclubs. Casinos still allow smoking on the gaming floors.

Taxes and Tipping
Prices displayed in the US do not include sales tax (9 percent in Orleans Parish). A 15 percent tip is standard for waiters and cab drivers; feel free to bump up that amount for excellent service, or in high-class establishments.
Check your restaurant bill to ascertain whether a standard tip has been added to the total. It's customary to tip porters $1 per bag; chambermaids $1–$2 per day; and helpful concierges about $5 for exceptional advice or booking services.

Time Zone
New Orleans is located in the Central Time zone, six hours behind Greenwich Mean Time; one hour behind New York City.

Travel Tip:
Bar culture is such an intrinsic part of New Orleans that it's hard *not* to bar hop when you're in town. When it comes to picking where to go, you'll see venues that have a cover charge—a flat fee to get in—and those that don't. Typically, if a bar doesn't charge a cover fee, it makes up that revenue by raising the drink prices. If there's live music, there may be a minimum drink requirement— you may even be required to purchase a drink with each new set.

DISCOVERING
NEW ORLEANS

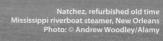

Natchez, refurbished old time
Mississippi riverboat steamer, New Orleans
Photo: © Andrew Woodley/Alamy

Most people visiting New Orleans head to the French Quarter and then don't go any further, but that doesn't mean you can't have an authentic experience in this neighborhood. You can find locals living, working, drinking and enjoying even the most tourist-heavy parts of the city. The key is to know where to go in New Orleans' oldest neighborhood.

The French Quarter, also known as the *Vieux Carre*, spans 12 blocks situated alongside the Mississippi River. The neighborhood runs from Canal Street to Esplanade Avenue and inland toward North Rampart Street. Candy-colored buildings line the street and if you look closely you'll see Spanish, French and Creole influences.

Right in the center of the neighborhood is Jackson Square. This is where you'll see most people posing in front of Andrew Jackson's statue, having their portrait done by a street artist, getting their tarot cards read and checking out the street performers. Take time to stop in the museums that line the square, namely the Cabildo and the Presbytere, both of which offer a good look at the city's history.

Aside from the museums, take my advice and hit up Jackson Square late at night. You can see all the monuments and the architecture and experience one of my favorite New Orleans institutions without the crowds. During the day, tourists wait on hour-long lines at Café du Monde, but around 3am, as the bars start to close, you'll find locals sitting down for a late-night *beignet*.

Speaking of long nights out, you can't talk about the French Quarter without mentioning drinking. The entire French Quarter is one of the only places where alcohol can be consumed in open containers on the street. Bourbon Street is the epicenter of the drinking, including local institutions like Pat O'Briens *(718 St. Peter St.)*, which invented the famous Hurricane cocktail and has a very popular dueling piano bar. For more civilized daytime drinking, head to the historic Napoleon House Bar and Cafe *(see p96)*. Grab a muffaletta (one of the few places in town to serve it hot) or a po-boy and wash it down with a Pimm's cup (or two).

View of Bourbon Street in the French Quarter Photo: © Michael J. Hipple/age fotostock

PETER'S TOP PICKS

 CULTURE

You might not get to New Orleans during Mardi Gras, and even if you're there at that time, stop at the Mardi Gras Museum located on the second floor of the Presbytere to get to know the history behind the debauchery. The exhibit highlights the full scope of activities and history of a New Orleans' Mardi Gras. **Presbytere (p 84)**

 GREEN SPACES

For a bit of quiet in this crowded district, head to Woldenberg Riverfront Park. There are lovely views of the river and some great outdoor concerts are held here. **Woldenberg Riverfront Park (p 88)**

 HISTORY

Voodoo in New Orleans is about as old as the city itself. Find out the history of this ancient practice and see artifacts from throughout New Orleans' history at the Voodoo Museum. **Historic Voodoo Museum (p 103)**

 STAY

The Bourbon Orleans Hotel has an historic past, including the Orleans Ballroom where some of the South's first mixed-race gatherings took place. **Bourbon Orleans Hotel (p 170)**

 SHOP

Check out Faulkner House Books for some of the best new, used and first-edition books in the city. **Faulkner House Books (p 193)**

 EAT

To find real Louisiana cooking check out K-Paul's Louisiana Kitchen for authentic Cajun food—blackened and delicious. **K-Paul's Louisiana Kitchen (p 176)**

 ENTERTAINMENT

Drop in at Preservation Hall where you'll hear old-school syncopated jazz from the Preservation Hall Jazz Band. **Preservation Hall (p 102)**

Location:
The square is bounded by Chartres, St. Philip, Decatur and St. Ann streets.

ASK PETER...

Q: I've heard all about the House of Blues having great jazz, but where can I find authentic jazz music without the tourists?
A: Opened in 1961, Preservation Hall is the place to go for authentic, old-school syncopated jazz. And the tradition keeps growing. Veteran musicians in their eighties mentor the younger prodigies, and often the younger musicians are the children of the older ones. Shows start filling up at 8pm every night and seating is limited. Once the rickety little chairs are gone, they're gone, and you'll be left standing in the back, catching quick glimpses of the musicians. So, get there very early for a good spot.

Jackson Square★★

The heart of early New Orleans was laid out in 1721 as a military parade ground known as Place d'Armes. In keeping with European town plans, the broad central plaza was surrounded on three sides by the parish church, the governor's residence and military barracks. To the southwest rolled the mighty Mississippi (levees block the river view today). Through the 18C the Place d'Armes hosted military drills, public meetings and ceremonial events; it also served as the site for public hangings. The square was renamed in the 1850s to honor Andrew Jackson (1767–1845), hero of the 1815 Battle of New Orleans and seventh US president. Today landscaped with formal gardens and surrounded by a cast-iron fence, Jackson Square forms a green oasis in the center of the French Quarter. Rearing at its center is a monumental bronze statue of Jackson astride his horse, dedicated in 1856.

Stately St. Louis Cathedral (occupying the first parish church's original site), the historic Cabildo and Presbytere (both house excellent museums) and the 1840s Pontalba Buildings surround the square on three sides. Musicians, street performers, artists, fortune tellers and craft vendors set up shop on Jackson Square's broad flagstone perimeter, mixing and mingling with an endless stream of tourists and shoppers to carry on the square's historic role as a public gathering place.

St. Louis Cathedral★

▶ *Allow 15min. 725 Chartres St.* ✆ *504-525-9585. www.saintlouiscathedral.org. Open year-round daily 9am–4pm (closed during Mass).*

What bride wouldn't want to get married in this iconic church, with its grand three-steepled white façade? (If you're planning a wedding in New Orleans, be advised that the waiting list is long!) The official seat of the Archdiocese of New Orleans was established as a parish in 1720 and ranks as the oldest continuously operating cathedral in the US. Dedicated in 1851, the present structure is actually the third church on this site (not counting a temporary wooden hut where New Orleans' earliest settlers worshiped). The first two-story wooden church was completed in 1727 but succumbed to the Great Fire of

Travel Tip:

PIRATE'S ALLEY

Notice the cobblestone alleyway on the left leading to Royal Street between the cathedral and its flanking buildings. This is Pirate's Alley, a picturesque walkway fronted by a few small businesses. Nobel Laureate author William Faulkner (1897-1962) lived and worked on the first floor of Number 624, and here wrote his first novel, *Soldiers' Pay* in 1925. Faulkner would no doubt approve of the Faulkner House bookstore *(see p193)*, which now occupies that space and specializes in rare and first editions—including those by Faulkner himself. Though privately owned, the house is open to tours by advance reservation (*504-586-1609*).

New Orleans is the setting for favorite American movies, plays and novels— not to mention renowned writers like Tennessee Williams and William Faulkner. So while you're here, why not see the city from the perspective of some of its most famous literary giants? Professor Kenneth Holditch's 2-hour literary walking tours take you down the narrow streets of Pirate's Alley and St. Peter's Street (where Williams wrote *A Streetcar Named Desire*) and to other literary landmarks. 504-949-9805.

1788. Don Andrés Almonester y Roxas, a wealthy Spanish real-estate developer, donated funds to rebuild the church (and the neighboring buildings) after the fire; this second structure was completed in 1794. Almonester's daughter, the Baroness Pontalba, funded a renovation and expansion of the church in 1849, during which the central tower collapsed, necessitating a near-total rebuild according to designs by French-born architect Jacques N.B. de Pouilly (completed in 1850). This present structure is built of wood and brick covered with stucco, many times buttressed, reinforced and strengthened over the decades to withstand the ravages of time and the elements. Designated a minor basilica in 1964, the cathedral is the mother church of the Archdiocese of New Orleans. Its façade, punctuated by its three precipitous steeples and embellished with Greek Revival porches and columns, is a beloved architectural icon and symbol of New Orleans.

Although the outside of the structure is grander than the inside, it's worth stepping in for a look. The clock in the central tower and a part of the façade wall are the only things surviving from the previous structure. In the sanctuary, ten stained-glass windows depict the life of King Louis IX of France, who was canonized a saint by the Catholic Church. Behind the cathedral lies St. Anthony's Close, a small pocket garden. Originally part of Orleans Street, which was the broad main thoroughfare of the early city, the land was acquired by the Church in 1831, and Orleans Street was halted at **Royal Street★★**. Legend has it that the park served for a time as a dueling ground before it was sanctified. Near Royal Street stands a modest memorial to the victims of yellow fever, which plagued the mosquito-infested city

Travel Tip:
It is possible to
explore New Orleans
during Mardi Gras
without it becoming
a stressful experience.
To avoid the crowds,
reserve a room in a
hotel well out of the
French Quarter, map
out the parade routes,
and start the day well-
fed and hydrated.
Dress appropriately
in layers, but don't let
that stop you from
dressing in costume
and incorporating
the Mardi Gras colors:
purple, green, and
gold. Also, even if
you have a planned
itinerary this is the
time to be flexible
and go with the flow;
revel in the city's well-
regulated chaos.

in the 18C and 19C. Behind it is a serene statue of Jesus, which lost a thumb and a finger during Hurricane Katrina.

Cabildo★★

◗ *Allow 1hr. 701 Chartres St.* ℘ *504-568-6968. http://lsm.crt.state.la.us. Open Tue–Sun 10am–4.30pm. $6.*
Adjacent to **St. Louis Cathedral★** fronting **Jackson Square★★**, the Cabildo was built by the Spanish government between 1795 and 1799 to house offices of the town council (*cabildo* in Spanish), and it continued to serve as New Orleans' city council headquarters until the 1850s. It was here, in 1803, that the Louisiana Purchase documents transferring ownership of the Louisiana Territory from France to the US were signed. Following the Civil War, the building housed the Louisiana Supreme Court; the landmark Plessy v. Ferguson case legalizing racial segregation in Louisiana was decided here in 1890. In 1911 the Louisiana State Museum acquired the aging structure and renovated it to house its collections. The Cabildo's most recent adventure occurred in 1988 when a fire erupted on the roof of the structure, damaging both the building and the historic collections within. The renovated building, complete with new and improved historical exhibits, reopened in 1994.

Now the flagship of the Louisiana State Museum complex, the Cabildo is one of the best spots to acquaint yourself with Louisiana's colorful, rambunctious history and culture. Excellent displays on the lower floor cover the early French explorations and the Native American groups that occupied the region prior to European settlement, along with the many challenges (diseases, floods) faced by the colonists as they struggled to establish a European-style society in the tropical swampland.

The Battle of New Orleans, the Civil War and the Reconstruction periods are presented on the upper level, along with cultural insights into Louisiana's music, architecture, economy, language, music and customs. In the Sala Capitular on the second floor, site of the historic Louisiana Purchase transfer, you'll find a death mask of Napoleon, one of only four made of the French Emperor upon his demise in 1861.

Presbytere★★

◗ *Allow 1hr. 751 Chartres St.* ℘ *504-5686968. http://lsm.crt.state.la.us. Open Tue–Sun 10am–4:30pm. $6.*
Located to the right of **St. Louis Cathedral★**, this c.1794

building was constructed on the site of the 1720 residence of the Capuchin monks who accompanied the first settlers to Louisiana. It was intended to serve as the rectory, or *presbytère*, of the wardens of the cathedral, although it functioned in various capacities throughout the 18C and early 19C. In 1911, like the **Cabildo★★**, the building was acquired by the Louisiana State Museum.

The sobering first-floor exhibit, Living with Hurricanes: Katrina and Beyond is an especially good way for visitors to New Orleans to understand the effect of hurricanes (and New Orleans' particular geographic vulnerability to them) on the Gulf Coast. It also paints a very clear picture of the extent to which Hurricane Katrina, which struck New Orleans on August 29, 2005, impacted the city and disrupted the lives of its residents. A wrenching artifact introduces the exhibit: Fats Domino's grand piano lying on its side covered with dried muck, exactly as it was found in the beloved musician's home after the floodwaters receded. The exhibit itself makes effective use of video footage and news broadcasts from the hours leading up to the storm, while audio testimonials accompanied by striking still photographs bring to life the experiences of emergency responders, ordinary citizen-heroes, medical personnel and storm refugees. A large graphic display shows exactly where and when floodwaters surged into the city as various levees failed. Other sections cover hurricanes of the past; the impact of Hurricane Rita, which devastated southwest Louisiana just a month after Katrina; hurricane preparedness; and disappearing Louisiana wetlands.

The Presbytere's second floor houses the extremely popular exhibit Mardi Gras: It's Carnival Time in Louisiana. It's a fun place to immerse yourself in the elaborate set of rituals—balls, parties, king cakes, krewes, parades—that takes place in New Orleans every year between Twelfth Night (twelve days after Christmas) and Fat Tuesday (the Tuesday before Ash Wednesday). Displays of jewel-encrusted costumes worn by Carnival royalty of the past are especially interesting, as is a timeline showing the development of "throws" (the beads, doubloons and other trinkets tossed by parade riders) from past to present. Don't miss the fascinating section about Mardi Gras as it is traditionally celebrated in rural areas of Acadiana; the Cajuns' rustic revelry is a far cry from the bead-centric hulaballoo of New Orleans.

Pontalba Buildings★

St. Peter St. and St. Ann St. bordering Jackson Square.

Considered by many historians as the first apartment buildings in the US, these red-brick Greek Revival row houses draped in filigreed wrought iron were built in 1850 for the Baroness Micaela Almonester Pontalba, the strong-willed heiress of 18C Spanish real-estate mogul Don Andrés Almonester y Roxas. After surviving a murder attempt by her father-in-law in France in 1834, the baroness, a shrewd businesswoman, returned to New Orleans determined to preserve the French Quarter (and along with it, her fortune) by constructing townhouses on her inherited properties flanking **Jackson Square★★**. The four-story buildings, designed by architect James Gallier and finished by Henry Howard, incorporated shops and storage space on the lower level with elegant residences above. The apartments quickly achieved a reputation as a desirable address for Creole society at a time when American settlers were establishing a presence in the neighborhoods across Canal Street.

There are two sets of Pontalba Buildings: the first, a group of 16 row houses on St. Peter Street, is known collectively as the Upper Pontalba, and is owned by the city of New Orleans; the state of Louisiana is the landlord of the Lower Pontalba buildings facing St. Ann Street across **Jackson Square★★**. The iron galleries adorning the façades sport intricate filigreework; see if you can spot the baroness' initials, A and P, incorporated into the central cartouches.

1850 House

❯ *Allow 15–30min. 523 St. Ann St., in the Lower Pontalba Building.* ℘ *504-568-6968. http://lsm.crt.state.la.us. Open year-round Tue–Sun 9am–5pm. Closed major holidays. $3.*
Part of the Louisiana State Museum complex, the 1850 House is the only apartment in the **Pontalba Buildings★** open to the public. From the first-floor entrance, which houses the museum gift shop, you can climb up to tour the residence above, restored to appear as it would have during New Orleans' antebellum period. Furnishings and decorations are faithful to the period, and the richly upholstered furniture, dinnerware, artwork and toys all give a good picture of the lifestyle of a mid-19C Creole family. Be sure to note, in one of the bedrooms, a portrait of Jenny Lind, the wildly popular Swedish opera singer who toured the US with P.T. Barnum in 1851 and gave several concerts in New Orleans, staying in one of the Pontalba Apartments during her visit.

Café du Monde

❯ *Allow 30min. 800 Decatur St.* ℘ *504-525-4544. www.cafedumonde.com. Open daily year-round.*
No visit to New Orleans is complete without a stop at this famous cafe draped with trademark green and white awnings at the corner of **Jackson Square★★**. Join the line of hopefuls vying for a table; once you're seated, examine the menu printed on the napkin holder before your waiter arrives. *Beignets* are what it's all about here—the tasty fried doughnuts (square, no hole) arrive three to an order, piping hot and drenched in powdered sugar. Go-withs include rich New Orleans-style *café au lait* made with

Travel Tip:
People will tell you that you must go to Café du Monde, but what they don't tell you is when to go. You don't want to go during the day when all the other tourists are crowding the area waiting for their *beignets* (fried pastries similar to funnel cake or doughnuts) and chicory coffee. Go late at night (think 3am) when the locals are wrapping up their night out.

chicory and served hot or iced, hot chocolate, milk or juice. The original stand opened in 1862 in the **French Market★**, and now operates 24 hours a day, closing only, as the menu notes, for "Christmas and some hurricanes." You can even step around to the rear of the building and peer in through a plate-glass window upon the endless conveyor of *beignets* as they're cut from dough strips and hurled into fryers.

Jackson Brewery

○ *Allow 30min. 600 Decatur St. ☎504-566-7245. www.jacksonbrewery.com. Open year-round Mon–Sat 9am–8pm, Sun 10am–7pm.*
This stately 1891 brew-house ranked among the largest independent breweries in the country in the 1960s, and churned out popular Jax beer for almost a century (the brewery switched to root beer and cola during Prohibition). Jax Brewery ceased operation in 1971, and in the 1980s the building was renovated as a popular riverfront mall. Today operating as the Shops at Jax, the building houses space for some 40 retailers, a food court and an upscale nightclub and bar.

Washington Artillery Park and the Moonwalk★

○ *Allow 30min. Decatur St. across from Jackson Square.*
For an iconic **view★★** of **Jackson Square★★** backdropped by **St. Louis Cathedral★**, climb the side ramps from Decatur Street to Washington Artillery Park, named for one of the oldest military units in the US. The cannon on display is a copy of one used by the field unit in the Civil War. To the rear extends a wonderful view of the Mississippi River as it curves past the French Quarter. The sidewalk amphitheater bordering Decatur Street is a good place to rest, people-watch and be entertained by an ever-changing lineup of street performers.
From the park you can stroll the Moonwalk, a boardwalk atop the levee, to take in views of the rolling Mississippi and historic Algiers Point on the opposite bank. In 1976 this scenic walkway, named for the former New Orleans mayor Maurice "Moon" Landrieu, replaced a more industrial-looking cargo wharf. Giant barges, tankers and riverboats glide past on the way to and from the Gulf of Mexico downriver; if you're lucky you may even spot a cruise ship departing for points south.

Riverfront Streetcar Line★

www.norta.com. Operates daily 7.30am–10.30pm. $1.25 (exact fare required).
A decidedly charming means of traveling between the French Quarter and the Warehouse District, the Riverfront Streetcar line extends from the foot of **Esplanade Avenue★** (adjacent to the **French Market★**) to just under the Mississippi River bridge at the New Orleans Convention Center. The red-painted cars—replicas of 1920s-era Perley Thomas streetcars—trundle back and forth atop the levee overlooking the Mississippi River. It takes about 15 minutes to ride from one end of the line to the other.

Woldenberg Riverfront Park★

○ *Allow 30min. Along the Mississippi River from St. Louis to Canal Sts.*
504-861-2537. www.auduboninstitute.org.

Thirteen acres of landscaped green space stretch from the **Jackson Brewery** to the **Audubon Aquarium of the Americas★★**, paralleling the Mississippi River with wonderful river views at every pace. Scattered throughout the park are shade trees, benches and sculptures, including Ida Kohlmeyer's whimsical Aquatic Colonnade, and John Scott's stainless-steel Ocean Song. The steamboats *Natchez* and *Creole Queen* dock here, and the beautiful expanse hosts frequent outdoor concerts and festivals.

Audubon Aquarium of the Americas★★

○ *Allow 2hr. 1 Canal St. 504-581-4629. www.auduboninstitute.org.*
Open Tue–Sun 10am–5pm. $19.95.

The slanted blue-green oculus overlooking the Mississippi River at the foot of Canal Street heralds a fascinating and fun array of exhibits that showcase aquatic life from North, Central and South America. Occupying a state-of-the-art facility that incorporates enormous tanks, aboveground habitats, play areas and an IMAX theater, the aquarium is a facility of the Audubon Nature Institute, which also operates the **Audubon Insectarium★** and the **Audubon Zoo★★**.

From the main entrance hall you'll wander through an underwater tunnel that penetrates the Caribbean Reef tank where fluttering rays, silvery tarpons and exotic tropical fish glide overhead and around colorful corals, immersing you in their watery world. From here climb up to the humid land of the Amazon Rainforest, where tropical plantings, waterfalls and a fun overhead walkway imitate the wild environment around the world's second-longest river. Tanks here house redtail catfish, red Pacus, piranhas and a huge green anaconda; steel your ears for the loud squawks of enormous macaws.

Additional sections on the second floor host an adorable colony of black-footed penguins; a fearsome-looking group of bonnethead and tiger sharks; tanks of seahorses, the anomalies of the aquatic world; and Buck and Emma, a pair of playful sea otters brought here from California. Kids shouldn't miss Adventure Island, a pirate-themed play area complete with a stingray touchpool full of friendly rays wait to be petted and fed. A giant white alligator is the star of the Mississippi River exhibit, which showcases riverine species like spotted gar, paddlefish and largemouth bass, all in a display area overlooking the actual river.

From here head down to the Gulf of Mexico exhibit, a wondrous 17ft-deep tank that replicates an offshore oil platform at quarter scale. Here you'll see red snappers, sea turtles, stingrays, alligator gars and more, some swimming in schools. The exhibit also features tanks of varied jellyfish. Shows in the facility's IMAX theater highlight the wonders of natural history; recent screenings included *Under the Sea 3D* and *Lions 3D—Roar of the Kalahari*.

VOODOO

New Orleans voodoo is heavily steeped in West African tradition, originating from what is now known as Benin, when African slaves were brought to the US. (There is a strong voodoo culture in the Caribbean as well, but those influences didn't appear in New Orleans until some decades later.)

In its earliest days, voodoo was practiced by slaves through spirituality, language, dance and culture, all reflecting deep African roots. Slaves were brought onto Louisisana plantations and forced to convert to Catholicism—the only legal religion in New Orleans. They quickly realized they could continue practicing their own faith by pairing African *loas* and *orishas* (elemental forces or spirits of the voodoo religion) with similar Catholic saints. This practice flourished in these tight-knit communities, and evolved as Creole culture and language took form in New Orleans.

The "golden age" of voodoo took place from the mid 1800s to mid 1900s, when voodoo queens brought this belief system into the spotlight. Perhaps the most famous of all was Marie Laveau, a Creole woman of color who was born into freedom in 1801. She was a "quadroon," of African, Spanish, French and Indian descent, who is thought to have worked tirelessly as a nurse and healer during the yellow fever epidemic.

Starting around 1930, the concept of "American voodoo" emerged, evolving from a religious and spiritual practice to a type of holistic healing art. Today, voodoo is most prominent as a tourist attraction, with shops, street performers, and fortune-tellers dominating the culture (items in shops are often imported from China!). Many practicing voodooists retreated into hiding, uncomfortable with this new form of practice.

It's hard to get away from the kitschy tourist side of voodoo. You'll see voodoo dolls, candles and tarot cards—not to mention fortune-tellers offering to cleanse your spirit—all over the city. But for a glimpse into the real history of voodoo, check out the New Orleans Historic Voodoo Museum *(see p103)*, a quirky little museum crammed with artifacts and images and staffed by experts who can share the stories of these ancient traditions. The museum also offers a walking cemetery tour where you can visit the grave of Marie Laveau, meet with a voodoo priestess, and learn the meaning behind voodoo rituals and objects.

LET THE GOOD TIMES ROLL!

Mardi Gras is more than beads, colorful parades and extravagant balls. The phrase "Mardi Gras" literally means "Fat Tuesday" in French and it marks the day before Ash Wednesday, the beginning of Lent. The term Fat Tuesday derives from the tradition to eat fat and lard in anticipation of a long period of fasting and sacrifice. Today the Mardi Gras festivities begin much earlier than the actual Tuesday before Lent. Celebrations start around January 6, just after the Christmas season is officially over and the party really heats up two weeks before Mardi Gras. Although Mardi Gras is celebrated in many cities around country, New Orleans is thought to best embody the idea of *laissez les bons temps roule* ("Let the good times roll!").

ASK PETER...

Q: What is the best way to see some of the famous cemeteries in New Orleans?
A: New Orleans' history comes alive in its cemeteries… so to speak. Learn the real stories of these local legends through an historical tour. New Orleans Spirit Tours takes you through the city's most famous cemetery, St. Louis No. 1, and shares the details of these architecturally significant tombs, the stories of its residents, and the influences of voodoo traditions. New Orleans' cemeteries can be a hotbed of petty crime, so you're best off going with an organized tour, especially if you plan to visit at night.

The Shops at Canal Place

333 Canal St. ☏504-522-9200. www.theshopsatcanalplace. com. Open Mon–Sat 10am–7pm, Sun noon–6pm.
With its soaring three-story atrium, its elegant, polished surfaces and sleekly designed storefronts, this glamorous multilevel shopping mall offers a quiet respite from the French Quarter clamor. Anchored by Saks Fifth Avenue department store, Canal Place features high-end retail outposts. The movie theater on the top floor takes dinner-and-a-movie to a whole new level with a gourmet cafe that serves small plates, snacks and cocktails for in-theater dining.

Audubon Insectarium★

▶ *Allow 90min. 423 Canal St. ☏504-410-2847. www.audubon-institute.org. Open Tue–Sun 10am–5pm. $15.95.*
Creeping, crawling, tunneling, flying—the denizens of the insect world are the focus of this award-winning entomology museum, the newest facility of the Audubon Nature Institute. Occupying part of the renovated lower floor of the massive gray **US Custom House** (1881), the kid-oriented museum uses hardcore science and state-of-the-art displays to entice visitors to explore the fascinating world of insects. Scale models and live specimens (including a hardworking colony of leafcutter ants and a giant Malaysian weevil) inhabit the Prehistoric Earth Hallway, which highlights the endurance and adaptability of the ancestors of some of today's insects. In the walk-through Underground Gallery, everything is supersized so you can see the

world from a bug's point of view. New Orleans and Louisiana form the framework for displays about mosquitoes, termites and other critters that complicate life for those of us who share their planet. Chef-facilitators in Bug Appétit give cooking demonstrations using insect ingredients; if you like, you can sample buggy treats like chocolate chirp cookies (made with grasshoppers) or six-legged salsa while learning about insects' role as a nutrient source in culinary cultures around the world. For a hands-on experience stop by Field Camp, where entomologists introduce you a variety of live specimens. In the Metamorphosis Gallery, a working lab, you'll see racks of various creatures in the process of transitioning from one life stage to the next; time it right and you may see a butterfly emerge from its chrysalis. In the Butterfly Gallery, a perennial favorite, you can walk about a calm, Asian-inspired space, admiring the graceful, fluttering creatures up close.

Travel Tip:
Learn to talk like a local. In New Orleans, you don't hop on a "trolley" because it's always referred to as streetcar. A "krewe" has nothing to do with street gangs, but are long-running organizations that host the parades and balls during Mardi Gras. There's no long "a" when you buy a box of "praw-leens." And if you've ever been in doubt about the correct pronunciation of the city, do as the locals do, and say "N'awlins."

Decatur Street

Busy Decatur Street runs from Canal Street across the river edge of the French Quarter. Souvenir and specialty stores and a few restaurants crowd each other along the blocks nearest Canal, while canned zydeco music blares forth from a bar or two. If you want to bring home a Mardi Gras mask, a ribald T-shirt, some choice beads, or the makings for your next costume, this is a good place to browse. Decatur Street crosses the foot of Jackson Square before continuing alongside the French Market downriver; this section boasts more specialty stores, better restaurants and a few choice jazz venues including the Palm Court Café (1204 Decatur St.).

Jean Lafitte National Historical Park Visitor Center★

❍ Allow 30min. 419 Decatur St. ℘ 504-589-2636. www.nps. gov/jela/Frenchquarter.htm. Open daily 9am–5pm.
Make a stop at this excellent visitor center a priority; it's a wonderful complement to any exploration of the French Quarter and a great way to get an understanding of the relationship between New Orleans' unique geography and its history. The park operates six sites located throughout New Orleans and Acadiana; each focuses on a different

Location:
Decatur Street
runs perpendicular
to Canal Street,
becoming Magazine
Street on the uptown
side of Canal.

aspect of regional culture, history or natural history. Here at the French Quarter visitor center, you'll learn about the various cultures (Native American, French, Spanish, African and Irish) that made up the early population of the city, and how their traditions created the particularities of language, music, food, architecture and traditions that make New Orleans such a vastly interesting place today.

Be sure to make your way around the "listening station," where you can hear samples of musical traditions like folk, jazz, brass bands, Cajun, zydeco and gospel.

New Orleans Jazz National Historic Park

◯ *Allow 15min. 916 N. Peters St.* ✆ *504-589-494.*
www.nps.gov/jazz. Open Tue–Sun 9am–5pm.

Preserving and celebrating New Orleans' historic role as the birthplace of jazz music, this modest park office and visitor center houses a jazz library, bookstore, a small performance venue and a well-stocked information desk where rangers can direct you to jazz-related sights around the city.

The park's rangers (many of them accomplished jazz musicians) organize walking tours and demonstrations, host jazz-related live performances and lectures, and maintain and operate Perseverance Hall *(Sat 9am–5pm)* in **Louis Armstrong Park** *(see p136)*, home to a weekly hands-on jam session where anyone can jump in to learn to perform in a traditional New Orleans brass band. The park offers brochures for self-guided tours of the Jazz Walk of Fame (across the river in Algiers Point) and Jazz History tours of several neighborhoods around the city. You can also access the park's collection of narrated tours by cell phone and mp3 download.

French Market★

◯ *Allow 1hr. 1008 N. St Peters St.* ✆ *504-596-3420.*
www.frenchmarket.org. Open daily 7am–7pm.

Extending downriver along the levee from **Jackson Square★★**, this marketplace complex was constructed in 1813 on a site used by Native Americans as their trading post. Through the 19C the bustling market attracted farmers, butchers and fishmongers serving the daily needs of New Orleans' Creole population. The buildings have been renovated many times in the decades since, and now house stores and restaurants extending over six blocks. As you move downriver away from **Jackson Square★★**, cross Ursuline Street to enter the Farmer's Market Building,

housing snack stands and fresh produce vendors; it's the perfect place to pick up traditional Big Easy foodstuffs like hot sauce, jambalaya seasoning and pralines. Farther on you'll enter the open-air Flea Market building, burgeoning with a superabundance of trinkets, souvenirs, apparel and accessories. The Decatur Street façade of the market overlooks tiny Latrobe Park, a pleasant seating area shaded by trees. If you're hungry, step across Decatur Street to the old Central Grocery *(923 Decatur St.)* and pick up a muffaletta, the pungent New Orleans sandwich made of Italian deli meats and cheeses layered on round bread and spiked with chopped-olive salad.

Old US Mint

◯ *Allow 30min. 400 Esplanade Ave. ℘ 504-568-6968. http://lsm.crt.state.la.us. Open year-round Tue–Sat 9am–5pm. $6.*

This National Historic Landmark building at the foot of **Esplanade Avenue★** has the distinction of being the only place to mint coins for both the US and the Confederacy. Completed in 1835, the imposing red-brick Greek Revival-style building was designed by prominent architect William Strickland, whose credits include the US Capitol in Washington, DC.

The mint began operations in 1838, after President Andrew Jackson lobbied for its establishment to help finance development of the nation's western frontier. After Louisiana seceded from the Union in 1861, the facility was used to house Rebel troops and to make coins for the Confederacy.

When the Federal army occupied New Orleans the following year, the mint was put back to work for the Federal government. It ceased operations once and for all in 1909, after turning out a sum total of about $300-million worth of gold and silver coins during its somewhat schizophrenic career. The building was transferred to the state and is now operated by the Louisiana State Museum. The first-floor displays trace the mint's history with photographs, coins (look for the rare Confederate half-dollar) and antique minting tools such as scales, balances and a massive coin press capable of exerting 12,000 pounds of pressure.

By 2013 the building's upper floor is slated to house the excellent jazz memorabilia collections of the New Orleans Jazz National Park; the collections include recordings, rare photographs and treasured instruments including Louis Armstrong's cornet and Dizzy Gillespie's trumpet.

Travel Tip:

The French Market is one of the oldest city markets in the country. Don't expect to pay by credit card and get ready to haggle over produce. At the weekend flea market, vendors know they are in a good position to overcharge a tourist, so think of list prices as the opening bid. More often than not, vendors will bargain with you, especially for large or multiple items.

Location:
Chartres Street
parallels Royal and
Decatur streets.
Uptown of Canal
Street, it connects
with Camp Street.

Chartres Street

This bustling commercial street crosses the Quarter past a mix of residential buildings, iconic restaurants and stores ranging from high-end to downscale, stocking items from luxury lingerie and handmade perfumes to funky antiques and novel accessories for the home. Le Petit Théâtre du Vieux Carré, a popular and well-regarded community theater ("little theater") founded in 1916, occupies the pink building at the intersection of St. Peter Street, on the corner of Jackson Square (the building was erected in 1922 and incorporated parts of a Spanish Colonial structure from the 1790s). Chartres Street passes directly between St. Louis Cathedral and Jackson Square with its welter of fortune tellers, musicians and street performers.

Old Ursuline Convent

◐ *Allow 20min. 1100 Chartres St. ☏ 504-529-3040. www.stlouiscathedral.org. Open Mon–Sat 10am–4pm. $5.*

The handsome complex of French Colonial-style buildings fronting Chartres Street ranks as the oldest structure in the Mississippi Valley. Erected by architect Ignace François Broutin and builder Claude Joseph Villars Debreuil between 1745 and 1752, the original complex (many times renovated and expanded) replaced an earlier compound built in 1734 to house a community of 12 Ursuline nuns who landed in New Orleans at the behest of sieur de Bienville. The city's founder had requested the presence of a religious order to provide medical care for the community's poor and to establish a school for girls. In addition to founding the city's first hospital, the nuns also established an orphanage, taking in the children of French colonists who perished during the Natchez massacre of 1729.

In 1824 the Ursulines relocated their community and school to newer quarters in uptown New Orleans, and the complex became the residence of the Archbishop of New Orleans. In the years since it has served variously as a priests' residence and even for a short time as the state capital.

Today it houses the archives and research center of the Archdiocese of New Orleans, and the restored first-floor rooms, church and rear garden are open for self-guided tours. Especially interesting are the sketches of various plans that detail the history of the structure, and a handwritten letter from President Thomas Jefferson, offering protection and assuring the Ursulines that the transfer of New Orleans to the US would not disrupt their mission in New Orleans. Adjacent to the convent, St. Mary's Church was built in 1845 as the chapel of the archbishops. Today the pretty church, where masses are still held daily, is also open for visits.

Beauregard-Keyes House and Garden★

➲ *Allow 45min. 1113 Chartres St. ℘504-523-7257. www.bkhouse.org. Visit by guided tour only year-round Mon–Sat 10am–3pm. $10.*

Well-to-do auctioneer Joseph Le Carpentier built this romantic home in the heart of the French Quarter in 1826, along with an unusual side garden (most French Quarter gardens were tucked away in walled courtyards).

The house is also distinctive for its Greek Revival elements like the pedimented front portico and the curving side staircases. In 1833 the property came into the possession of John A. Merle, Switzerland's consul in New Orleans, and his wife. Madame Merle planned and planted a formal French parterre garden here, enclosing it with brick walls outfitted with grille windows, to give passersby a glimpse of the greenery within.

The house takes its name from two of its later owners, however: Confederate general Pierre G.T. Beauregard—the commander who ordered the first cannon shot at Fort Sumter—who rented the home and lived here briefly after the Civil War; and prolific American writer Frances Parkinson Keyes, who restored both the house and garden to their antebellum condition in the 1940s and lived here until her death in 1970.

Knowledgeable docents lead tours highlighting the stories of the home's various occupants. Keyes' studio contains many of her manuscripts. You'll also see her doll and costume collections here as well as Beauregard family heirlooms and portraits.

Napoleon House Bar and Cafe

500 Chartres St. ℘504-524-9752. www.napoleonhouse.com.
This grand corner townhouse, graced with upper-story dormers and a central octagonal cupola, was built in 1814 for New Orleans' first mayor, Nicholas Girod, a Napoleon sympathizer who, as legend has it, offered the second-floor apartment as a refuge to the exiled French emperor. Napoleon never actually came here—he died before he

Travel Tip:
Although most people associate New Orleans with *beignets* and po-boys, the Culinary History Tour covers all that, and much more. The walking and tasting tours take you to historic restaurants whose food has shaped the New Orleans culture—and explains all the differences between Cajun and Creole food. Yes, you're on a tour, but you're visiting many of the city's most established restaurants in one day and you don't have to score a reservation or wait for hours to get a table.

FRANCES PARKINSON KEYES

Born in Charlottesville, Virginia where her father headed the Greek department at the University of Virginia, Frances Parkinson Keyes (1885-1970) published her first novel, *Old Grey Homestead* in 1919. Her husband, Senator Henry Wilder Keyes, died in 1938, after which time Frances began spending winters in New Orleans. There she devoted herself to writing and to restoring the French Quarter house she purchased in 1944.

Ignoring curious fans, who came daily to peer through her windows, Keyes eventually set up her study in the home's former slave quarters. She wrote more than 20 of her 51 books at the house, including *Dinner At Antoine's*, *The Chess Players* and *Blue Camellia*.

could take Girod up on his offer—but the name and the legend stuck, and today the house is best known as one of the French Quarter's most atmospheric bar/restaurants. It's hard to beat the place for ambience—dark and a little dingy, with peeling paint, chipped plaster, wooden beams and low lighting from various mismatched fixtures.

The lush courtyard is a good spot to order the house' signature drink, a Pimm's Cup, listen to soothing classical or jazz music and take a break from your French Quarter wanderings.

New Orleans Pharmacy Museum

◐ *Allow 30min. 514 Chartres St. ☎ 504-565-8027. www.pharmacymuseum.org. Open year-round Tue–Fri 10am–2pm; Sat 10am–5pm. $5.*

Apothecary shop of the nation's first licensed pharmacist, Louis J. Dufilho Jr., this 1823 building passed through several owners and even served as a paper warehouse before being purchased by the city and opened as a pharmacy museum. Today it houses a fascinating, and sometimes grim, collection of Civil War-era surgical tools, rare patent medications, live leeches and blood-letting instruments. There are plenty of "miracle" cures at hand, including the aphrodisiac Spanish Fly and Lydia Pinkham's famous vitamins that promised "a baby in every bottle," all displayed in

Travel Tip:

New Orleans is renowned for its cocktails, and the Pimm's Cup at Napoleon House Bar and Cafe is famous. Other venues to get the best include the Sazerac Bar inside Roosevelt Hotel— order a potent sazerac or a more refreshing Ramos Gin Fizz. The Carousel Bar inside Hotel Monteleone is the birthplace of the Vieux Carré, made with rye whiskey, cognac and bitters.

gorgeous antique mahogany cabinets.

Note the massive 1855 Italian marble soda fountain; donated to the collection by the St. Louis College of Pharmacy, the fountain pays homage to the tradition of soda fountains in drugstores, one that dates back to the 1830s when pharmacists would mix bitter-tasting medicines with phosphates and flavorings to make them go down easier. The newly renovated walled courtyard is planted with traditional medicinal herbs.

Maspero's Exchange

440 Chartres St. ✆ 504-524-8990.
www.pierremasperosrestaurant.com.

The two-story gray building at the corner of Chartres and Toulouse streets *(1788)*, now a popular restaurant, was the site of a coffee house and bustling exchange market where slaves were bought and sold through the mid-19C. It's also reputed to be the site of secret meetings where citizens and leaders such as Andrew Jackson and pirate Jean Lafitte met to plan the city's defense against British invaders before the Battle of New Orleans.

Travel Tip:
Every year, the New Orleans Culinary and Cultural Preservation Society organizes Tales of the Cocktail, the country's premier mixology festival celebrating classic drinks and modern creations. Tickets can be bought online: www.talesof thecocktail.com.

BRULATOUR PATIO

Popularly known as the Brulatour Patio *(520 Royal St.)*, the small paved space behind Seignouret House was built by Francois Seignouret in 1816 as a place to keep horses and carriages. During the 1930s, the courtyard became home to the New Orleans Art League, where it displayed original paintings by local artists. Architecturally, it's one of the most historic and recognizable landmarks in the French Quarter with pronounced arches, a mezzanine and a sweeping staircase. From 1948 until 1998, the patio was open to the public and regularly featured in the media. Since then, it has been sold to the Monteleone family and is no longer open for public visits. The family has plans to develop the buildings surrounding the patio into a retail business, which means it could be open once again very soon.

Location:
Royal Street parallels
Bourbon and Chartres
streets, hooking
up with St. Charles
Avenue when it
crosses Canal Street.
The blocks between
St. Louis and St. Anne
streets are closed
to traffic daily in
the afternoon.

Royal Street★★

Parallel to and one block away from bawdy Bourbon Street, Royal Street is better known for upscale elegance than downscale partying. Some of the French Quarter's loveliest mansions (some graced with intricately whorled galleries of wrought and cast iron) line the street; many date from the Spanish Colonial era and have been owned by the same families for generations. Shopping (and window-shopping) is the main draw for visitors here, as Royal Street boasts a noble array of art galleries and antique shops of the highest order, most of them lining the blocks between Iberville Street and Orleans Avenue.

Rising near the center of the Quarter is the massive and elegant Omni Royal Orleans hotel *(see p171)*. The street is a welcoming place for a leisurely stroll, with stops to browse through showrooms for art and antiques; to peek through carriageways at interior courtyards; to gaze upward at plant-festooned balconies; or to take in the stylings of the street performers who set up shop on the barricaded blocks between St. Louis and St. Ann streets.

Exchange Alley

This charming lane extending from Canal to Conti streets between Royal and Chartres streets is one of the few French Quarter streets that was not part of Adrien de Pauger's original plan for the city. The alley was carved out in the 1830s as an approach for the grandiose St. Louis Hotel, outpost of Creole society in the early 19C. Today graced by stylish lampposts, the lane boasts picturesque façades and pleasant cafes.

Louisiana Supreme Court Building

◗ *Allow 30min. 400 Royal St.* ✆ *504-310-2588. www.lasc.org. Open Mon–Fri 9am–5pm; guided tours available by appointment.*

The massive white marble Beaux-Arts style pile occupying the entire block between Royal, Conti, Chartres and St. Louis streets was completed in 1910 to house the Louisiana Supreme Court and the Orleans Parish Civil District Court. It's a striking example of the American Beaux-Arts style, although the builders were severely criticized for having razed several fine old Creole buildings to clear the

Travel Tip:
Antoine's *(see p177)* is
the oldest family-run
restaurant in the
country and it's best
known for inventing
oysters Rockefeller.
You'll find all sorts
of old-timey dishes
still on the menu
such as Baked Alaska.
Reservations at this
elegant restaurant
fill up fast, but try to
score a table for the
Sunday jazz brunch.

ST. LOUIS HOTEL

In 1838, at the height of the cultural rivalry between
established Creole and newly arrived American residents of
New Orleans, the doors opened on a grand new hotel on St.
Louis Street between Royal and Chartres streets. Designed
by Frenchman J.N.B. de Pouilly, the Creoles' architect of
choice, the lavish four-story structure was intended as a
business and social center to boost the reputation (and
property values) of the French Quarter against the ascendant
popularity of the American Sector across Canal Street. Its
huge central rotunda was the business center of the Quarter
as merchants, aristocrats and auctioneers gathered to
buy, sell and trade everything from real estate to stocks to
slaves. The hotel business faltered after the Civil War (during
which it served as a military hospital); the building fell into
ruin in the early 20C and was completely destroyed by the
great hurricane of 1915. In 1960 the structure was rebuilt,
designed by architects Arthur Davis and Samuel Wilson Jr,
with architectural nods to its predecessor including its famed
arches and Spanish wrought-iron railings. It now operates as
the elegant 346-room Omni Royal Orleans, carrying on the
tradition of grand French Quarter hotels.

site. A massive renovation was completed in 2004; today
the Fourth Circuit Court, a law library and judicial offices
occupy the building in addition to the state Supreme
Court. The Royal Street entrance accesses a law museum
on the first floor; the building also houses a fascinating collection of rare books.

Historic New Orleans Collection★

533 Royal St. ☎ 504-523-4662. www.hnoc.org.
Open year-round Tue–Sat 9:30am–4:30pm, Sun 1:30am–
4:30pm. Guided tours of residence and history galleries
available ($5); downstairs gallery free.

This private archive is housed in a beautifully restored
18C Spanish Colonial manse that managed to survive the
city's 1794 fire intact. Changing exhibits fill the first-floor
Williams Gallery, and an incredible group of maps, historic
documents, drawings and sketches can be viewed on a
guided tour of the 1792 Merieult House, which includes
the Louisiana History Galleries upstairs. Compiling the Historic New Orleans Collection was the passionate project

of the late General L. Kemper Williams and his wife, Leila, French Quarter preservationists who spent a lifetime chronicling their city's illustrious past. They purchased their residence, an 1889 Trapolin townhouse, in 1938 and lived there until 1964. After the general's death in 1971, the Williams' home was opened to the public.

The research collection is especially strong in documents relating to the Battle of New Orleans and the War of 1812 in the South, including rare books, maps and plans that collectively tell the story of one of the greatest military upsets of all time. If time permits, take the tour of the Williams' residence, decked out with gorgeous early-20C Louisiana antiques and Chinese porcelains. Boasting some 6,000 city-related documents, the research center *(410 Chartres St.; ✆ 504-598-7171)*, is staffed by helpful and knowledgeable history hounds, who can track down documents and materials relating to famous floods and fires, infamous town citizens like voodoo queen Marie Laveau, and architectural plans of some of the city's most famous buildings.

LaBranche Buildings
700 Royal St. at St. Peter St.
Visitors to the French Quarter routinely train their cameras on the lovely LaBranche buildings rising majestically along Royal Street at the corner of St. Peter Street. Built in 1840, they are the epitome of Creole elegance. There are actually three LaBranche buildings; the three-story brick townhouses were built as investment properties by the wealthy widow of a Creole sugarcane planter, and are justly famed for their intricate cast-iron balconies, often draped with plants (and, during Carnival season, beads). Look for the figures of oak leaves and acorns entwined in the curlicued ironwork.

Madame John's Legacy
632 Dumaine St. ✆ 504-568-6968. http://lsm.crt.state.la.us. Not open to the public.
This raised Creole cottage, one of the few 18C survivors in the Quarter, earned its enduring fame thanks to writer George Washington Cable, who used the house in his novella *Madame John's Legacy*, the story of how a quadroon, or mixed-race, mistress used her inheritance from her white lover. Separated by an L-shaped courtyard, the home's three buildings include a two-story *garçonnière*—a stand alone apartment that was used for older children or bachelors.

From the front, note that the brick ground level is actually a basement; the main living area occupied the upper level. Houses such as this were common throughout the French Quarter in the 18C. Now the property of the Louisiana State Museum, the residence is currently open only for special events.

Gallier House★
❍ *Allow 1hr. 1132 Royal St. ✆ 504-525-5661. www.hgghh.org. Open by guided tour only year-round Mon & Fri 10am–2pm, Sat noon–3pm. $10; combination tickets available with Hermann-Grima House.*

Noted New Orleans architect James Gallier, Jr., whose architect father designed **Gallier Hall**★ *(see p110)*, built this side-hall, Italianate townhouse as his own residence in 1857. Gallier the younger and his father also designed the **Pontalba Buildings**★, the old French Opera House (which burned down in 1919) and the original St. Charles Hotel.

The Gallier House has been lovingly restored and is grandly furnished in the style of an upper-middle-class family in the 1860s. Notable for its wrought-iron arches on the second-floor galleries outside, and inside for its Corinthian columns, etched-glass skylight and gas chandeliers, the house is open to visitors by guided tour. Docents lead groups through the interior garden, the elegant carriageway and the restored slave quarters.

Take a moment to look through the carriageway; it may be the only one in the city with a carriage parked in it. Anne Rice fans should note that this was the house the author had in mind when she described Louis and Lestat's residence in *Interview with a Vampire*.

LaLaurie Mansion

1140 Royal St.

A dark reputation shadows the elegant building at the corner of Royal and Gov. Nicholls streets. The mansion, built in 1832, was home to the wealthy socialite LaLaurie family who lived here until 1834 when, according to newspaper reports, a fire broke out in the residence and responders discovered a number of slaves who had been imprisoned and apparently tortured. As the story goes, a mob of enraged citizens attacked the home, forcing the family to flee. The house has changed hands many times, and now figures on most lists of haunted sites in New Orleans.

Bourbon Street★

Year-round but especially at Mardi Gras time, Bourbon Street teems with cocktail-toting revelers who come to celebrate, to drown their sorrows or simply to indulge in the pleasures of this unabashedly hedonistic city. The scene along Bourbon Street almost any night of the week is one of concentrated, dedicated party-

Travel Tip:
In 2011, New Orleans became a bicycle-friendly city. The city recently added more bicycle lanes, racks and other cycle-friendly amenities, so it's easy to get around. Opt out of hailing a cab and instead rent a bike in the French Quarter through Ride This Bike. www.ride thisbike.com.

Location:

Bourbon Street parallels Royal and Dauphine streets, becoming Carondelet Street on the uptown side of Canal Street. Much of Bourbon is blocked off to vehicles daily, starting late afternoon.

ing; it's the modern-day culmination of New Orleane-ans' historic dedication to their motto, *"Laissez les bons temps rouler!"* **Lights flash, music booms and hawkers stand in doorways touting the dubious wanton pleasures within. If you're seeking a less rowdy nook, take a quick peek into Musical Legends Park (311 Bourbon St.), site of charming statues of Pete Fountain, Al Hirt, Fats Domino and other contributors to the city's musical character.**

Near the center of the street, the Bourbon Orleans Hotel *(see p170)* **ranks among the oldest and most storied hostelries in the French Quarter; its grand ballroom hosted social events as early as 1817.**

Preservation Hall★

◗ *Allow 1hr. 726 St. Peter St. ☏ 504-522-2841. http://preservationhall.com. Open nightly 8–11pm. $12.*

From the outside this modest French Quarter building doesn't bear the slightest resemblance to a concert hall. But it's the sound, not the look, that draws throngs nightly to the private-home-turned-performance-space to hear rollicking sets of traditional New Orleans-style jazz. Opened in 1961, Preservation Hall was founded to give local musicians a place to play New Orleans jazz, and to preserve traditional jazz as rock and modern jazz rose in popularity. Louis Armstrong called it the place "where you'll find all the greats," and his words are as true today as ever. On any given night you'll hear veteran musicians joining forces with up-and-coming artists to thrill rapt audiences of jazz aficionados (and perhaps, soon-to-be aficionados). Bands perform three sets each night, starting at 8:15, 9:15 and 10:15. Sets last about 45 minutes; entrance tickets are good for one set. Folks start lining up early to snag one of the few seats (benches, actually); most of the audience ends up on the floor or standing in the back. Bring the kids and prepare for a boisterous good time—this is one of most family-friendly jazz venues in town.

Travel Tip:

Breast baring during Mardi Gras is not as common as you may think… and it's actually illegal (you could be prosecuted if spotted by police). Try to stay away from the crowds on the ground on Bourbon Street. Instead try to get up on a balcony to watch the mayhem and have a few drinks with the locals mocking the questionably clothed tourists.

Hermann-Grima House★

◗ *Allow 1hr. 820 St. Louis St. ☏ 504-525-5661. www.hgghh.org. Visit by guided tour only year-round Mon, Tue, Thu & Fri 10am–2pm, Sat noon–3pm. $10; combination tickets available with Gallier House.*

This lovely home offers the opportunity to enter the world behind the French Quarter façades. The symmetrical, Federal-style brick mansion was built in 1831, long after the Spanish Colonial era that produced the majority of the French Quarter's architecture, so it stands out dramatically from the neighboring homes (although its iron balcony is a decidedly Creole flourish). Built in 1831 for German businessman Samuel Hermann and later owned by the Grima family for five generations, the house offers a peek into the lives of a wealthy Creole family living in antebellum New Orleans.

The handsome mansion with its courtyard garden (another Creole feature) boasts the only horse stable and functional outdoor kitchen in the Quarter. Its American design, complete with a center hall and double-hung windows, was revolutionary at the time.

The house was converted as a house museum in 1924 and its historic restoration was meticulous. Knowledgeable docents make this one of the city's most historically accurate tours. At Halloween, the house is draped in black bunting and docents explain 19C mourning customs.

Historic Voodoo Museum

◉ *Allow 15–30min. 724 Dumaine St. ℘ 504-680-0128. www.voodoomuseum.com. Open daily 10am–6pm. $7.*

Step into this modest museum arrayed in the rooms of a former French Quarter shop a few paces off Bourbon Street and enter into the mystical, mysterious world of voodoo, the charismatic spiritual practice that originated in West Africa and was carried here by slaves. Over time, voodoo traditions in New Orleans mingled with those of other European colonies such as Saint-Domingue (now Haiti) and with those of Native Americans to form a hodgepodge of ideas and practices that played (and continue to play) a role alongside Western religions in the spiritual lives of New Orleaneans.

As the museum makes clear, its mission is to illustrate, not to propagate, so expect no voodoo practitioners trying to hex you (or sell you a *gris-gris*). In the anteroom gaze up at a large portrait of Marie Laveau, New Orleans' famed 19C voodoo priestess and spiritual leader. A Creole Catholic hairdresser, Madame Laveau was sought out by believers as a healer, fortune-teller, and practitioner of voodoo, and became the focus of a cultlike following during her lifetime.

The museum has an intriguing collection of masks, ritual objects, voodoo dolls, paintings and *gris-gris*—charms made of natural materials that, when combined, are believed to confer powers on the owner.

Lafitte's Blacksmith Shop

941 Bourbon St. ℘ 504-593-9761. www.lafittesblacksmithshop.com.

Located a few blocks from the louder stretches of Bourbon Street, Lafitte's occupies one of the oldest Creole cottages in the city. Now a dingily atmospheric watering hole favored by locals, Lafitte's was constructed around 1772, more than a decade before the 1788 fire that destroyed most of the city; some of the façade's plaster topcoat has artfully worn away to reveal the traditional *briquet-entre-poteaux* (brick-between-posts) construction.

Gas lamps and candles keep the interior dark and moody. Legend has it that the building was once home to the family of the infamous pirate, Jean Lafitte, who ran a legitimate blacksmith shop up front and sold his illegal booty to fencers out the back door. Like most things Lafitte, the story is unsubstantiated, but it makes for a good yarn over an afternoon drink.

Musée Conti★

○ *Allow 30min. 917 Conti St. ℰ 504-525-2605.*
www.neworleanswaxmuseum.com. Open Mon, Fri & Sat 10am–4pm. $7.

Wax museums tend to be populated by statues of celebrities of the present or the recent past. This one takes a different tack—its 154 lifelike wax figures animate cunningly staged tableaux that bring approximately 300 years of New Orleans history to life. The city's history boasts no shortage of colorful personages and intriguing events; as you stroll past the scenes you'll see Napoleon in his bathtub having an argument with his brothers; Marie Laveau selling a charm to a wealthy young woman; the signing of the Louisiana Purchase; slaves being sold at auction; and a complex (and somewhat gory) scene from the Battle of New Orleans.

Costumes are historically accurate; the hair on the figures is human (inserted strand by strand), and overall the museum provides an entertaining way to learn about the twists and turns of New Orleans' history and culture. Be sure to spend some time examining the miniature diorama of a Mardi Gras Parade along Royal Street c.1900. Beyond the history section, a "haunted dungeon" includes a few mild frights populated by the likes of Dracula and the Wolf Man.

DINNER AND JAZZ
...LIKE A LOCAL

Everyone knows that New Orleans is the birthplace of jazz, and the improvised syncopated ragtime rhythms capture perfectly the laid-back city vibe. This city is one where locals love to get up and dance—New Orleans' venues attract such top-notch jazz performers that even its hotels becomes a local scene. Ask about the "jazz table" at Mélange Restaurant inside the Ritz-Carlton New Orleans (*921 Canal Street*), and spend an evening at the Royal Sonesta Hotel where Irvin Mayfield's Jazz Playhouse (*300 Bourbon Street*) has nightly shows. For fantastic jazz and great New Orleans cuisine, you won't want to miss these local haunts:

Palm Court Jazz Café
(1204 Decatur Street)
Check out this fully restored early 19C building where you can experience traditional New Orleans food with live jazz. The Palm Court often showcases five and six-piece jazz bands. The best part: there's a different band performing here every day of the week.

Funky Pirate
(610 Bourbon Street)
Don't come here looking for fine dining; but do come for some of the best live music in the city. There is music at the bar every evening, and New Orleans bands are featured on Sunday and Monday nights. You'll see it's one of

the of the quirkier bars in the city as soon as you walk through the doors—it's entirely done up in pirate décor.

Bombay Club
(830 Conti Street)
Another great spot for authentic jazz music. Not only can you listen to live jazz bands (from trios to quartets to groups of five or more) on weekends, but there is also a piano player filling the place with music each week night. Bombay Club also offers a menu of over one hundred different martinis.

Fritzel's Jazz Pub
(733 Bourbon Street)
A local institution since 1969, this New Orleans hangout showcases

traditional jazz played in an intimate and unpretentious setting. Local favorite Tim Laughlin and his Quartet are regularly featured at this pub.

Arnaud's
(813 Bienville Street)
This restaurant is known for its quintessential New Orleans cuisine and its weekly jazz brunch. But for more than fine dining and brunch, ask to be taken into the Mardi Gras museum upstairs, where there is a priceless collection of dazzling costumes and vintage photographs on display.

DISCOVERING

CBD AND THE WAREHOUSE ARTS DISTRICT

There's more to art in New Orleans than vendors hawking street art in the French Quarter and the historic works shown in museums. Want to see where contemporary art in New Orleans is made and where artists live? Then head to the revitalized warehouse district, known as the "SoHo of the South."

The neighborhood began as an industrial zone in the 19C, its warehouses were built to store grain, coffee, and other imported goods shipped through the port. In 1976 the neighborhood had an initial facelift with the opening of the Contemporary Arts Center. The 278sq m/3,000sq ft center has art on display as well as theater and dance performances and it fueled the fire for the area's revitalization, followed by the 1984 World's Fair. The area's abandoned warehouses became the home to contemporary art spaces, studios and galleries.

Most of the art galleries are located on Julia Street (aka Gallery Row). The galleries in the neighborhood host an evening Art Walk on the first Saturday of every month, where you can mingle with local and international artists showcasing their latest works. Today the chic arts district also has some of the city's top restaurants: does the name Emeril Lagasse ring a bell? *This New Orleans icon paved the way for foodie's when he opened Emeril's, (see p178)*.

Beyond Julia Street, a very different kind of art awaits at the New Orleans Glassworks and Printmaking Studio *(727 Magazine St.; www.neworleansglassworks.com)*. This isn't just about passive art appreciation. Master glass artists showcase their techniques, but you can also participate in a short class to make your own glass beads or other crafts.

Nearby, the National World War II Museum (formerly the D-Day Museum) is the multi-million-dollar brainchild of Stephen Ambrose, with tens of thousands of artifacts and exhibitions telling the many stories of the war and its heroes.

Looking up the length of Canal Street from top of the Trade Centre
Photo: © Sylvia Pitcher Photolibrary/Alamy

PETER'S TOP PICKS

 CULTURE

Head to the Ogden Museum for their vast collection of Southern art. **Ogden Museum of Southern Art (p 115)**

 GREEN SPACES

Explore the Mississippi at Algiers Point where you will find picturesque views and can take a ride on the water. **Algiers Point (p 112)**

 HISTORY

Check out the National World War II Museum to learn about the events of WWII and New Orleans' role. **National World War II Museum (p 116)**

 STAY

The Renaissance Arts Hotel is located in a historic warehouse, so you don't even have to walk out of the hotel lobby to see great art. **Renaissance New Orleans Arts Hotel (p 171)**

 SHOP

Shop at the Riverwalk Marketplace. Extending all the way from Julia Street to Canal Street, this riverfront street features jewelry, T-shirts and New Orleans souvenirs. **Riverwalk Marketplace (p 119)**

 EAT

The best place to find authentic Southern po-boys is Mother's restaurant. It can get very crowded at lunchtime, but it's worth the wait. My now favorite sandwich is served here: the "debris po-boy," which is loaded with unbelievably delicious bits of leftover meat. Emeril's restaurant is another neighborhood classic, perfect for a chic evening meal. **Mother's (p 178) Emeril's (p 178)**

 ENTERTAINMENT

Interested in Cajun music and dancing? There's no better way to explore this part of New Orleans than at Mulate's where Cajun is the only thing on the menu. **Mulate's (p 187)**

fast-food restaurants, a gaze up the boulevard still brings to mind its classy 20C heyday as a high-end shopping destination. At the foot of Canal Street, between the Hilton Hotel and the **Audubon Aquarium★★** *(see p88)*, you'll find the Canal Street Ferry landing, serving the town of Algiers across the river *(see sidebar p112)*.

Canal Street Line
www.norta.com. $1.25 (exact fare required).
The first streetcar line up Canal Street was established around the late 1830s, about the same time as the **St. Charles Avenue streetcar★★** line. Service was halted in the 1960s due to low demand, but in 2004 the line was refurbished and reopened. Today the red streetcars (copies of the original Perley cars, but with modern amenities) rumble up and down the entire length of Canal Street past the retail, medical and eventually residential sectors farther away from the river. At Carrollton Avenue the line splits off in two directions (look for the direction indicator at the top of the car). The Cemeteries branch heads all the way to the end of Canal Street where it intersects with City Park Avenue (historic cemeteries surround the terminus). The City Park-Museums branch heads up Carrollton Avenue to its terminus near the Lelong Avenue entrance to **City Park★** *(see p147)*, with easy access to the **New Orleans Museum of Art★** *(see p148)*. It takes about a half-hour to ride either branch end to end.

Roosevelt Hotel
❍ *Allow 15min. 123 Baronne St.* ✆ *504-648-1200. www.therooseveltneworleans.com.*
One of the *grande dames* of historic New Orleans hostelries, the Roosevelt is well worth a stop to get a taste of a particularly colorful aspect of New Orleans history. Opened here in the early 1920s, the hotel has hosted a glittering list of celebrities from the worlds of entertainment and politics including many US presidents. It's best known among Louisianians, however, as the New Orleans headquarters for controversial politician Huey P. Long, who maintained a suite here during his stint as a US senator in the 1930s. Walk through the magnificent coffered lobby, which stretches all the way through the building; near the University Place entrance you'll find an unusual and ornate conical pendulum clock, created for the Paris Exhibition in 1867. For a quintessential New Orleans experience, order a Sazerac cocktail (made with whiskey, bitters and simple syrup) or a Ramos Gin Fizz (gin, citrus juice, orange flower water, egg white, cream and sugar) in the historic Art Deco Sazerac Bar, and sip away while admiring the Social Realist murals created by Paul Ninas.

Church of the Immaculate Conception
❍ *Allow 15min. 130 Baronne St.* ✆ *504-529-1477. www.jesuitchurch.net.*
Completed in 1929, the beautiful "Jesuit Church," as it is known, was established by the Society of Jesus, the first religious order to accompany settlers

Travel Tip:
Between April
and June, take
advantage of
Wednesdays at
the Square.
Every Wednesday
Lafayette Square is
transformed into
a block party with
free concerts, food,
beer and soda.
The concerts
take place from
5–7:30pm, bring a
blanket and hang
out on the square
with the locals.

to New Orleans in 1725. The building sports an abundance of Moorish flourishes including the bronze exterior doors, the domed cupolas and exterior stonework, the ironwork pews and twisted columns, and the chandeliers. Be sure to admire the stained-glass windows, portraying Jesuit saints, which were crafted in Germany and France.

Lafayette Square

Bounded by St. Charles Ave. and Camp St., between Girod and Poydras streets.

Named for the French hero of the Revolutionary War, the Marquis de Lafayette, this square facing **Gallier Hall★** in today's Central Business District was the center of life for Americans living in New Orleans in the early 19C. The expanse of green, laid out in 1788, is the city's second oldest; only **Jackson Square★★** predates it. Among the statues that grace the square are images of Benjamin Franklin, statesman Henry Clay and local philanthropist John McDonough, whose belief that slaves should be educated led him to bankroll the city's free public schools.

Gallier Hall★

545 St. Charles Ave. Not open to the public.

You might find it odd that a building modeled on the Parthenon in Athens, Greece, symbolized all that was American in New Orleans, but that was, in fact, the case. At the time Gallier Hall was being constructed on **Lafayette**

JOHN MCDONOGH "THE MISER"

John McDonogh was a controversial philanthropist who left much of his wealth to fund schools for poor white and freed black children in New Orleans and Baltimore. A slave owner himself, he became active in the American Colonization Society, which facilitated black slaves to emigrate back to Africa. He also operated a scheme on his plantations whereby the slaves could "earn" their freedom over a number of years by working during leisure time. After his death in 1950, the New Orleans' education system benefited from his will and more than 30 "McDonogh schools" were built in and around the city. The schools became a lightning rod for desegregation protests in the 1950s, and in the 1970s, many were renamed in an effort to remove slaveholder names from public schools. Today, only a handful still bear his name.

WHAT'S IN A NAME?

Credit for the design of Gallier Hall goes to Irish architect James Gallier, Sr. Ironically, before coming to New Orleans, Gallier changed his name from Gallagher to Gallier in the hope of being better accepted by the city's Creole society. Apparently it worked, since Gallier's later commissions included the 1858 French Opera House (which burned down in the early 19C) and the majestic Pontalba Buildings on Jackson Square in the French Quarter, residence of choice for Creole society in the 19C.

Square (1845-53), the area west of Canal Street was the epicenter of the American population in New Orleans. This stately Greek Revival structure represented the fact that the Yankees were here to stay, much to the chagrin of their Gallic neighbors in the French Quarter just downriver. Made of Tuckahoe marble and fronted by massive double Ionic columns supporting figures of Justice, Liberty and Commerce, Gallier Hall served as the city hall for more than a century, shifting the city's base of power from the Creole-dominated French Quarter to the American Sector.

Today the building functions as a performance and reception space. Over the years, various New Orleans' VIPs, from Jefferson Davis and General P.G.T. Beauregard to local musical legend Ernie K-Doe (2001), have lain in state here. During Mardi Gras, the mayor of New Orleans traditionally watches the parades from the Gallier Hall steps, where he is toasted by the king or queen of each passing procession and symbolically transfers dominion over the city (just for the day) to Rex, King of Carnival.

Harrah's Casino

228 Poydras St. ✆ 504-533-6000. www.harrahsneworleans.com. Open 24hr daily year-round.

The massive building angling onto the foot of Canal Street opened in 1999 as the only land-based gaming facility with table games in the state—other casinos in Louisiana occupy riverboats, and only slot machines operate at the Fair Grounds Race Course *(see p191)*. The building occupies a wedge-shaped property covering several blocks, with entrances on both Canal and Poydras streets, and the main gaming floor is enormous.

Warehouse Arts District

Once storage central for the massive quantities of cotton, sugar and coffee that were shipped from the port of New Orleans, this district lost its sense of purpose as the city's shipping operations moved farther upriver. By the 1970s into the early 1980s as the wharves were

Location:
Bounded by
St. Charles Avenue,
Lafayette Street,
Convention Center
Boulevard and
the Pontchartrain
Expressway (H-90).

**Buses and
Streetcars:**
St. Charles Avenue
streetcar. Buses 5
Marigny–Bywater,
10 Tchoupitoulas or
11 Magazine.

torn down to make way for riverfront development, this area of abandoned warehouses became a no-man's land of crumbling industrial buildings. The opening of the Contemporary Arts Center in 1976 sparked a renaissance, and galleries began creeping slowly into the downtown backwater. The 1984 Louisiana World's Fair further called attention to the neighborhood, which was ripe for development. Soon 19C warehouses were being transformed into lofts, offices, galleries and upscale eateries. Today the Warehouse Arts District shines as the hub of the arts and culture scene in New Orleans, with art galleries clustered along Julia Street.

Civil War Museum★

◗ *Allow 1hr. 929 Camp St.* ☎ *504-523-4522. $7. Open Tue–Sat10am–4pm. www.confederatemuseum.com.*
Louisiana's oldest museum is home to the second-largest collection of Confederate memorabilia in the US, second only to the Museum of the Confederacy in Richmond, Virginia. Architect Thomas Sully designed this striking red-stone Romanesque building, with its beautiful interior cypress woodwork and 24ft ceiling, in 1891. Inside, more than 500 rare photographs offer a fascinating insight into early photography, with tintypes, ambrotypes, daguerreotypes, and *cartes de visites* showing portraits of Confederate officers and soldiers. Display cases along the sides feature uniforms, armaments and personal belongings, some from well-known Louisiana Confederate figures including General P.G.T. Beauregard and Franklin Gardner. Carefully preserved original battle flags line the walls; you'll also

ACROSS THE RIVER: ALGIERS POINT

A quick visit to picturesque Algiers Point on the West Bank of the Mississippi is a great way to take a break from the bustle of the French Quarter and the CBD. It's easy, fun and free to get there by ferry from the Canal Street Ferry landing. Ferries depart every 30min; the ride across is brief, but you'll love the views, especially on the return trip. Before you go, be sure to contact the New Orleans Jazz National Historical Park *(see p59)* for information about the Jazz Walk of Fame, a series of commemorative markers along the Algiers riverfront celebrating the musicians who made New Orleans the birthplace of jazz.

CIVIL WAR 1861-65

New Orleans played a huge role in the Civil War and the city's capture by Union soldiers was a pivotal moment in the war.

As the largest city in the Confederacy, New Orleans' location at the mouth of the Mississippi made it a highly strategic port city to export goods like cotton, tobacco, and sugar. Besides being a hub of commerce, there was also the New Orleans Mint, where much of the United States money was printed. By 1850, it was the sixth-largest city in the US and the largest in the Southern states. So when Louisiana voted to secede in 1861, it's no surprise that the Union army made capturing New Orleans its prime objective.

New Orleans supplied thousands of Confederate troops to the war effort, and its slave-driven industries made it one of the wealthiest cities in the south. On April 16, 1862, Captain David G. Farragut, in command of the Union's West Gulf Blockading Squadron, led an attack of the Mississippi's two greatest forts: Fort Jackson and Fort St. Philip. After more than a week of constant battle, the Union fleet demolished the ports. Once they made it through the ports, they arrived at the gates of New Orleans and conquered it without any further confrontation. Although the battle was devastating for the defensive ports on the Mississippi, the city itself was left relatively unscathed, which is why the city maintains its antebellum charm and pre-colonial architecture.

Given that the Union Army entered the city without much confrontation, there are few Civil War landmarks in New Orleans proper. You can check out the **New Orleans Civil War Museum** at the Confederate Memorial Hall *(see opposite)* where visitors can explore hundreds of artifacts from the war, including Confederate uniforms, original battle flags and a large collection of original Civil War portraiture and Southern art. In addition, there's the **Cabildo** *(see p84)*, part of the Louisiana State Museum complex in Jackson Square. This National Historic Monument served as the post-war home of the Louisiana Supreme Court, and has been meticulously restored to its original, authentic state. Beyond the museums, there are the cemeteries honoring those who lost their lives in war. Inside **Greenwood Cemetery** on City Park Avenue is a Confederate tomb that marks the mass grave of hundreds of Confederate soldiers. **Metairie Cemetery** *(see p152)* contains the remains of Gens. P.G.T. Beauregard, John B. Hood and Richard Taylor, as well as many other notables.

MERCEDES-BENZ SUPERDOME

1501 Girod St. General information: ☎ 504-587-3663.
Box office: ☎ 504-587-3822. www.superdome.com.

Looming like a giant metal spaceship at the edge of the CBD, "the Dome" was considered at the cutting-edge of arena design when it opened in 1975; it has been many times expanded and renovated in the years since. In 2011 Mercedes-Benz acquired the naming rights to the famed sports venue, and it was officially renamed. Home to the New Orleans Saints football team, the venue also hosts the annual Allstate Sugar Bowl and, every four years, the BCS national championship game determining the top college football team in the country. Six Superbowl championships and several men's and women's Final Four NCAA championships have been played here, and the Dome has staged memorable rock concerts by top-tier talent including the Rolling Stones, David Bowie, Pink Floyd, Paul McCartney and U2. It also hosts the main performance events of the extremely popular annual Essence Music Festival. In between sporting events, rock concerts and music festivals the dome is put into use for traveling rodeos, monster truck rallies and the like.

The Superdome and the events held within it make the news constantly, but never more so than in the days before and immediately after Hurricane Katrina *(see p33)*, when it was designated a "shelter of last resort" by the New Orleans mayoral administration. An estimated 30,000 people crowded into the facility to wait out the storm, many of them visitors to the city whose hotels had shut down, along with residents lacking the means to obey the mandatory evacuation order issued prior to the storm. Katrina's winds peeled off the Superdome's outer roof layer, ripped holes in the roof, cut off the electrical power and shut down water supplies to the facility, creating unendurable conditions for those sheltered within.

Following the storm, the Superdome was closed for a year for cleaning, renovations and repair (if you're attending an event in the Dome, look for the photographic chronology of the damage and repairs in the 200-level lobby above Gate A). Work was completed in time to host the New Orleans Saints 2006 season opener against the Atlanta Falcons, a game the Saints won in spades, rejuvenating the morale of the recovering city and replacing the memories of the dome as a scene of human suffering.

Superdome Fast Facts

- The imposing steel dome is 27 stories high.
- The building covers a 52-acre footprint.
- The Superdome seats 73,208 fans when it's filled to capacity.
- The dome is the world's largest continuous unsupported roof.
- The roof area extends over 9.7acres.

find an exceptional number of antique swords, guns and artillery including rare LeMat revolvers. A raised, dais like platform at the rear of the main hall is devoted to personal memorabilia from Jefferson Davis, President of the Confederacy; the items were transferred to the museum by Davis' widow upon his demise in 1889.

Ogden Museum of Southern Art

◑ *Allow 1hr. 925 Camp St. ☎504-539-9600. www.ogdenmuseum.org. Open year-round Wed–Mon 10am–5pm (Thu until 8:30pm). $10.*

The "O," as the Ogden Museum bills itself, is the place to gain an appreciation for Southern art and the American South. A striking 67,000sq ft complex affiliated with the Smithsonian Institution, the museum is home to one of the largest and most impressive assemblages of Southern art anywhere.

The Ogden celebrates the South's vivid spirit and patchwork of cultures through its exhibits, but also through an ongoing program of lectures, films and music. Named for businessman and philanthropist Roger H. Ogden, who donated the 1,200 pieces that form the core of the collection, the museum features works by artists in 15 states and the District of Columbia. When you first walk into the Ogden's dramatic, four-story atrium with its floating staircase, you'll know you're in for a truly engaging experience.

Wander the museum's 20 galleries, where works from the permanent collection as well as traveling shows are organized in chronologically and thematically arranged exhibits that chart major trends in the development of Southern art from the 18C to the 21C.

ART AND CULTURE IN THE AMERICAN SOUTH

It wasn't until recently that Southern Art was recognized as a distinct genre in the art world. Rather than highlighting just one form, it's comprised of several different movements from all over the American South, from Folk Art to Southern Expressionism to Modernism— and as an offshoot of Civil War-era portraiture. Check out one of the largest collections in the country at the Ogden Museum of Southern Art, a museum that has helped define and identify Southern visuals arts and culture. The collection has revived long-forgotten Southern artists and helps preserve the unique history of the South.

ASK PETER...

Q: Where should I stay if I want to explore the Warehouse Arts District?

A: You can get the best of both worlds at the Renaissance Arts Hotel, located inside a historic warehouse built in the early 20C. If you're in the area for the art, you don't even have to walk out of the hotel to find some of the best Southern Art in the area. In 2003, the hotel partnered with the Arthur Roger Gallery to open The Project Space, a huge gallery located on the first floor of the hotel.

Travel Tip:
For a real wartime
historical experience,
you can't beat the old
Warehouse District.
Don't just focus on
the Civil War: Learn
all about World War II
and the city's crucial
role in the war at the
World War II Museum.
Museum-only
entrance is at $19 per
adult, but military
in uniform get in for
free—or at a deep
discount with an ID.

Travel Tip:
Chef Daniel Link's
Cajun-style restaurant
Cochon has become
a "hard to get" dinner
reservation in town.
So if you want to have
a taste of Cochon
without the hassle of
making reservations,
head around the
corner during the
day for lunch at
Cochon Butcher *(900
Tchoupitoulas Street)*.
It's run by the same
people with the
same Cajun-inspired
menu, but it's geared
towards the lunch
crowd with authentic
appetizers and
gourmet sandwiches.

National World War II Museum★★

> Allow 3hr. 945 Magazine St. (entrance on Andrew Higgins Dr.). ℘ 504-528-1944. www.nationalww2museum.org. Open daily 9am–5pm. $19. Please note: Some sections of the museum contain graphic images of wartime death and destruction, and may not be suitable for young children.

This sobering but ultimately inspiring museum occupying a state-of-the-art facility in the Warehouse District presents the American experience of the most wide-ranging and transformative armed conflict in modern history. The museum was founded in 2000 as the **National D-Day Museum**, with a focus on the amphibious landing operations in Normandy on June 6, 1944 that turned the tide of the war. In 2004 a major addition expanded the display areas to cover the entire scope of the conflict in Europe and the Pacific, and the museum was renamed the National World War II Museum. The year 2009 brought the opening of a new facility across the street, housing an award-winning multimedia presentation, a performance venue and a restaurant. The museum continues its growth, with plans for three more pavilions to be completed in 2015 to further its mission of educating today's generations about the reasons for the war, how it was fought and its relevance today.

Enter the grand Louisiana Memorial Pavilion where you'll see large artifacts including a restored C-47 troop carrier aircraft and a Higgins boat, one of the shallow-draft 36-passenger transports—designed and built in New Orleans—credited by General Dwight D. Eisenhower with winning the war by enabling amphibious landings. From here you'll head up to the second floor, which details the expansionist policies of Germany, Italy and Japan in the 1930s, the bombing of Pearl Harbor in 1941, and the changes in the lives of ordinary Americans as their nation mobilized for war.

The third floor is entirely devoted to the Allied invasion of Normandy, dubbed "Operation Overlord," with sections on Hitler's defenses in Europe; the Allied leaders who planned and executed the invasion; deception techniques employed to confuse the enemy; the tension-fraught decision to proceed; and detailed accounts of the struggle to prevail at each of the Normandy beaches. Throughout, fiber-optic maps, photographs and videos paint a clear picture of the enormously complicated and critical invasion; mini-theaters scattered among the exhibits provide a closer look at various battles; and audio stations deliver

oral histories recorded by veterans and civilians. The exhibit continues with the progress of the war in the months following D-Day, the march to Berlin, and the surrender of German armed forces on VE-Day, May 7, 1945.

An extensive second-floor section details the war in the Pacific theater, with exhibits on the many D-Days (amphibious landings) in the South Sea islands and Japan. Throughout, video stations continuously screen short films highlighting personal histories and major conflicts such as the battles of Midway, the Philippines and the Leyte Gulf. This section ends with a moving treatment of the US decision to drop atomic bombs on the Japanese cities of Hiroshima and Nagasaki, and Japan's subsequent surrender in August 1945. Across the street, the museum's theater screens an emotion-packed 4-D presentation Beyond all Boundaries *(45min)*, featuring immersive special effects that plunge the viewer into the story of this war that changed the world.

Visitors can peer into (but not enter) the windows of the Restoration Pavilion, where pieces from the museum's ever-expanding collection of large artifacts including boats, vehicles and weapons, undergo restoration.

Contemporary Arts Center★

◑ *Allow 30min. 900 Camp St. at St. Joseph St.* ☏ *504-528-3800. www.cacno.org. Galleries open Thu–Sun 11am–4pm. $5.*

Founded in 1976, the Contemporary Arts Center (CAC) spurred the Warehouse District's renaissance as a center for visual art and culture in New Orleans. Dedicated to showcasing contemporary work by both up-and-coming and established visual and performing artists, this light-filled, beautifully renovated former warehouse space houses more than 10,000sq ft of gallery space, two theaters with a lively schedule of productions by established and emerging playwrights, musical programming and even all-star jam sessions. As a multidisciplinary arts center the CAC organizes exhibits and performances to appeal to different sectors of the community. Everyone, from sophisticated art buffs to children, can find something to enjoy here. Kid-centric shows regularly sell out, as did the recent Darwin the Dinosaur, combining puppetry, electroluminescent light and dance.

Contemporary visual arts exhibits are always noteworthy. CAC is well respected nationally, and its exhibits often travel around the country. Recent highlights include NOLA NOW, bringing together works by 35 local artists producing work in the challenged economic and sociopolitical environment of New Orleans. When you enter the lobby, be sure to notice the museum's front desk, created by sculptor Gene Koss as an undulating wave of glass plates.

Louisiana Children's Museum★

◑ *Allow 2hr. 420 Julia St.* ☏ *504-523-1357. www.lcm.org. Open Tue–Sat 9:30am–4.30pm, Sun noon–4:30pm. $6.*

Hands-on learning equals hands-on fun at this spunky children's museum, where kids from toddlers to age twelve are encouraged to discover the world throughout 45,000sq ft of learn-by-doing exhibits. Role-playing rules

Travel Tip:
New Orleans can be a very kid-friendly city, if you know where to go. For starters, riding on a streetcar is always a fun—and affordable—way to get around and see the city from a different perspective. The Louisiana Children's Museum has interactive exhibits for toddlers and young ones, and the Crescent City Lights Youth Theater puts on stage productions for kids ages three and up.

ASK PETER...

Q: Where can I learn how to make New Orleans-style cuisine?
A: You can learn to cook in the Central Business District at Crescent City Cooks. Locally owned and operated, the school has classes on traditional New Orleans cuisine, a cafe with baked goods and a retail store featuring items like Louisiana-style cooking utensils, spices, and recipes. You can take group, private, or semi-private classes daily. www.crescentcitycooks.com.

upstairs at Little Winn-Dixie, a pint-sized grocery store complete with dairy cases and cashiers; Kid's Cafe, for budding chefs-to-be; and Little Port of New Orleans where you can climb aboard a play tugboat or track a barge's cargo on an interactive global map.

Creativity rules at Art Trek, a miniature art studio, and at New Orleans: Proud to Call it Home, where model houses, floor plans and materials make it fun to learn about and recreate the city's architecture. Downstairs, you can lift, tug, pull and drag while getting to know the workings of various simple machines. Kids can also get charged up by a psychedelic-looking plasma ball, or step inside a giant bubble to see a rainbow of colors.

Riverwalk Marketplace

◑ *Allow 1hr. 500 Port of New Orleans Pl. ☎ 504-522-1555. www.riverwalkmarketplace.com. Open Mon–Sat 10am–7pm, Sun noon–6pm.*

Extending along the riverfront from the foot of Julia Street all the way to (and under) the Hilton Hotel at the foot of Canal Street, the Riverwalk unites a good assortment of popular retail chain stores along with purveyors of T-shirts, hot sauce, jewelry and Mardi Gras trinkets. The food court is an excellent spot to relax with a beverage or a local treat while watching the action on the river.

Southern Food and Beverage Museum

◑ *Allow 1hr. In the Riverwalk. ☎ 504-569-0405. http://southernfood.org. Open Mon–Sat 10am–7pm, Sun noon–6pm. $10.*

Foodie visitors salivate upon entering this remarkable small museum celebrating the multilayered culinary culture of the southern US, with a definite emphasis on New Orleans. Here you'll learn everything you need to know about many of the regional foodstuffs, recipes and beverages that can be difficult to locate outside New Orleans but so wonderful to indulge in while you're here.

The central gallery is dedicated to New Orleans' beloved Leah Chase, chef-owner of famed Dooky Chase restaurant. Here you'll find a wealth of information about coffee, chicory, sugar, meat products, seafood, produce and grains, and the ways in which New Orleans' diverse ethnicities applied tradition, innovation and experience to transform these simple local ingredients into iconic treats like gumbo, calas, *beignets*, jambalaya, *étouffée*, pralines, *boudin*, muffalettas and *café brulôt*.

A separate gallery houses the Museum of the American Cocktail, with a colorfully told history of liquor in the US, all illustrated by beautifully labeled bottles and glamorous cocktail trays. Note the astounding collection of absinthe spoons.

Preservation Resource Center

▶ *Allow 10min. 923 Tchoupitoulas St. ☎ 504-581-7032. www.prcno.org. Open Mon–Fri 9am–4:30pm, Sat noon–4:30pm.*

Fans of historic architecture should plan a quick stop at the visiting space of this organization dedicated to helping New Orleans homeowners preserve their architectural treasures. Among other information, the center offers maps and brochures to guide you through all of the city's architecturally significant neighborhoods.

Blaine Kern's Mardi Gras World★

▶ *Allow 1hr. 1380 Port of New Orleans Pl. ☎ 504-361-7821. www.mardigrasworld.com. Visit by guided tour only daily 9:30am–4:30pm. $19.95.*

If you can't visit New Orleans during Mardi Gras, you can at least get a taste of parade magic here. In the cavernous warehouse next to the upriver end of the New Orleans Convention Center, parade floats are created, refitted and repaired by Blaine Kern Studios, as they have been since 1947. Guided tours begin with a short film about Carnival (along with a slice of tasty king cake), then proceed through a historical exhibit before exploring the craft stores, artists' studios and warehouse where giant floats sit in silent storage throughout the year.

Along the way you'll learn about how krewes (as parading organizations are called) are formed and financed and how floats are reused and refitted according to changing themes. Signature floats—those that appear year after year—are brought to this warehouse for repair purposes; if you're lucky you may get an up-close look at beloved signature floats like the Leviathan (Krewe of Orpheus), the Bacchagator (Krewe of Bacchus), or the Boeuf Gras, symbol of the Krewe of Rex.

Travel Tip:

To drink like a local, head to the Rusty Nail *(1100 Constance Street; www.therustynail.biz).* Trust me you truly have to be a local to find it. It's tucked underneath the Cotton Mill Condo's and Crescent City Connection bridge, hidden in a corner. Known for its Scotch selection, the bar is also hopping in the day during football season. Root for the Saints and drink from the Bloody Mary bar.

GALLERY ROW
...LIKE A LOCAL

It's easy to explore the Warehouse Arts District like a local because that's exactly where you'll find the locals hanging out. Julia Street between Camp Street and Tchoupitoulas Street is the place to shop for cutting-edge contemporary art in New Orleans. Anchored by the innovative Contemporary Arts Center on Camp Street, this swath of the neighborhood showcases some of the region's finest artists, at their grittiest and most passionate. Most change their shows several times a year; check websites first to see what's hanging during your visit, or simply wander in at will. Most open Tuesday–Saturday.

On the first Saturday of every month is the city's premier **Art Walk event**. In the evening hours, locals walk among restored warehouse galleries to explore their latest exhibits and meet with the artists and gallery owners. From Southern art to contemporary crafts to the hands-on Children's Museum, there are more than a dozen galleries that open their doors to the public from 6pm to 9pm. The streets are lined with live brass brands, Zydeco and R&B musicians and food vendors selling mouthwatering treats.

Julia Street is also home to one of the most anticipated annual events in the city (no, not Mardi Gras!). It's **White Linen Night**, a massive block party where locals don their finest whites to celebrate New Orleans arts. This is one of the city's off-season events, taking place on the first Saturday of August.
Translation? It's hot, humid and crowded! So do as the locals do and pack your lightest whites before setting out to discover the vibrant visual art and live music. You can cool off with a cocktail at one of the many curbside bars, sit down for a full Cajun-style meal, or grab a cone at the New Orleans Ice Cream Company. The night ends at the Contemporary Arts Center after-party and fund-raiser with more art exhibitions and live music.

Jammin' on Julia is a springtime street party to raise funds for the The New Orleans Arts District, when the museums and galleries open their doors once again for strolling art aficionados, with live music, specialty cocktails, and outdoor dining. And the weather is much cooler, so no white clothes needed!

Best of all, the Warehouse Arts District is a designated Louisiana Cultural District, which means there is no sales tax tacked on to original works of art.

Here's a sampling of what you'll find on Gallery Row:

LeMieux Gallery *332 Julia St. 504-522-5988. www.lemieux galleries.com.* Presents "Third Coast art," work by Gulf Coast artists from Louisiana to Florida.

Soren-Christensen Gallery *400 Julia St. 504-569-9501. www.sorengallery.com.* Showcases paintings and sculpture by a stable of national and international artists.

Arthur Roger Gallery *432–434 Julia St. 504-522-1999. www.arthurrogergallery.com.* A leader in both regional and national contemporary art, as well as a powerful force on the New Orleans gallery scene.

Heriard-Cimino Gallery *440 Julia St. 504-525-7300. www.heriard-cimino.com.* Carries work by mid-career artists with established reputations, many from Louisiana.

Gallery Bienvenu *518 Julia St. 504-525-0518. www.gallerybienvenu.com.* Abstract and figurative paintings and sculpture from a thoughtfully selected cohort of emerging and mid-career artists from the US and abroad.

Ariodante Contemporary Craft Gallery *535 Julia St. 504-524-3233. http://ariodantegallery.com.* Features upscale crafts from mostly Gulf Coast region artists, at approachable prices.

Jean Bragg Gallery of Southern Art *600 Julia St. 504-895-7375. www.jeanbragg.com.* Louisiana paintings and pottery are the focus at this gallery re-established here in 2005. Jean Bragg is an important member of the arts community and her gallery hosts a different contemporary exhibition each month.

M. Francis Gallery *604 Julia St. 504-931-1935. www.mfrancisgallery.com.* The evolution of African American art and culture is on show at this inspiring and vibrant art "space." Programs and events (some for children) are held as well as exhibitions.

George Schmidt *626 Julia St. 504-592-0206. www.georgeschmidt.com.* Presents lively canvases that the gallery's namesake (who works and lives here) describes as "history painting, narrative art and other reactionary work on paper and canvas."

GARDEN DISTRICT AND UPTOWN

The Garden District may be residential, but that doesn't mean you should overlook it. For starters, it's far from your average residential neighborhood. I'm not talking about apartment complexes or small ranch houses. No, I'm talking about some of the most historic and grand Southern mansions in the city. In fact, the Garden District is part of a larger designated National Historic Landmark area, noted for the collection of homes representing architecture styles from antebellum to the early 20C. The leafy neighborhood was once inhabited by wealthy Southerners who did not want to live close to the Creole community in the French Quarter. Many of the 19C homes are still impeccably maintained and there are several notable and historic structures, including a handful of celebrity-owned homes. The Garden District boasts the fascinating and evocative Lafayette Cemetery, bounded by Washington Avenue, Prytania Street, Sixth Street and Coliseum Street. As one of the oldest above-ground cemeteries it does attract tourists, but it remains a peaceful place to stroll.

Visiting the Uptown District you're more likely feel like you're in a quaint village and not a cosmopolitan American city. It has its share of 19C houses and independent shops and also benefits from Audubon Park and the famed Zoological Gardens.

Magazine Street is the commercial part of the Garden District, filled with antique shops, art galleries, chain stores, cafes and locally owned restaurants. Parts of the six-mile stretch are perfect for a stroll: there's an appealing-if-funky stretch (coffeehouses, thrift stores, bars) from Felicity to Jackson, then it starts getting gradually more upscale as you proceed uptown. From Jefferson uptown through Nashville is pretty well-to-do (gourmet groceries, elegant clothing and decorating boutiques, nicer restaurants, spas and salons). The 11 Magazine bus runs all the way from Canal Street to the end of Audubon Park, so that's really the best way to visit the street from the French Quarter, hopping on and off. You could also take the St. Charles Avenue streetcar uptown from the French Quarter, then hop off and walk (7–10 blocks) down one of the main connecting streets i.e. Jackson, Louisiana, Napoleon, Jefferson, Nashville or State.

White mansion in traditional style in New Orleans' Garden District
Photo: © Natalia Bratslavsky/Bigstockphoto.com

PETER'S TOP PICKS

 CULTURE

The Latter Memorial Library is housed on the grounds of several prominent New Orleans family homes, so it naturally offers a lot of city history. **Latter Memorial Library** (p **131**)

 GREEN SPACES

Audubon Park, on the site of a former sugar plantation, is a can't miss when visiting the neighborhood. Bring your own picnic lunch and enjoy people watching. For a local's experience, head over to Coliseum Square in the Lower Garden District (closer to downtown), where you'll see people walking their dogs, or sitting out under the park's giant oak trees. **Audubon Park** (p **128**) **Coliseum Square** (p **129**)

 HISTORY

Lafayette Cemetery was established in 1833 and has been a burial ground for city residents through a Yellow Fever epidemic and Civil War. Save Our Cemeteries offers an excellent tour *(see p57)*. **Lafayette Cemetery** (p **126**)

 STAY

For a more homey experience, check out Sully Mansion Bed & Breakfast. It's walking distance from Magazine Street. **Sully Mansion Bed & Breakfast** (p **173**)

 SHOP

Magazine Street is a leisurely shopping experience with a lot of small independent stores and renovated warehouses to explore. **Magazine Street** (p **125** & p **195**)

 ENTERTAINMENT

Head way off the beaten path to Carrollton in the Uptown District, to the ever-so-divey Maple Leaf Bar. It was one of the first bars to re-open after Katrina and remains a great venue for live music seven nights a week. **Maple Leaf Bar** (p **187**)

Location:

St. Charles Street begins at Canal Street, runs west to Lee Circle (where it becomes St. Charles Avenue) and continues all the way uptown.

Buses and Streetcars:

St. Charles Avenue streetcar.

Travel Tip:

One of the most famous roast beef po-boy sandwiches in the city was at the Parasol Bar. The original owners sold it and moved three blocks down the street to Traceys (*2604 Magazine Street*) between Magazine Street and 3rd Street. The owners brought all their recipes with them and now if you want the famous Parasol's sandwiches, you have to go to Traceys.

St. Charles Avenue★★

Apart from the historic French Quarter, perhaps nothing symbolizes New Orleans more persuasively than the lovely boulevard that curves for four glorious miles from Lee Circle to Carrollton Avenue. Enormous live oak trees overhang it, antebelleum mansions line its flanks and historic streetcars rumble up and down its neutral ground (New Orleans-speak for the central median). Come Carnival season, some of New Orlean's most venerable krewes stage their parades along the stretch from Napoleon Avenue to downtown, tossing beads and other trinkets to throngs of delighted paradegoers (look for evidence of past parades dangling from trees and wires overhead).

Architecture buffs can drink in a panoply of styles including Greek Revival, Queen Anne, Beaux-Arts, Georgian Revival and Richardson Romanesque. Some of the architectural highlights include the Byzantine Revival Touro Synagogue (no 4224), the Colonial Revival façade of the Academy of the Sacred Heart (no 4521); the magnificent Richardson Romanesque Brown Mansion (no 4717); the Colonial Revival Wedding Cake House (no 5809); and the Georgian Revival Zemurray House (no 7000), now owned by Tulane University as its president's home.

St. Charles Avenue Streetcar★★

◗ *Allow 45min.* ✆ *504-827-7802. www.norta.com. Operates 24hrs/day (see website for schedule). $1.25 (exact fare required).*

Built for commuters between New Orleans and the then-suburb of Carrollton in 1835, the St. Charles Avenue streetcar line is the oldest continuously operated street railway line in the world today (the original cars were pulled by steam locomotive; the line was electrified in 1893). Designated a National Historic Landmark, the line runs from Canal Street along St. Charles Street to Lee Circle, then all the way to the end of St. Charles Avenue before making the bend onto Carrollton Avenue and terminating at Carrollton and Claiborne (a total of 7.5 miles). A one-way trip takes about 45 minutes during low traffic times (about 90 minutes during rush hour). Hopping aboard the cars and gliding past the beautiful homes of St. Charles Avenue is an easy, scenic way to travel from the **French**

MAGAZINE STREET ...LIKE A LOCAL

By turns colorful, rundown, funky, hip, upscale and downscale, Magazine Street undergoes several metamorphoses on its journey from Canal Street to Audubon Park uptown. The street lies between (and parallels the curves of) the Mississippi River and St. Charles Avenue, passing through various residential and commercial districts; the most interesting and walkable lie upriver of the Warehouse District. As you drive or walk the blocks (ranging from funky and working-class around the Lower Garden District to more upscale as you move toward Audubon Park), you'll pass restaurants, coffee shops, designer boutiques, day spas, second-hand stores, music shops, upscale import furniture showrooms, and gift shops of every stripe. There are a few spots that are die-hard local favorites—the best are locally owned and operated. More stores are listed in Your Stay in New Orleans (see p195–196).

Sucré

(3025 Magazine Street)
This "sweet boutique" showcases New Orleans' French influence in terms of pastry. Think macaroons that are works of art. There's also cupcakes, chocolates and other sweet treats.

Rendez-Vous Tavern

(3101 Magazine Street)
Loved by sports fans, this bar has 11 huge screens, an Internet jukebox and video poker machines; it's a man cave turned bar.

Mahony

(3454 Magazine Street)
An ever-popular spot for for po-boys. Here's a tip: there will probably be a wait at lunchtime, so go at off times or just chill at the bar and people watch.

Fleurty Girl

(3117 Magazine Street)
Opened by a New Orleans native who used her income tax money to start a T-shirt line. You can get anything you can think of that has to do with New Orleans, but it's much more than just a souvenir shop.

Funky Monkey

(3127 Magazine Street)
For a more vintage look, check out this store. It's a clothing exchange store that mixes new, used and vintage clothing for men and women with hipster styles. You can also find custom-made T-shirts and other more quirky items.

The Bulldog

(3236 Magazine Street)
This restaurant and bar has built a following with draft beers and excellent bar food. With more than 50 beers on tap and 100 more available in bottle form, the place is known for variety. But drinking here could almost be considered philanthropic. The Bulldog donates to the SPCA for every collectable pint glass returned to the bar.

Hazelnut

(5515 Magazine Street)
China, books, ceramics and other elegant gifts. The store's classic Southern charm is reminiscent of another era, and get this, one of the owners is *Mad Man* star Bryan Batt.

WALKING TOUR

Garden District★★★

Developed in the mid-19C by American entrepreneurs riding the tide of a formidable boom in cotton, sugar, shipping and finance, the Garden District boasts mansions of awe-inspiring size and beauty. Departing from French and Creole traditions, the styles here favor Victorian, Italianate and Greek Revival, entrancing lovers of noteworthy architecture *(see p35)*.

» *Begin at the Rink, an historic shopping arcade at the corner of Prytania St. and Washington Ave. From here, cross Prytania to the Washington Ave. entrance of Lafayette Cemetery.*

Lafayette Cemetery

1400 Washington Ave. http://lafayettecemetery.org.
Open Mon–Fri 7am–2:30pm, Sat 7am–noon.
Established here in the 1830s, this cemetery rewards slow wandering, to admire the beauty of its funerary architecture and the remarkable diversity of its deceased. Note the many graves of yellow fever and malaria victims as well as those of Civil War notables from both sides of the conflict.

Commander's Palace

1403 Washington Ave.
Established in 1883, this bright blue, turreted Victorian structure opposite the cemetery is a jewel in the Brennan family culinary crown, perennially ranked among the nation's top fine dining restaurants *(see p181)*.

» *Backtrack to Prytania St. and turn right.*

Colonel Robert Short's House

1448 Fourth St.
The elaborate cast-iron fence cordoning this grand Italianate villa *(1859)* designed by Henry Howard ranks among the loveliest architectural ironwork in the city; look for the rare cornstalk motif.

» *Continue down Prytania and turn right on Third St.*

Robinson House

1415 Third St.
Architects Henry Howard and James Gallier Jr. completed this striking mansion in 1865 for tobacco merchant Walter Robinson. Thanks to water collected on the roof, and carried by gravity into the home's water closets, its residents enjoyed an early form of indoor plumbing.

Musson House

1331 Third St.
Sided in pink and embellished with frothing cast-iron balconies, this corner villa *(1850)* was built for cotton broker Michel Musson, uncle of painter Edgar Degas.

Payne-Strachen House
1134 First St.
Jefferson Davis, former president of the Confederacy, passed away while visiting a friend at this five-bay Greek Revival home, built in 1849 for cotton broker Jacob Payne.

Rosegate
1239 First St.
Designed by James Calrow for wholesaling magnate Albert Brevard, this lovely double-galleried villa was purchased by famed novelist Anne Rice in 1989, and figured prominently in her book *The Witching Hour.*

Morris House
1331 First St.
A spectacular iron gallery adorns the two-story façade of this fanciful Italianate villa (1869).

Toby's Corner
2340 Prytania St.
Thought to be the oldest home in the Garden District, this Greek Revival mansion was built in 1838 for Philadelphia wheelwright Thomas Toby.

Bradish Johnson House and Louise S. McGehee School
2343 Prytania St.
Sugar magnate Bradish Johnson spent $100,000—close to $1.5 million today—to build this Second Empire-style mansion in 1872. Since 1929, the building has been home to the private Louise S. McGehee School for girls.

» *Continue to Camp St. and turn left to the intersection of First St.*

» *Continue toward Prytania St. on First St.*

» *Turn right on Prytania St.*

ANNE RICE

Novelist Anne Rice is synonymous with New Orleans. She spent her childhood and teenage years in the city and returned as an adult. Her love for the city is evident in her novels, particularly in the iconic *Vampire Chronicles* series. Although there are no longer organized tours focusing on her literary landmarks, most Garden District Tours will point out her former home at 1239 First Street (she moved to California in 2005 after the death of her husband). You can roam around Lafayette Cemetery, which inspired her as a child and was featured prominently in *Interview with a Vampire*.

Travel Tip:
A meal at Commander's Palace is a must, especially for its famous bread pudding souffle with whiskey sauce. Bow-tied waiters will serve you here, so go smart. To save money go for lunch instead of dinner and you'll get two courses starting at $16, plus 25 cent martinis!

Location:
Bounded by Louisiana Avenue, S. Claiborne Avenue, Leonidas Street and the Mississippi River.
Buses and Streetcars:
Buses 32 Leonidas (to the Riverbend), 11 Magazine, 10 Tchoupitoulas (to Audubon Park) or 15 Freret (to the universities).
St. Charles Avenue streetcar.

Quarter★★★ to the **Garden District★★★** and **Uptown★** sights such as the **Audubon Zoo★★**, Tulane University and the Riverbend.

Uptown★

"Uptown" is an umbrella term that describes the areas upriver from Louisiana Avenue all the way to the Riverbend (the neighborhood between Audubon Park and the bend of the Mississippi), and between Claiborne Avenue and the river. Students, young professionals, bohemian hipsters and New Orleans high society all make their homes here. Along St. Charles Avenue and the broader streets that intersect it (Napoleon, Jefferson, Nashville and State) you'll find mansions of jaw-dropping size and beauty, many of which have been owned by the same families for generations. Distinguished Tulane and Loyola Universities are located in the universities area across from beautiful Audubon Park, location of the famed Audubon Zoo.

Audubon Park★★

Bounded by St. Charles Ave., Walnut & Calhoun streets and the Mississippi River. www.auduboninstitute.org. Open daily 5am–10pm.

Across **Magazine Street★** from the zoo lies Audubon Park. Formerly the site of a 400-acre sugar plantation, this space served as a Union encampment during the Civil War and as the site of the 1884 World's Cotton Centennial, which sparked residential development of uptown New Orleans. A nephew of Frederick Law Olmsted designed

ASK PETER...

Q: Is there any way to get a peek into private gardens?
A: In the spring, don't miss the Secret Garden Tour. The guided tour gives visitors a look into the private gardens of homes in Uptown New Orleans. Operated by volunteers, the Secret Garden Tour raises funds for brain injury programs throughout the state of Louisiana. www.secretgardenstour.org.

BIRD ISLAND

The east side of Audubon Park is home to Ochsner Island, known to locals as "Bird Island." In recent years herons, egrets and cormorants have been seen nesting in trees above the lagoon, and the rookery has been a popular site for birdwatching. However, 2011 saw a decline in the number of birds that returned, and in the spring, all the birds mysteriously abandoned their nests. Numerous theories abound, including human disturbances, animal predators and a storm. It is hoped that the following years will see a return of New Orleans' feathered friends.

THE IRISH CHANNEL

Bounded by Magazine Street and the Mississippi River, Louisiana Avenue and the Central Business District, the Irish Channel is so named because of a mass influx of immigrants from Ireland during the 1800s, many of whom established the area as a solid, working-class neighborhood of modest, single-story homes, many of them classic shotguns *(see sidebar p141)*.

As was true in most big cities during the 19C, the Irish were considered lowly laborers and were employed for the most dangerous of jobs, including digging the 6 mile New Basin Canal, which was to link the Mississippi River to Lake Pontchartrain. According to local lore, the Irish are responsible for a distinctive variant of the New Orleans accent, which sounds more Brooklynese than Southern.

A lively **St. Patrick's Day Parade** still rolls down Magazine Street through the neighborhood each year on the Saturday before or after March 16, usually starting out from **St. Alphonsus Roman Catholic Church** on Constance Street (between Josephine and St. Andrews streets), where services used to be held in both Gaelic and English. In addition to the standard New Orleans parade throws (the beads are green and white, of course), float riders toss cabbages and potatoes to the throngs of spectators; sharp reflexes are a must to dodge or catch the flying vegetables.

Downriver from the Garden District, on the downtown side of Jackson Avenue, lies the neighborhood known as the **Lower Garden District**. The area was laid out in 1807 (predating the Garden District) by architect Barthelemy Lafon, who incorporated plenty of parks and green spaces into his plan, and named the streets intersecting St. Charles Avenue for the nine Muses of Greek mythology. Several of Lafon's parks were sacrificed in the mid-20C to make way for the Mississippi River bridge onramps, but a few remain, most notably **Coliseum Square**, a lovely wedge-shaped green space with an energetic fountain along Coliseum Street. Nicely restored two-story Italianate and Greek Revival homes surround the square, many of them rivaling those in the Garden District in terms of size and beauty. Other Lower Garden District streets are a bit grittier, reflecting the neighborhood's decline in the decades after World War II, but revival is steady, thanks to the efforts of determined neighborhood organizations and preservationist groups. A particularly funky stretch of Magazine Street bounds the Lower Garden District to the south.

PLANTATION HOMES

Georgia may have Tara from *Gone with the Wind*, but Louisiana has one of the largest concentrations of elegant, antebellum plantation homes. Plantation homes line the banks of the Mississippi River and many are open to the public as museums, hotels or restaurants.

Although there is no real architectural definition of antebellum homes (the term antebellum refers to the pre-war period), they tend to be symmetrical and boxy with grand pillars and columns. Most homes also feature central entrances in both the front and back of the house and a prominent balcony. Interiors feature grand entryways, a sweeping staircase and formal ballroom once used to host elaborate parties. A typical plantation home also included vegetable gardens, chicken coops, pig pens, and barns—after all, they were agricultural centers.

The grandeur of the plantation homes emphasize the wealth and prestige of the landowners, who made their money by producing large quantities of products like cotton, tobacco and sugarcane. To many of the slaves at the time, plantation homes were referred to as "the big house," not only because of the size of the home, but also what the home represented—the power of the owners who resided there.

Tours are available year round at many of the plantation homes. Two of my favorites include:

The **Destrehan Plantation** *(see p157)* is run by a not-for-profit organization. Outside the metro area, but the closest large plantation to the city, it's ideal for visitors. There are costumed tours, museum exhibits, craft lessons and Folk Art. The plantation displays an original document signed by Thomas Jefferson that you can't miss.

The **Laura Plantation** in Vacherie *(see p159)* deviates from other homes as it's built in a more French-Creole style and was owned and operated by a Creole family. The property was recently renovated after a fire and the architectural detail has been meticulously preserved. In addition to the architecture, this former sugarcane plantation also has a cultural and literary legacy as "the American home of Br'er rabbit" from Joel Chandler Harris' work. Like the Destrehan Planation, there are organized activities and guided tour options.

the park's original landscaping. Droves of joggers, walkers, rollerbladers and bikers take their daily exercise along a 1.8-mile oak-lined path that winds around the section between **St. Charles Avenue★★** and Magazine Street, past several playground areas and a pretty golf course. South of Magazine Street, the expanses around and behind the zoo are home to tennis courts, riding stables and a broad riverside expanse of sports fields and picnic areas known as "The Fly."

Audubon Zoological Gardens★★

◑ *Allow 4 hrs. 6500 Magazine St.* ✆ *504-581-4629. www.auduboninstitute.org. Open Tue–Fri 10am–4pm; weekends 10am–5pm. $14.95.*

With its lush tropical landscaping and 58 natural habitats featuring exotic animals from around the globe, this beautifully designed zoo is a treat. Established here early in the 20C, the zoo completed its most recent facelift in 2002 and consistently ranks among the finest of its kind in the US. Play areas, live stage shows, animal feedings and special fee-based exhibits boost the entertainment factor; the zoo is enormously popular with residents and visitors alike.

Some of the zoo's most attention-getting inhabitants include a playful troupe of orangutans and siamangs (you may hear the siamangs' whoops from the parking lot); King Rex and King Zulu, a pair of noble white tigers; and Panya and Jean, a charming pair of African elephants known to greet visitors near their habitat. In the Louisiana Swamp exhibit, which wins rave reviews for its pitch-perfect depiction of life on the bayou, you'll cross an elevated boardwalk over a colony of alligators while raccoons and bears nest overhead. The swamp's aquarium facility boasts catfish, nutria and rare white alligators.

Fearsome jaguars rule the Mayan-themed Jaguar Jungle exhibit, and a herd of giraffes snack right near the viewing platform in African Savanna, opposite Monkey Hill, an artificial hill outfitted as a playground where youngsters can roll and tumble. In the Reptile House, don't miss the chance to see a rare Komodo dragon. In addition to animal exhibits, the zoo boasts a variety of fee-based exhibits and play areas including the Zoo Train, a white tram that chugs around the facility; the Cool Zoo splash park; and Dinosaur Adventure, populated by a dozen animatronic dinosaurs.

Latter Memorial Library

◑ *Allow 10min. 5120 St. Charles Ave.* ✆ *504-596-2625. http://nutrias.org. Open Mon–Thu 9am–6pm, weekends noon–5pm.*

Crowning a raised site, the stately library occupies the former

ASK PETER...

Q: Where can I go to spend the afternoon outdoors?
A: For fresh air, head about 6 miles from the center of New Orleans to Audubon Park. The park is an old plantation site converted into a nature preserve which is popular among walkers and joggers. Go for a 2-mile walk under live oaks and Spanish moss. There's also the famed zoo and a recently redesigned golf course.

Travel Tip:
Those looking for a taste of college life (and college partying) in New Orleans should head to The Boot *(1039 Broadway Street)* for last call. The Boot is a notorious dive bar right in the shadow of Tulane University that seems to pride itself on its cheap drinks and being open after all the other bars close. "Three for one Fridays" and "50 cent shot night" are just some of the specials it runs during the week.

MAPLE STREET BOOKSHOP

This much-loved New Orleans literary institution was founded in 1964. The original local bookstore can be found a few blocks past Loyola and Tulane Universities. Narrow aisles are crammed with shelves full of books and titles by local authors are particularly well represented. There's a little lounge for quiet reading that adds to the quaint ambiance, as well as old posters and newspaper cuttings anywhere there's wall space. New books can be found at 7529 Maple Street and used and rare titles are next door at 7523. There are now also branches in Bayou St. John *(3141 Ponce de Leon)* and Faubourg Marigny *(New Orleans Healing Center, 2732 St. Claude Avenue)*. Find time to support this neighborhood business and "Fight the Stupids!" (the store's long-standing motto). www.maplestreetbookshop.com.

home *(1907)* of several prominent New Orleans families before being donated to the city in 1948 for use as a branch library. As such, it offers a rare opportunity to enter a **St. Charles Avenue★★** home. Even though the interiors have been refitted to house the stacks, the downstairs reading rooms retain their original décor, including mirrors, mahogany woodwork and elaborate fresco ceilings.

Loyola University

⊙ *Allow 15min. 6363 St. Charles Ave. www.loyno.edu.*
The castle like façade of Loyola University, heralded by noble Holy Name of Jesus Church, forms an impressive quadrangle fronting **St. Charles Avenue★★**. The central building, Marquette Hall, houses the university's administrative offices. Gaze upward at the church's crenelated tower (inspired by England's Canterbury Cathedral) before stepping in to admire the rich stained glass windows and massive marble altar. Loyola University, a Jesuit institution, was established at this site in 1904.

Tulane University

⊙ *Allow 1hr. 6823 St. Charles Ave. www.tulane.edu.*
Prestigious Tulane University was founded in 1834 as the Medical University of Louisiana in the aftermath of a yellow fever epidemic. The main campus is a presence uptown, its noble stone façades forming a gracious semicircle fronting **Audubon Park★★**. It's pleasant to stroll through campus, taking in the handsome university buildings.

Travel Tip:
The Maple Leaf Bar is located in the Carrollton neighborhood near Tulane University. The bar is one of the longest continually operating music venues in the city (dating back to 1974). Today this cool hang-out is known for music of all genres as well as poetry and prose readings.

RIVERBEND

When the St. Charles Avenue streetcar reaches the uptown end of the avenue, it makes a hard right onto Carrollton Avenue and continues to its terminus at Carrollton and Claiborne avenues. The area where it makes that turn is commonly known as the Riverbend (although in truth, it's the streetcar line that bends, not the river at this point). The neighborhood originally developed in the early 1880s as the town of **Carrollton**, a suburb that formed at the intersection of two commuter rail lines heading east to downtown New Orleans and north to Lake Pontchartrain. Then a village in a rural area, Carrollton thrived as a middle-class suburb and served for a time as the seat of Jefferson Parish until it was annexed by the ever-spreading city of New Orleans in 1884.

Today the Riverbend area bustles with day spas, boutiques, ice-cream shops, coffee houses and small restaurants. Most are unique, but you'll find a few outposts of well-known chains here too. Stroll along the lower end of Carrollton, along Hampson Street and around the pretty park behind the small modern shopping mall. The Riverbend is a favored hangout for Tulane and Loyola students and faculty, many of whom live along the streets intersecting St. Charles and Carrollton Avenues. If you're exploring the area in the morning or late evening, the venerable **Camelia Grill** makes a perfect stop; their Chef Special omelets, cheeseburgers and milkshakes are always in demand by locals. The neighborhood also offers easy access to the biking/jogging path atop the river levee.

Walk (or ride the streetcar) a few blocks up Carrollton to **Oak Street**, another funky New Orleans enclave that is gaining in popularity and hipness while somehow retaining the feel of a classic neighborhood shopping street from the 1950s (Haase's Shoes has been selling footwear to New Orleans uptowners since 1921). The blocks make for a great stroll by day if you're seeking ultrahip resale shops, craft studios or home design stores. By night, live music rolls forth every night from **Maple Leaf Bar** (no 8316), hosting some of New Orleans' best-known bands as well as touring national acts. Two doors down, at **Jacques-Imo's Café** (no 8324), the sign proclaiming "Warm Beer, Lousy Food, Poor Service" doesn't seem to discourage the crowds in search of rollicking fun from queuing up for tables in the cramped main room or out on the sidewalk. If you're in search of more upscale fare, one New Orleans' culinary star that twinkles in the area is **Brigtsen's** (see p180).

DISCOVERING
TREMÉ AND FAUBOURG MARIGNY

Walking east from the tourist driven French Quarter gives you a different take on the city. The Tremé and Faubourg Marigny neighborhoods have a historic past as the original location for Creole settlers. At the turn of the 19C, French-speaking freed black slaves, working class whites, and other immigrants settled in the area.

Tremé is arguably the oldest African American neighborhood in the country—it was definitely the first neighborhood where freed slaves were able to own property, and many free persons of color had land here. Tremé has several museums dedicated to African American life, history and culture, including The African American Museum and The Backstreet Cultural Museum where visitors can see artifacts from New Orleans traditions such as Mardi Gras and jazz music. The neigborhood is home to the Louis Armstrong Park, dedicated to the famous jazz musician, as well as St. Louis Cemetery No 1, the final resting place of many of New Orleans' prominent figures.

Close to Tremé is the second-largest neighborhood in New Orleans, Faubourg Marigny. The neighborhood has gone through several different incarnations, but a visit is a world away from the typical New Orleans tourist experience. After the 1950s, crime and neglect took over Faubourg Marigny as many middle class people moved away. In the 1970s, the area and its natural beauty started to draw people back and the neighborhood began a renaissance. Today, Faubourg Marigny is an artist-friendly neighborhood with newly renovated buildings, painted in rich, vibrant colors.

While there's a heavy residential component to the neighborhood, there are some notable attractions, particularly the nightlife along Frenchman Street. Local favorite low-key restaurants include Elizabeth's *(601 Gallier Street)* serving "real food, done real good" and Gene's Po-Boys *(1040 Elysian Fields Avenue)*, which is the prime neighborhood sanwich spot.

St. Louis Cemetery No. 1 Photo: © Irene Abdou/Alamy

PETER'S TOP PICKS

 GREEN SPACES

Check out the Louis Armstrong Park for outdoor activities and historical landmarks like Congo Square. **Louis Armstrong Park** (p **136**)

 HISTORY

To learn about the rich history of the African American population in New Orleans and beyond, check out the African American Museum. **African American Museum** (p **138**)

 STAY

The Frenchmen is one of the city's older hotels. The rooms are smaller, but you will definitely feel a part of the city's history. **The Frenchmen** (p **173**)

 SHOP

Purchasing or window-shopping, you'll love the American Aquatic Gardens. A nursery and gift store, this place is a must-see and a must-shop. **American Aquatic Gardens** (p **195**)

 EAT

Dooky Chase is a longtime New Orleans institution where you'll discover some of the best Creole gumbo in town. Flooded after Hurricane Katrina, owner Leah Chase lived outside the restaurant in a trailer while the community rallied to help her reopen the business. Its doors are open again, but on a limited schedule, so go for lunch between Tuesday and Friday. **Dooky Chase** (p **181**)

 ENTERTAINMENT

It might mean a cab journey, but Sweet Lorraines and down-home jazz music that draws devoted locals every week is worth it. **Sweet Lorraines** (p **188**)

Location:
Bounded by
Rampart Street,
Esplanade Avenue,
Claiborne Avenue
and Canal Street.
**Buses and
Streetcars:**
91 Jackson-
Esplanade to
Rampart Street.
5 Marigny-Bywater
to Frenchmen
Street. Canal
Street streetcar to
Rampart Street.

Tremé

Deemed the oldest African-American neighborhood in the US, Tremé (pronounced truh-MAY) is noteworthy in that people of color worked, owned property and prospered here as early as the 1700s, a time when most blacks in the American South were enslaved. The neighborhood spawned several early civil-rights movements, some pre-dating the Civil War. Tremé was the location of the (now demolished) home of shoemaker Homer Plessy, whose 1892 act of civil disobedience brought about the US Supreme Court's landmark Plessy v. Ferguson case. Having bounced back from a period of decline in the 1990s, the neighborhood has seen steady gentrification in recent years, and its fame exploded in 2010 when it became the setting and subject of a popular television series.

Louis Armstrong Park

▶ *Allow 30min. 835 N. Rampart St.*

A broad arch fronting Rampart Street heralds the entrance to Louis Armstrong Park. The nicely landscaped green space is home to several historical sites and cultural venues, including New Orleans Municipal Auditorium and the **Mahalia Jackson Theater for the Performing Arts** *(see p183)*. The park benefitted from a facelift begun in 2010 and its lagoons, paths, statues and bridges make it an attractive, welcoming spot for a day-time stroll.

Just left of the arched entrance lies **Congo Square**, commemorating the spot where slaves, free blacks and native Americans gathered on Sundays as early as the 1700s to trade and sell handmade goods, to socialize and eat, and to drum and dance. These weekly gatherings kept African traditions

Travel Tip:
New Orleans music isn't all about jazz and zydeco. It has a long tradition in opera, dating back to the late 17C. The official New Orleans Opera was founded in 1943. Head to the Mahalia Jackson Theater, which replaced the original French Opera House that burned in 1919. Both classic and contemporary performances can be found here.

LOUIS ARMSTRONG 1901-71

New Orleans is the birthplace of one of the founding fathers of jazz, Louis Armstrong. Born into poverty, Armstrong got his first trumpet aged seven and his musical debut was in New Orleans in 1931. He went on to become the first solo trumpeter and vocalist to base his style on improvisation and he took this style of music and introduced it to the world. Today, there are two statues in New Orleans to honor Louis Armstrong's legacy: One at Algiers Ferry Landing, and the other in the park named for him on North Rampart Street.

TREMÉ JAZZ MUSICIANS

Tremé has given rise to early jazz musicians and bands who helped shaped the genre. In fact, the neighborhood has been a hotbed of jazz culture since before there was even a name for the style, and it remains a destination for enthusiasts today.

Tremé native **Alphonse Picou** was a Creole clarinetist who came to define early jazz. He played in the band of Buddy Boden, one of the founders of early jazz. Though Picou left Tremé for a short stint in Chicago, his heart was in New Orleans and he remained in the city for most of this life. He weathered the Great Depression as a metalsmith, but returned to music in the 1940s when he opened a bar on St. Philip and Claiborne streets. His 1961 funeral was among the largest ever held in the city and, to some, marked the end of an era.

The jazz trombonist **Lucien Barbarin**, who makes his home in Tremé as well, famously stayed put after Hurricane Katrina in 2005 saying, "I'm going to stay because I was born and raised there and I'm going to pass away there. We name drinks after hurricanes. We should be used to this." The neighborhood is also home to "The King of Tremé" virtuoso drummer **Shannon Powell**. Born in 1962, Powell is a regular at the city's Jazz Fest. Today he plays with the Preservation Hall Jazz Band in addition to leading his own quartet with Jason Marsalis, Steve Masakowski, and Roland Guerin.

Jazz trumpeter, singer, and composer **Kermit Ruffins** founded Rebirth Brass Band in 1983 while at Clark High School in the neighborhood. Joe's Cozy Corner in Tremé is often considered the birthplace of the band. The band is known for having incorporated traditional New Orleans Brass Band Music with funk, soul, jazz, and hip hop influences.

European jazz musicians such as Henry Ragas and Louis Prima have also lived in Tremé. Learn about the neighborhoods cultural and historic sites through a walking tour with the New Orleans African American Museum *(http://noaam.org/tours)*, and get a personal tour of the neighborhood's jazz influences on a tour with French Quarter Phantoms *(www.french quarterphantoms.com/)*. And a fun fact? Tremé is home to the world's only laundromat that's been inducted into the Rock and Roll Hall of Fame. That's right, the building that once housed the J&M Studios, founded by New Orleans music engineer and studio owner, Cosimo Matassa, is now a laundromat—but the structure was named a Rock and Roll landmark in 2010.

alive. Opposite the St. Phillip Street entrance in the northeast corner of the park you'll find several historic structures maintained by the **New Orleans Jazz National Historical Park** *(see p92)*. If you visit on Saturday around 11am, be sure to drop by **Perseverance Hall** to watch nascent jazz musi-

ASK PETER...
Q: Where can I see New Orleans' up and coming artists?
A: St. Claude Avenue is the epicenter of New Orleans' cutting-edge arts scene that's truly off the beaten path. Known locally as the St. Claude Art District (SCAD), it's home to edgy art studios and collectives, as well as the University of New Orleans St. Claude Gallery. Every second Saturday of the month an art walk takes place where you can meet the artists and listen to live music while mingling with the locals.

cians jam with their elders at the park's Music For All Ages programs, an only-in-New-Orleans spectacle well worth seeing.

African American Museum

◐ *Allow 30min. 1418 Gov. Nicholls St. ℘ 504-566-1136. www.noaam.org. Open Wed–Sat 11am–4pm. $7.*

The African-American experience, in Tremé and elsewhere, is the focus of this worthwhile small museum and cultural center. Visitors are invited to explore landscaped gardens and historic buildings, including a beautifully restored villa that blends Creole and American elements. Come here to take in thoughtfully curated rotating exhibitions detailing various aspects of African-American art, culture and history. Recent exhibits highlighted works by Dutreuil Barjon, a prominent Creole furniture artisan in 19C New Orleans; glorious quilts by New Orleans quilt artists; and "Drapeto-mania: the Disease of Freedom," a stirring exploration of documents and objects related to slave oppression.

St. Louis Cemetery No 1★

◐ *Allow 30min. 425 Basin St. Open Mon–Sat 9am–3pm, Sun noon–3pm (hours vary).*

This historic cemetery opened in 1789 and has been in continuous use ever since as the resting place for final remains of ordinary citizens as well as prominent figures of New Orleans history. Crowded with high tombs and laced with narrow paths, the cemetery is best visited with a group or on a guided tour. Just inside the entrance turn left past the wall of "oven vaults," then turn right, where you'll spy a tomb covered with markings, mostly triple Xs. This is the Glapion family tomb, supposed repository of the remains of Marie Laveau, Voodoo Queen of New Orleans; the markings and offerings are left in supplication by believers who continue to seek her intercession.

Across Basin Street you'll see the rear entrance to **Our Lady of Guadalupe Church** *(411 N. Rampart St.; ℘ 504-525-1551; www.judeshrine.com).* The small church was dedicated in 1827 as a mortuary chapel for the parish church of St. Louis (at the time it was feared that the corpses of yellow fever victims were infectious and unsafe to bring into the main church for funerals). It's therefore older than the existing **St. Louis Cathedral★**.

St. Augustine Catholic Church

◐ *Allow 15min. 1210 Gov. Nicholls St. ☎ 504-525-5934.*
www.staugustinecatholicchurch-neworleans.org.
Open for Mass (Sun 10am) and by appointment.

The second-oldest black Catholic parish in the US, St. Augustine was established here in 1841, mostly thanks to the efforts of Tremé's free black residents. Outside, along the church's sidewall lies the **Tomb of the Unknown Slave**, a large cross propped sideways and draped with iron shackles. The stirring shrine commemorates Africans everywhere who died separated from home and culture because of slavery. Within the handsome building, designed by French architect J.N.B. de Pouilly (also credited with **St. Louis Cathedral★**), you'll find graceful African flourishes and a beautiful wood altar made from a branching tree trunk.

Backstreet Cultural Museum

◐ *Allow 30min. 1116 St. Claude Ave. ☎ 504-522-4806.*
www.backstreetmuseum.org. Open Tue–Sat 10am–5pm. $8.

This small private museum opens a window onto the world of the Mardi Gras Indians, a somewhat secretive subculture part African and part American Indian, hard to understand and entirely unique to New Orleans *(see sidebar p67)*. The Backstreet Museum's collection of Mardi Gras Indian suits forms a glorious display of folk art; the brilliantly colored creations of beads, feathers and canvas can cost upward of $10,000 and are produced entirely by hand. Other mementos describe second-line parades, jazz funerals and New Orleaneans' general penchant for parading in the streets at every opportunity.

ON SCREEN TREMÉ

The media has paid particular attention to the Faubourg Tremé neighborhood in recent years. Tremé is often the location chosen for film and television about the city after Katrina. In 2010, HBO started airing popular drama series *Treme*, which follows the lives of residents as they rebuild their lives after the hurricane. The neighborhood is also the subject of *Faugbourg Tremé: The Untold Story of Black New Orleans*, a 2008 documentary which tells the story of Tremé before and after the storm through the eyes of local writers, musicians and artists.

Travel Tip:
See the sights from another perspective when you take a bicycle tour through the city with the Confederacy of Cruisers. The Original Creole Tour takes you through the Marigny and Tremé neighborhoods on two wheels, exploring the narrow streets at a leisurely pace and getting to meet the locals along the way. www.confederacyof cruisers.com.

Travel Tip:
For real-life stories about New Orleans natives before, during and after Katrina, pick up a copy of *Nine Lives: Life and Death in New Orleans*. Then go meet JoAnn Guidos, one of the people profiled in the book at her famous Kajun's Pub restaurant *(2256 St. Claude Ave.)*. She owns a truly eclectic bar (open 24hrs) with a neighborhood atmosphere and affordable drinks.

JAZZ OUTSIDE THE FRENCH QUARTER ...LIKE A LOCAL

Many people mistakenly think the French Quarter is the only place to go to hear the best jazz in the city. Think again. Many locals actually leave the French Quarter to seek out some of the best rhythm and blues music in Tremé and Marigny. The neighborhoods are known for eclectic restaurants and authentic music clubs.

Situated directly adjacent to Faubourg Marigny sits Frenchmen Street, a two block stretch of dive bars with old rickety stages. You won't see huge amp systems or sophisticated sound productions in any of the bars along the two block strip, but the wood stages create the right ambiance for appreciating jazz. This is the street to visit if you want to hear practically every type of rhythm and blues music. Experience everything from jazz to blues to reggae, and as an added bonus, the drinks are dirt-cheap.

Check out the **Spotted Cat** *(see p189)*, a hole in the wall type of establishment where you'll mingle with jazz aficionados. At the Spotted Cat, you could be standing next to someone having a conversation and the next thing you know they are up on stage playing some of the best jazz music you've ever heard.

On the other end of the spectrum, though just a few doors down is **Snug Harbor Jazz Bistro** *(see p188)*, a restaurant-bar where established musicians show up to entertain the masses. Ellis Marsalis, regarded by many as the premier modern jazz pianist in New Orleans regularly appears at the venue. If you are lucky, you will catch the 78-year old pianist tickling the ivories. My advice is to head over before or after dinner since the food is thought to be satisfactory at best.

The street also has some great smoke-free clubs, which is rare since New Orleans does not have a law forbidding smoking inside. **The Maison** *(see p188)* and **d.b.a** *(see p188)* have voluntarily enacted a smoke-free policy, so you can enjoy the sounds of great jazz without having to deal with a smoky room.

Faubourg Marigny

This vibrant neighborhood on the east edge of the French Quarter was named for 18C aristocrat and good-time guy Bernard de Marigny de Mandeville, who at the tender age of 15 inherited the plantation that once defined the district. In 1806, thanks to his mounting gambling debts, Marigny began to sell off parcels of land at a good price to *"les hommes de couleur libres"* (free men of color) instead of to American developers. Thus New Orleans' first suburb (*faubourg* in French) was born. Younger urban dwellers have moved into the area in droves in recent years, fixing up their shotgun houses, hanging out in corner coffee shops and trolling the neighborhood art galleries.

Frenchmen Street

Between Esplanade Ave. and Washington Square.
www.frenchmenst.com. The Marigny enjoys an enduring reputation as one of New Orleans' hottest music club scenes, home to dozens of nightclubs and restaurants. Frenchmen Street, the Marigny's main artery, is chockablock with cafes, bookstores and restaurants that draw crowds, perfect for an evening stroll and a meal. Live music pours forth from a dozen clubs, most of which stage well-known local bands although national and international talent often play gigs here too. If you're here on Friday, try to snag a table at **Snug Harbor** (*626 Frenchmen St.*) to catch a set with beloved pianist Ellis Marsalis.

SHOTGUN HOUSES

Found in many New Orleans neighborhoods, especially in Faubourg Marigny, Mid-City and the Irish Channel, shotgun houses made good use of narrow lots. Typically one-room wide, the shotgun house with its long row of back-to-back rooms and no hallway probably evolved on Haitian sugar plantations. It was said that if you were to fire a gun through the front door of one of these structures, the shot would pass unimpeded through the line of rooms and go right out the back. Some houses sport a second story, or "camelback," at the rear of the house. The high ceilings and open design of these houses draw the heat up and keep the air circulating, always a good thing in the Crescent City's humid summer climate.

Location: Bounded by Esplanade and Elysian Fields avenues, the Mississippi River and Rampart Street. **Buses and Streetcars:** 5 Marigny to Frenchmen Street.

Travel Tip:
Orange Couch Coffee (*2339 Royal Street*) is a trendy coffee shop that serves coffee and pastries. But it's also home to a delectable treat that you wouldn't expect to see here: Japanese mochi ice-cream (sticky rice wrapped around small balls of smooth ice cream). Lychee shakes and Vietnamese coffee round out the Asian-inspired menu. www.theorange couchcoffee.com

Travel Tip:
The Old New Orleans Rum Distillery (*2815 Frenchman St.; ℘504-945-9400; www.new orleansrum.com*) has award-winning rums made from Louisiana sugar-cane molasses. You can tour the distillery and take part in a tasting. It's at the far end of Frenchman St., so take a taxi or call to arrange a pick up from the Quarter.

AFTER KATRINA

When the levees walling New Orleans' drainage canals failed during Hurricane Katrina *(see p33)*, nearly 80 percent of the city was inundated with water pushed in from surge-swollen Lake Pontchartrain to the north and the Gulf of Mexico waterways to the south. Wrenching images of the catastrophic flooding of entire communities—and the chaotic rescue and evacuation of residents who had stayed in the city through the storm—grabbed news headlines. The eyes of the world have turned elsewhere in the years since the disaster, but in New Orleans, Katrina is not yet in the past. Recovery and rebuilding are ongoing, and will be for years to come.

It's worth noting that floodwaters never reached most of the areas that draw visitors to New Orleans. The French Quarter, St. Charles Avenue, Magazine Street, the Garden District, some of the Warehouse District and parts of uptown escaped the waters thanks to their location atop "the sliver by the river," local parlance for the naturally high ground close to the Mississippi River. Residents cleared out of these areas before and immediately after the storm, to be sure, but many returned fairly quickly to rebuild and resume their lives, erasing most traces of storm damage.

However, recovery has been uneven in the residential neighborhoods that bore the brunt of the flooding—those closest to the levee breaks along the Lake Pontchartrain drainage canals, the Industrial Canal and the Mississsppi River Gulf Outlet (MRGO). Residents have been slow to repopulate Gentilly, Eastern New Orleans, and the poverty-stricken streets of the lower Ninth Ward, all areas where homes, schools, shopping malls and medical facilities were decimated. For some, deciding to return to these places has meant coming back to a ruined house, no job, no services and no community. In certain areas, the slow return has dampened political and economic will to rebuild. But a large and resilient Vietnamese community is re-established in Eastern New Orleans, as are many middle-class African Americans, though not in the same numbers as before the flood. The middle-class neighborhoods of Lakeview are scarred, but well on the way back up. The communities of neighboring St. Bernard Parish, which lies on a finger of land between the Mississippi River and the MRGO, were entirely inundated but persist in the mighty struggle to rebuild.

In the months after Katrina, the state of Louisiana implemented multiple federally funded **recovery programs** intended to compensate residents for uninsured damages to their homes, create incentives to develop rental property, and encourage businesses to resettle or move to the area. These programs have met with varying degrees of success. New Orleans' economy, already suffering from a slow drain of company headquarters pre-Katrina (mostly in the oil and gas industry), lost thousands more jobs in the aftermath, and continues working to recreate employment opportunities. According to the 2010 census, New Orleans' population now stands at 80 percent of what it was in 2000, with the biggest reductions in the numbers of African Americans living in the city.

On the upside, New Orleans' many hotels and convention spaces have been completely restored, and even expanded. There are now more restaurants in the city than there were pre-Katrina, so visitors these days will have an even harder time deciding whether to eat at an old-line Creole dining mecca, a beloved neighborhood dive or a trendy hot spot helmed by a celebrity chef. The **New Orleans Saints** and the **New Orleans Hornets** returned to renovated (and packed) arenas after spending the season after Katrina playing at other venues; the Saints' thrilling September 2006 victory against the Atlanta Falcons in their first home game back in the Superdome is one of residents' most cherished post-Katrina memories. And an even more telling note, Mardi Gras is alive and well; the city's parading krewes (all privately funded, mostly by New Orleans citizens) are back and going strong, rolling parades through the streets at Carnival time among surging crowds of delighted visitors.

The disaster spawned an outpouring of help in the form of money, manpower and expertise from individuals and groups both locally and from around the US. Below are a few of the many, many organizations that welcome involvement in continuing the work of rebuilding New Orleans.

Make It Right

www.makeitrightnola.org.
Founded by actor Brad Pitt, Make It Right builds sustainable, affordable homes for working class families in the lower Ninth Ward.

Women of the Storm

www.womenofthestorm.net.
Founded by a diverse group of New Orleans women affected by Katrina, this political action group seeks to educate government leaders and the media about the issues affecting New Orleans and the Gulf Coast such as housing, safe levees and coastal restoration.

New Orleans Habitat Musicians' Village

www.nolamusiciansvillage.org.
The brainchild of musicians Harry Connick Jr. and Branford Marsalis (both New Orleans native sons), Musicians' Village is creating homes and a community for local musicians and their families.

Volunteer New Orleans

www.volunteerneworleans.com.
The New Orleans branch of Volunteers of America coordinates unaffiliated volunteers desiring to donate time and expertise to the rebuilding effort.

Don't just go to where locals party and shop. Instead, see where they live. Mid-City is a predominantly residential section of New Orleans, so it doesn't contain as many tourist attractions as other parts of the city.

Mid-City isn't always deserted by tourists. I'm sure you've heard of the New Orleans Jazz & Heritage Festival. Well guess what? It's in Mid-City. So for a week and a half in the spring, this part of town is where everyone is. Visitors also flock to Mid-City around Halloween for the Voodoo Experience—a major concert festival. The rest of the year the neighborhood doesn't have the same crowds, but the charm of the suburb easily makes up for its lack of notable landmarks.

Mid-City got its name as the midway point between the Mississippi River and Lake Pontchartrain. It got its start when engineer Albert Baldwin Wood developed the screw pump, which drained water from the land situated below sea level. Before this innovation, Mid-City was simply a swampland that continuously flooded. Within the neighborhood, the area by the Fair grounds race track and the nearby portion of Esplanade Avenue is known as Bayou St. John or Esplanade Ridge. The old Bayou can be seen near City Park and is a calm long strip of water that trails through the neighborhood.

Lumberyards and turpentine works still exist along Canal Street, which was originally dug in 1832. Canal Street, one of the most important thoroughfares in the entire city, goes directly through Mid-City and streetcars line the busy street. For local eats: Mandina's Restaurant *(see p181)*, which fuses Creole with Italian cuisine, including traditional New Orleans red bean dishes every Monday. For more true New Orleans dining experiences, make your way to Esplanade Avenue where the shops and restaurants in the 3000–3200 blocks are a staple for residents.

Mid-City is also home to the New Orleans Museum of Art (NOMA) in City Park, a Neoclassical Beaux Arts-style museum. The museum just celebrated its centennial in 2011, and what a century its been. With a $200 million collection spanning more than 4,000 years of art history, it's a can't miss for art lovers everywhere.

Members of the C T C Steppers at the 2008 New Orleans
Jazz Heritage Festival Photo: © Ninette Maumus/Alamy

PETER'S TOP PICKS

CULTURE

NOMA boasts impressive collections and a stunning sculpture garden. **New Orleans Museum of Art** (p **148**)

GREEN SPACES

New Orleans City Park is twice the size of New York City's Central Park and the highlight here are the mature live oaks, best seen on a ramble through the Botanical Garden. **City Park** (p **147**) **Botanical Garden** (p **149**)

HISTORY

Longue Vue House and Gardens offers a wonderful glimpse into various movements of the 20C. The gardens, started in 1934, are a particular highlight— the current house was rebuilt to reflect the design of the gardens! Don't miss the majestic Duelling Oak in the City Park; the site of countless duels in the early days of New Orleans. **Longue Vue House and Gardens** (p **151**) **Duelling Oak** (p **148**)

STAY

Looking for an authentic antebellum home to stay in? Rathbone Mansions takes you back to early 19C New Orleans. **Rathbone Mansions** (p **174**)

SHOP

Tony Metairie Road is a little bit removed from the more touristy areas downtown and in the French Quarter, but it offers great, original finds. **Old Metairie** (p **152**)

EAT

Sunday Brunch at the exclusive Ralph's on the Park is a must. They have a kids brunch menu too! **Ralph's on the Park** (p **182**)

Location:
The avenue runs
from the French
Quarter to
City Park.
**Buses and
Streetcars:**
Bus 91 Jackson
Esplanade.

Esplanade Avenue★

Gracious, tree-lined Esplanade Avenue leads from the French Quarter all the way up to City Park, tracing part of a relatively high "ridge" of land—if such a thing can be said to exist in low-lying New Orleans. Native Americans used this high ground as a portage between the Mississippi River and Bayou St. John (which connected with Lake Pont-chartrain). As New Orleans expanded out from the French Quarter in the early 19C, wealthy Creole families built mansions in the area, which became known as Esplanade Ridge, and the avenue became the main thoroughfare of Creole society. Although some sections of Esplanade Avenue have deteriorated, many others retain their Creole period elegance. A drive from the Quarter to the park passes some lovely 19C homes, many of them noteworthy examples of the Italianate style.

Degas House

◐ *Allow 90min. 2306 Esplanade Ave.* ✆ *504-821-5009. www.degashouse.com. Guided tours by appointment. $12.50.*
Rising gracefully on the west side of Esplanade Avenue near North Tonti Street, this nicely restored Italianate home was the scene of an extended visit by French painter **Edgar Degas**. The artist's uncle, Michael Musson, owned a cotton-brokerage business downtown, and Degas lived here with his American relatives, creating 22 paintings during his year-long sojourn from 1872 to 1873. The house appears as it did during Degas' time, and now operates as a bed-and-breakfast inn. Tours of the property are available by advance reservation.

New Orleans Fair grounds

1751 Gentilly Blvd. ✆ *504-944-5515. www.fairgrounds racecourse.com. Casino open daily 9am–midnight; grounds and grand-stand open for races and events only. Free for casino; $5 for grandstand.*
The horse race track first laid out on this spot in 1852 is touted as the oldest still-operating racing site in the US. The handsome grandstand and clubhouse overlooking the one-mile dirt track replace the original facility, which were destroyed in a fire in 1993. Thoroughbred race meets are held here from Thanksgiving to March, and the grounds are the site of the hugely popular annual **New Orleans Jazz & Heritage Festival** (Jazz Fest) in late April/early May *(see p65)*. The facility also operates year-round as a slots casino.

Bayou St. John

This slow-moving finger of water originating in present-day Mid-City channeled water from the surrounding swampland into Lake Pontchartrain and formed part of a trade route—Native Americans and later merchants brought goods in by boat, then portaged them along the Esplanade ridge to the Mississippi River. Today the picturesque channel is traversed by several bridges and flanked by a charming residential neighborhood of the same name.

Pitot House

◑ *Allow 45min for guided tour. 1440 Moss St. ☏ 504-482-0312. www.louisianalandmarks.org. Open Wed–Sat 10am–3pm. $7.*

This genteel residence overlooking Bayou St. John was constructed in 1799 (its original site was a block away) and in 1805 was acquired by James Pitot, New Orleans' first mayor. Several owners occupied the house over the decades (including a convent of nuns), altering it as they came and went. Tours of the home, now authentically restored to its original appearance by the Louisiana Landmarks Society, focus on its architectural history and the features (deep balconies and louvered shutters for shade, facing doors and windows for cross-ventilation) that allowed residents to tolerate Louisiana's heat and humidity in the days before air-conditioning.

City Park★

Situated in the north-central part of New Orleans near Lake Pontchartrain, this 1,300-acre park is the fifth-largest swath of urban greenery in America (it's twice the size of New York City's Central Park). The land, formerly part of a large plantation that overlooked Bayou St. John, was gifted to the city in 1854, and encompasses lush green lawns, sparkling lagoons and noble stands of trees (some of the live oaks are over 600 years old). During the 1930s WPA workers built roadways, bridges, fountains, a bandstand and a peristyle replete with Classical Greek flourishes. New Orleans' art museum, botanical garden, a small amusement park, paddleboat house and picnic shelters lie in the

Travel Tip:

Alligators may look like swamp monsters, but in New Orleans, they are an entirely acceptable form of meat. The city's proximity to the bayou, in which there lives a surplus of gators, make hunting the reptiles common. Alligator meat is white with a mild flavor and firm texture. You can easily find it deep fried in bite-sized pieces at roadside stands. Many locals prefer to eat it in sausage form, or in alligator sauce *piquante*, which is pieces of alligator tail meat in a spicy Cajun sauce.

Location:

Main park entrances on at Lelong Avenue from Esplanade Avenue; Anseman Avenue from City Park Avenue; Friederichs Avenue from Wisner Boulevard and Victory Avenue and Roosevelt Mall Boulevard from Marconi Drive.

Buses and Streetcars: Bus 91 Jackson-Esplanade to City Park Avenue. Canal Streetcar 48–City Park/Museum.

ASK PETER...

Q: I'm headed to the City Park area, what's there to do?

A: Once you've taken time to stroll the botanical garden and visit the Museum of Art, across from the park entrance is Ralph's on the Park, a Cajun/Creole restaurant in a beautifully restored historic building where the Sunday brunch can't be beat. City Park also features… a haunted golf course. Yes, that's right, the City Park Golf Course seems to have a ghost lingering around the 18th hole. So unless you're feeling brave, maybe it's time to play a nine-hole game instead.

section nearest Esplanade Avenue; on the far side of I-610 you'll find a state-of-the-art tennis facility, riding stables, sports fields and a forest and arboretum with nature trails (the forest is making a comeback after being decimated by Hurricane Katrina floodwaters). To the left of the art museum and sculpture garden entrance stands the majestic **Dueling Oak**, a glorious live oak tree that was the setting for innumerable 19C duels, the favored means of settling *affaires d'honneur* in Creole society. *1 Palm Dr.* ℘*504-482-4888.* www.neworleanscitypark.com.

New Orleans Museum of Art★

◗ *Allow 2hr. 1 Collins Diboll Cir.* ℘*504-658-4100. www.noma.org. Open year-round Tue–Sun 10am–5pm (Fri 9pm). $10 (Wed free).*

Standing majestically at City Park's main entrance at the head of **Esplanade Avenue★**, the New Orleans art museum (today nicknamed NOMA) was founded in 1911 in a dignified Beaux-Arts building. A steady stream of acquisitions, many of them from local benefactors, necessitated expanding the original facility in 1993 with a rear addition, bringing the total exhibition space to 46 galleries on three levels.

Today the museum's permanent collection totals more than 40,000 works from an impressive array of major artistic genres and movements. Particular strengths include Western European art from the medieval period through the 20C (look for paintings by Monet, Manet, Pisarro and Degas); arts of the Americas, including pieces from pre-Columbian Mexico and fine Spanish Colonial paintings from

FABERGÉ

Born in Saint Petersburg, Russia, in 1846, Peter Carl Fabergé is best known for his Fabergé eggs, which were designed to symbolize rebirth and love. So what does Fabergé have to do with New Orleans? Following a temporary exhibit of one of the most important private collections in the United States, *Fabergé from the Hodges Family Collection*, the New Orleans Museum of Art has opened a permanent Fabergé Gallery. The exhibition was made possible by a group of Southern collectors and includes Fabergé Easter eggs, miniature Fabergé eggs as part of jewelry and a clock that was owned by the last Tsarina of Russia.

Peru; Indian and Asian art, with Chinese jades and more than 300 Japanese Edo-period screens and scrolls; African and Oceanic art, including bronzes and figures in wood and terra-cotta from the Republic of Benin and the West African Yoruba culture and totem figures from Micronesia; and modern American art, including a survey of works by 19C and 20C Louisiana artists. The museum also boasts a fabulous collection of glittering pieces by renowned Russian jeweler Peter Carl Fabergé (including three Imperial Easter eggs); intriguing English portrait miniatures from the 17C–19C; two period rooms featuring decorative arts of the of American Colonial and Federal periods; and an astounding assortment of porcelain and fine art glass.

The grounds around the main museum building hold the museum's showpiece **Sculpture Garden★** *(open daily 10am–4:45pm)*, a rolling, 5-acre forested site with lawns, paths, a pretty lagoon, footbridges and more than 50 sculptures by prominent contemporary artists from North and Latin America, Europe, Japan and Israel. Works are by turn inspiring, thought-provoking and simply beautiful; all are greatly enhanced by the lovely setting. Prominent artists represented here include Claes Oldenburg, Jacques Lipchitz, Barbara Hepworth, Jaume Plensa, Auguste Rodin, George Segal, René Magritte, Isamu Noguchi, Henry Moore and George Rodrigue.

New Orleans Botanical Garden★

◐ *Allow 60min.* ☏ *504-483-9386. http://garden.neworleans citypark.com. Open year-round Tue–Sun 10am–4:30pm. $6.*

Built by WPA workers during the Depression, the botanical garden opened as the City Park Rose Garden in 1936, and was reborn in the 1980s as the New Orleans Botanical Garden. Badly damaged by floodwaters after Hurricane Katrina, the garden is now restored to glory, and visitors can delight in strolling the paths beneath a canopy of moss-draped live oaks, admiring more than 2,000 varieties of plants flourishing in theme gardens. Sculptures, many of them by WPA artist Enrique Alferez, grace many a nook and vista. Special features worth noting include a lush tropical garden; a butterfly garden; a bamboo-filled Japanese garden; and cacti thriving in 1930s-era brick greenhouses.

Beneath the spectacular glass dome of the conservatory you'll find a tropical rain forest garden and a living fossil garden of prehistoric plants. Be sure to stroll all the way back to the wonderful **New Orleans Train Garden**, where

Travel Tip:
The Sculpture Garden's entrance is located at the Pavilion of the Two Sisters on Victory Avenue in City Park, behind the New Orleans Museum of Art. Free parking is available along Victory Ave and the Victory Avenue parking lot.

STREETCARS
...LIKE A LOCAL

New Orleans has managed to embrace new technology while keeping the nostalgia of its historic roots. Case in point: the public transportation system. It's a pedestrian-friendly city, but there are numerous bus routes and tons of cabs that can take you anywhere you want. But for a really authentic take of the city and the past look into the streetcar lines. They're not trolleys filled with tourists as in other places—locals swear by the streetcars.

If you're looking to go back to the time of speakeasies and Louis Armstrong, be sure to hop onto the oldest operating streetcar: the St. Charles Avenue line. Decked with authentic mahogany seats and brass fittings, the streetcar continues to transport the public while maintaining the quality fixtures. Taking this route you can stray away from the French Quarter for a bit and explore the Central Business District, go through Uptown, Garden District, Lafayette Cemetery, as well as Loyola and Tulane University—and of course, right through Mid-City. This is one of the most scenic rides in the city, and it's also a leisurely route; from beginning to end it takes about 40 minutes. If you're in a rush, opt for the speedier Magazine Bus Route which parallels the St. Charles Avenue line.

The Canal Street line generally has a healthy balance of both tourists and locals. It starts off at the French Market on Esplanade Avenue, goes through the Central Business District, into Mid-City. This is a great opportunity to check out NOMA (New Orleans Museum of Art) as well as the Sydney and Walda Bestoff Sculpture Garden: two cultural landmarks of New Orleans.

The final and most recent addition to the streetcar line is the Riverfront line which was inaugurated in 1988. It runs 2 miles from the French Market to the cruise ship terminal giving travelers an opportunity to sit back, relax and you guessed it… enjoy the riverfront of the Mississippi River.

Each one-way trip costs $1.25 (exact change only) with transfers available for $.25. But you can purchase a $3 Jazzy Pass from a bus driver or a streetcar conductor, as well as from various hotels and drug stores around the city. The pass means you can hop on and off the streetcars and transfer for free. The card can be dipped into the fare machine, so there's no digging around for spare change.

miniature trains and streetcars chug past scale models of city neighborhoods, complete with landmarks like St. Louis Cathedral and mansions of the Garden District *(trains run Thu–Sun 10am–2pm, weather permitting)*.

Carousel Gardens and Storyland

◗ *Allow 2hr. 𝄞 504-483-9432. www.neworleanscitypark. com/carousel_gardens.html. Open Thu–Sun in summer; weekends spring and fall; hours vary; $3 entrance only, $20 unlimited rides.*

This charming, kid-oriented amusement park boasts a nice assortment of timeless, state fair-type thrill rides (Scrambler, Tilt-A-Whirl, Ferris Wheel, Bumper Cars) plus an antique Looff carousel and other tame thrills, all in a lovely setting beneath City Park's live oaks. Younger kids make a beeline for Storyland, a fairytale-themed play area where wolves pop out of chimneys, cows jump over moons and Mother Goose flies overhead. It's a delightful place to run, climb, scamper and slide in Cinderella's pumpkin, Jack and Jill's hill, Old King Cole's castle and a welter of colorful toadstools.

Location:
Sights lie on either side of City Park Avenue, which becomes Metairie Road as it proceeds west into Metairie. To get to the cemetery, turn right alongside the I-10 onramp and follow signs to Lakelawn Metairie Funeral Home.

Buses and Streetcars: Canal Streetcar–Cemeteries (walk to Longue Vue is less than a mile from the terminus).

Bordering Metairie

City Park Avenue, which traces City Park's southern boundary, continues west to become Metairie Road after it crosses into the suburb of Metairie. Historic cemeteries (worth a peek to see the aboveground tombs of noteworthy New Orleaneans) lie on either side of it at the intersection of Canal Boulevard, endpoint of the Canal streetcar line. Continuing west, Metairie Road winds through the tony shopping district of Old Metairie after passing the turnoff to lovely Longue Vue.

Longue Vue House and Gardens★

◗ *Allow 1hr. 7 Bamboo Rd. 𝄞 504-488-5488. www.longuevue.com. House visit by guided tour only year-round Tue–Sat 10am–5pm, Sun 1–5pm (last tour 4pm). House $10; gardens only $7.*

Often called the Versailles of New Orleans, this palatial Mid-City estate was created from 1939 to 1942 by the late philanthropists Edgar Bloom Stern, a New Orleans

businessman and cotton broker, and his wife, Sears Roebuck heiress Edith Rosenwald Stern. The Greek Revival-style mansion, designed for the Sterns by architects William and Geoffrey Platt, is surrounded by eight acres of lovely gardens. Renowned landscape architect Ellen Biddle Shipman is responsible for the gardens; she also gets credit for part of the interior design, which features fine American and English antiques, French and Oriental carpets, and a noteworthy collection of 18C English creamware. Inside the house, three stories and 20 rooms filled with antiques and contemporary art include the Oriental-style **dining room** with its Chinese rice-paper screens, and the **drawing room**, where the likes of Eleanor Roosevelt, Jack Benny, Pablo Casals and John F. Kennedy were entertained. The home's interior conveys a sense of a conservative upper-crust life-style from the 1930s and 1940s, one that supported the likes of a Flower-Arranging Room and a Wrapping Room, used only to open mail and wrap presents.

While Ellen Biddle Shipman was influenced by formal gardens in Europe, the eight acres of plots she created for the Sterns have a more intimate feel. Standouts include the **Wild Garden**, planted with wildflowers and Louisiana iris, and the magnificent **Spanish Court**, inspired by the 14C Generalife Gardens in Grenada, Spain. Stroll the ambling forest paths, inhale the aroma of magnolias, camellias, roses, sweet olives, and oleanders, and listen to the lyrical sound of water splashing in fountains. Kids love the **Discovery Garden**, where they can run to their hearts' content, dig for worms and navigate an herb maze.

Metairie Cemetery★

◗ *Allow 1hr. 5100 Pontchartrain Blvd. ☏504-486-6331. www.lakelawnmetairie.com. Open daily 7am–5pm.*

This historic cemetery was established on grounds formerly occupied by the Metairie Race Course; the track's oval shape is evident in the cemetery's layout. Self-guided tours are available at the funeral home, and give insights into the monumental tombs and funerary architecture that are among the most elaborate in New Orleans. The list of burials here is long and notewor-

OLD METAIRIE

Old Metairie is a little community far removed from the more touristy areas of downtown New Orleans. The oak tree-lined shady Metairie Road was once Metairie Ridge; used by Native American Indians and French settlers as a road. The strip was first paved in the 1920s and bisects the oldest suburb of New Orleans, nestled in between residential neighborhoods peppered with English Tudor, Greek Revival and Mission Revival homes. Metairie Road boasts upscale boutiques, jewelry stores, coffee houses and up-and-coming restaurants, plus it's home to Sal's Sno-Balls *(1823 Metairie Road)*, a family business that has been serving some of New Orleans' best shaved ice since 1960.

NEW ORLEANS CEMETERIES

New Orleans is a city on a swamp that is built below sea-level, which makes digging and burial a tricky business. Years ago, it was necessary to drill holes in wooden coffins and weigh them down with rocks before burial, and even then a good rain might have them popping out of the ground. Naturally, aboveground burial became common and now New Orleans is home to over 30 cemeteries filled with aboveground tombs and mausoleums. Even one of the newer locations, Metairie Cemetery, which is built on much higher ground than the older ones, has above-ground tombs as dictated by style and tradition. Cemeteries are often referred to as "cities of the dead," with tombs ranging from very ornate to simple structures. Of more than 30 historic cemeteries around the city, five are currently on the National Register.

The most well known of all, St. Louis Cemetery No 1 is on Basin St., within walking distance of downtown and the French Quarter. Here you can visit the tomb of **Marie Laveau**, the "voodoo queen of New Orleans." Leave a small "X" on her tomb in return for her blessing. Before you go, check out the tombs of Homer Plessy (of Plessy v. Ferguson fame) and the family of impressionist painter Edgar Degas.

Outside of the well-trafficked St. Louis Cemetery No 1, some cemeteries are literally small stone cities that provide ample opportunity for muggers and thieves to hide. Visit during daylight hours and your best bet is to go in with a group tour; you'll find safety in numbers and learn a lot. The non-profit organization **Save Our Cemeteries** *(see p57)* offers tours on a first-come, first-served basis. Each tour is a little over one hour and they run whatever the weather. Tours of Lafayette Cemetery in the historic Garden District leave from the entrance to the cemetery at Washington Avenue (across from Commander's Palace) at 10:30am Monday, Wednesday, Friday and Saturday. Tours of St. Louis Cemetery No 1 leave from inside the lobby of Basin Street Station at 501 Basin Street at 10am every Friday, Saturday and Sunday. Group tours of St. Louis Cemetery No 2, the Canal Street cemeteries, and Metairie Cemetery can be arranged by request.

thy, including celebrities from the worlds of music (Louis Prima, Al Hirt), the military (P.G.T. Beauregard, John Bell Hood) and sports (Mel Ott). Confederate President Jefferson Davis was interred here in the elaborate Army of Northern Virginia tomb upon his death in 1889, but his remains were relocated in 1893 to Richmond, Virginia.

New Orleans is one of my favorite cities, but it's not the largest. So for a vivid contrast to the compact city, take a day or two to go out a little bit further and explore the outlying areas of the Big Easy.

In case you didn't know, New Orleans is smack dab in the middle of Cajun country. If you want to get a feel for Cajun life, just follow the smell of the iconic crawfish boil or take part in a traditional *boucherie* (that's a pig cookout) where you might even be asked to lend a hand.

Just a short drive northwest from the city is the state capital of Baton Rouge, which is also home of the Louisiana State University and the Tigers football team. Joining in the tailgating festivities on a Saturday game day is a rite of passage for those who live in the area.

In New Orleans you may have heard the locals tell tales about the swamps and the bayous, but if you venture outside of New Orleans proper you have the chance to witness them firsthand. Take a boat or airboat tour into the swamps *(see p59)* and learn about the vast, unique eco-system that makes up the Mississippi River Delta area. You may even see a gator or two.

The past is ever-present in Southern Louisiana, and nowhere more so than the River Road on the way to Baton Rouge. The banks of the Mississippi are lined with majestic antebellum plantation homes open to the public. Join a tour, or better yet hire a car to travel along either bank at a leisurely pace. Handsome paddlewheel riverboats ply the Mississippi and you can choose from a relaxed lunch or jazz dinner cruise, or a day cruise to Chalmette Battlefield.

Beyond these tourist-driven experiences, taking time to experience life outside the city gives you a taste of what the rest of Louisiana is about. And guess what, there's more than gator and souvenirs.

Old State Capitol Building, Baton Rouge Photo: © Andre Jenny/age fotostock

PETER'S TOP PICKS

 CULTURE

Visit the Acadian Cultural Center to get a feel for traditional and contemporary Cajun life. **Acadian Cultural Center (p 164)**

 GREEN SPACES

Get out of the city and take a tour of swamps and wetlands that are rich in bird and wildlife. **Swamp tours (p 59, 162)**

 HISTORY

Venture an hour and a half outside the city to see the regal "White Castle" Nottoway Plantation, one of the largest antebellum mansions in the South **Nottoway Plantation (p 161)**

 STAY

When venturing into Cajun country, stay at The Juliet Hotel, a boutique hotel located close to all the area's activities. **The Juliet Hotel (p 174)**

 EAT

Head to Café des Amis at Breaux Bridge to check out authentic Cajun food. The popular Saturday morning zydeco breakfast is a real treat with outstanding food AND live music. **Café des Amis (p 182) Paraje Arevalo (p 34)**

 ENTERTAINMENT

It's always fun to watch the LSU fans go crazy. Head to Baton Rouge to watch the Tigers and experience the passion and intensity that surrounds the state's beloved college team. **Louisiana State University Tigers (p 160)**

ASK PETER...

Q: Where can I visit in the lower Ninth Ward?

A: An army of volunteers is helping to rebuild the district, but there is a long way to go. Tours of the devastated areas are a safe way to learn more about the destruction caused by Katrina, but if you have your own transport you might feel less conspicuous going independently. Stick to St. Claude Avenue and go in the daytime to see the quirky bars and theaters. As well as the steamboat houses (see opposite), check out the *House of Dance and Feathers* (1317 Tupelo Street), a museum focusing on the culture of the Mardi Gras Indians.

Location:
5mi south-east of New Orleans in Chalmette.
Directions: Go east on Route 46 to park entrance at 8606 W. St. Bernard Highway.

STEAMBOAT HOUSES

Twin steamboat houses, designed to resemble steamboats, were first built by husband and wife team, Milton and Mary Doullet in 1905. The two were riverboat pilots and were inspired by the Japanese pavilion at the St. Louis World's Fair. In 1912, their son, Paul, built its neighboring counterpart. The interiors of the houses are coated with ceramic, and the wraps around the porches are covered in white tile casings. This makes the houses extraordinarily flood proof and ensured that the Steamboat Houses sustained minimal damage during Hurricane Katrina, suffering superficial wind damage only. You can see these houses in the Lower Ninth Ward, on Egania Street at numbers 400 and 503.

Chalmette Battlefield and National Cemetery★

At this riverside battlefield on January 8 1815, General Andrew Jackson and a force of around 5,000 fighters successfully defended New Orleans against a British invasion of around 8,000 soldiers. The battle, which brought together wealthy Creoles, Acadian farmers, free men of color, Native American tribes and even pirates to fight alongside Jackson's militia for a common cause, was the final major confrontation of the War of 1812. The American victory secured US ownership of the Louisiana Territory and made a hero of Jackson, who went on to become the seventh US president.

Visitor Center

◗ *Allow 1hr. 8606 W. St. Bernard Hwy., Chalmette. ✆ 504-281-0510. www.nps.gov/jela. Open daily 9am–4:30pm.*
In the visitor center, displays and audiovisual presentations lay out the events leading up to the confrontation, and clearly illustrate the various strategies employed by Jackson and Major General Sir Edward Pakenham, the British commander. A 1.5-mile road leads past key battle sites; the low dike fringing the battlefield represents the redoubt dug by the Americans to defend their positions. Adjacent

to the battlefield lies the quiet Chalmette National Cemetery; stroll through to see graves of soldiers from conflicts ranging from the War of 1812 to the war in Vietnam.

River Road East Bank Plantations★★

One of the finest assortments of antebellum plantation homes in the South lies along the historic River Road between New Orleans and Baton Rouge. During the area's 19C plantation heyday, more than 2,000 plantations thrived here, and the Mississippi more resembled a street than a waterway, with steamboats pulling up to the large, elegant residences fronting the riverbanks on both sides. Today you'll drive past oil refineries and chemical plants as you travel along the route to visit the gracious survivors of another time, preserved amid all the modern industry.

Destrehan★★

● *Allow 90min. 13034 River Rd. (Hwy. 48), Destrehan.* ℘ *985-764-9315. www.destrehanplantation.org. Visit by guided tour only daily 9am–4pm. $15.*

Completed in 1790 as the heart of a 6,000-acre indigo (later sugarcane) plantation, this raised Creole-style manor is considered the oldest documented plantation house in the Mississippi Valley. During the early 18C the property stretched all the way from the Mississippi River to Lake Pontchartrain. In 1793, the plantation was purchased by Jean Noel Destrehan who, with his brother-in-law Etienne de Boré, perfected the process of granulating sugar. The house was expanded in 1810, and Greek Revival ornamental details were added in 1839 to conform to antebellum tastes. In the Jefferson Room, you'll find a document signed in 1804 by Thomas Jefferson. Historic craft demonstrations (indigo-dyeing, candlemaking) by costumed interpreters take place daily.

Location:
The River Road mostly follows the curve of the Mississippi River; state and local route numbers change along the way.
Directions: From New Orleans take I-10 west toward Baton Rouge, then I-310 south; exit at Highway 48 in Destrehan and follow signs for Destrehan Plantation. To get from Destrehan to San Francisco, follow Highway 48 west to Norco and follow signs to Highway 61 north. Stay on Highway 61 about 10 miles, then turn left on Route 53 to the town of Reserve. Turn right on Route 44, the River Road, and follow signs about 4 miles to San Francisco. From San Francisco, continue west on the River Road about 30 miles, following signs to Burnside and Houmas House.

San Francisco★

▶ *Allow 1hr. 2646 Hwy. 44 (River Rd.), Garyville. ☎ 985-535-2341. www.sanfranciscoplantation.org. Open daily 9am–4pm. $15.*

The eye-catching exterior style of this ebulliently decorated plantation house *(1856)*, with its latticework, scrolled cornices, and balustraded captain's walk, was dubbed "Steamboat Gothic" for its fancied resemblance to riverboats passing on the Mississippi.

The home's name is thought to come from the nickname bestowed on it by one of its former owners, Valsin Marmillon, who claimed that the expense of running the plantation left him *"sans frusquin"* (without a penny), an expression that later morphed into "San Francisco."

The interior has been restored to around 1860, and contains a fine collection of period antiques.

Houmas House★

▶ *Allow 1hr. 40136 Hwy. 942 (River Rd.), Burnside. ☎ 225-473-9380. www.houmashouse.com. House visit by guided tour only Mon–Tue 9:30am–5pm, Wed–Sun 9:30am–7pm. $20 house and gardens, $10 gardens only (self-guided).*

This stately plantation home gained its name from the land upon which it was built, which was originally owned by the Houmas Indians. It pairs a modest four-room house *(1790)* with an 1840 Greek Revival mansion built for John Smith Preston, a son-in-law of Revolutionary War hero Wade Hampton. The exquisite gardens nurture native Louisiana and exotic tropical plants.

River Road West Bank Plantations★★

Heading upriver on the West Bank from New Orleans toward Baton Rouge you'll encounter Oak Alley, Laura and Nottoway plantations, each illuminating a different aspect of this region's economic development, history and architecture. Preservation of the River Road plantations began with the restoration of Oak Alley in the 1920s. As on the East Bank, as you proceed you'll wend your way past sugarcane fields of varying heights (harvest time begins in September) that recall the region's historic prosperity.

Location:

The River Road follows the West Bank of the Mississippi River; route and highway numbers change as the route heads west.

Directions:

To get to Laura Plantation, take I-10 west toward Baton Rouge; exit at Route 641 south toward Gramercy. Continue south on Route 3213 over the Mississippi River and take the Highway 18 ramp; continue west about 4 miles toward Vacherie, following signs for River Road Plantations and Laura. From Oak Alley, continue west on Route 18 about 3.5 miles. To get to Nottoway, continue to follow the bends of the river west on Route 18, through Donaldsonville. The River Road becomes Route 405; continue on it to White Castle and Nottoway; the distance from Oak Alley is about 43 miles.

8

Laura★★

▶ *Allow 90min. 2247 Hwy. 18, Vacherie. ☎ 225-265-7690. www.lauraplantation.com. Visit by guided tour only daily 10am–4pm. $18.*

The Creole culture of New Orleans and the lower Mississippi Valley are the focus of excellent guided tours of this colorfully painted raised Creole cottage *(1805)*, beautifully restored after having survived a devastating fire in 2004. The story of this sugar-cane plantation is remarkable in that it was operated largely by the women of the Duparc and Locoul families for 84 years. Guided tours of the plantation *(and of the French Quarter by sister organization Le Monde Creole, see Sightseeing p57)* offer insights into Creole lifestyle and culture based on Laura Locoul's personal memoirs.

Also on the site are 12 historic outbuildings, including original slave cabins where, in the 1870s, the African folktales of Br'er Rabbit were first recorded.

Oak Alley★★

▶ *Allow 90min. 3645 Hwy. 18, Vacherie. ☎ 225-265-2151. www.oakalleyplantation.com. House visit by guided tour only daily 9am–5pm (last tour 4:30pm). $18.*

Named for the gracious quarter-mile-long *allée* of 28 live oak trees that approaches it on the river side, this stately

Travel Tip:
You can take a formal tour of Oak Alley and visit the museum, but you can also head to the restaurant that is open daily for breakfast and lunch in a cottage located on the grounds. Don't forget to try the famous mint julep!

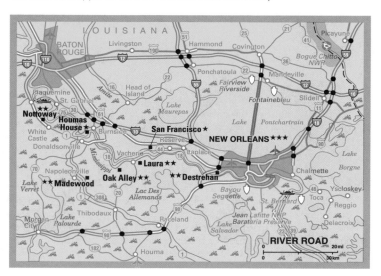

FOOTBALL FANS

While you are in New Orleans head to Baton Rouge to watch the **Lousiana State University** football team and experience the devoted fans.

The South takes college sports seriously and the only conference that matters is the SEC. All of the national powerhouses are a part of this southern centered conference and it is considered by many to be the best in the land. LSU played in the BCS National Championship in 2012, and despite a dismal performance, the school is expected to be a contender for the national championship again next year. But win or lose, a Saturday game day excursion out to Baton Rouge is an almost religious experience, a required ritual to take part in the amazing tailgating scene.

Tailgates are usually a good place to soak up the culture of a team and at Tiger Stadium they go all out. Hundreds of people get to the stadium days in advance in anticipation of a big game and the quality of food at the tailgates is legendary. Expect to find anything from standard burgers and hot dogs to Cajun specialties. Alligator or gumbo as you tailgate, why not?

While walking through the parking lot you will hear shouts of "Tiger Bait" being directed at visiting opponent's fans. Rivals including Tulane's Green Wave, Ole Miss' Rebels, Auburn Tigers, Alabama Crimson Tide, Arkansas Razorbacks and the Florida Gators have all been tiger bait. The term is a nod towards the school's famous mascot Mike the Tiger. You can even go see Mike the Tiger in person. Since 1936 LSU has had a real life Bengal tiger present at home games and you can find the most recent version of Mike, now Mike VI, parked out in front of the opponent's locker room on game days.

If you want to see the players up close make sure to line up with the thousands of other fans who take part in the "March Down the Hill." Before they enter the stadium, the players and coaches walk from the Pete Maravich Assembly Center down to the stadium and are cheered on by the fans that line the walkway.

Greek Revival mansion was completed in 1839 as the heart of a flourishing sugarcane plantation. (The trees predate the house by more than a century.) A total of 28 massive columns support the two-story gallery surrounding the house. Guided tours by costumed interpreters cover the home's elegant interior, furnished with fine period antiques.

Nottoway★★

○ *Allow 90min. 31025 Hwy. 1, White Castle. ☎225-527-6884. www.nottoway.com. Visit by guided tour only daily 9am–4pm. $20 house, $8 grounds only (self-guided).*

Largest plantation home in the South,, this ornate white mansion (1859) on the Mississippi displays a fanciful mix of Greek Revival and Italianate styles. Designed by Henry Howard for Virginia sugarcane planter John Hampden Randolph and his family, the 53,000sq ft house boasts 64 rooms sporting elegant appointments that speak to the enormous wealth of successful plantations during the antebellum years. The stately white ballroom boasts curved window panes and shutters, a great extravagance for the day. The historic Nottoway property was recently expanded with modern facilities and amenties; today it is a popular conference center and resort.

Travel Tip:
Consider renting a car for longer excursions. Most plantation homes, Baton Rouge and Cajun country are anywhere from an hour and a half to two hours one-way and the taxi fare would be pretty steep! Rent your own car for a few days and explore all the unexpected attractions along the way.

Baton Rouge★

Incorporated in 1817, this busy port and university city on the banks of the Mississippi has been Louisiana's state capital since 1849. Its colorful name comes from a red stick placed by local Native Americans to mark a hunting boundary; the *"baton rouge"* **was spotted and noted by Pierre Le Moyne during his exploration of the region in 1699. Baton Rouge is home to the sprawling campus of Louisiana State University. LSU figures prominently in Baton Rouge life, particularly during football season, when home games of the LSU Tigers dominate the campus areas surrounding the massive stadium.**

Location:
81 miles (about an hour and a half) northwest of downtown New Orleans.
Directions:
Take the Pontchartrain Expressway (I-10) west toward Baton Rouge, and follow I-110 North (I-10W continues to Lafayette and Cajun Country). For downtown sights, exit at North Boulevard (exit 1C) .

State Capitol and Gardens★

○ *Allow 30min. State Capitol Dr. at N. 4th St. ☎225-342-7317. http://crt.louisiana.gov/tourism/capitol. Tower open 8am–4:30pm.*

Louisiana's State Capitol building, a striking 34-story Art Deco skyscraper (1932), is the tallest state capitol in the US. It dominates the surrounding landscape, as was the intention of its creator, the controversial and redoubtable governor Huey P. Long. (Long was buried in the Capitol's garden after being assassinated in 1935.) Views from the

ASK PETER...

Q: Is there a beach close to New Orleans?
A: New Orleans is not known for its beaches. Due to the multiple rivers that run through the area, many of the coastal lines are muddy. White sandy beaches are at least 3 hours away. Head to Alabama and the Gulf Shores, or further east to the famous Pensacola Beach, which draws a bit of a crowd.

Travel Tip:

Have you ever wondered how to make Tabasco sauce? If so check out the Tabasco museum and factory on Avery Island, a nature preserve 140 miles west of New Orleans. The museum and factory tour teach you everything there is to know about how the spicy sauce is produced. The 170-acre setting is a wildlife refuge that is waiting to be explored.
www.tabasco.com/main.cfm.

spire's 27th-floor observation gallery encompass the river and the Pentagon barracks, established in 1819 to house a US army garrison serving the southwestern US. The **Old Arsenal** (1838) to the east contains a small military museum.

Old State Capitol

◗ *Allow 30min.100 North Blvd. ☏ 225-342-0500. www.sos.la.gov. Open Tue–Sat 9am–4pm.*
It was in the main chamber of this castle like, Gothic Revival-style structure *(1850)* that state representatives in 1861 voted to withdraw from the Union and form a separate nation (which existed for four weeks before joining the Confederacy). Today you'll find entertaining displays about Louisiana's colorful political history arrayed around the main level.

A concrete promenade along the east bank of the river near the Old State Capitol leads past riverboat casinos and the **USS Kidd**, a decommissioned World War II destroyer. Nearby you'll find the **Louisiana Art and Science Museum** *(100 River Rd., ☏ 225-344-5272; open Tue–Fri 10am–3pm, Sat 10am–5pm, Sun 1–4pm; $7)* with changing displays of regional culture and a planetarium theater.

Louisiana State Museum★

◗ *Allow 90min. 660 N. 4th St. ☏ 225-342-5428. http://lsm.crt.state.la.us. Open Tue–Sat 10am–5pm.*
The sleek new building across from the capitol complex contains colorful, fun exhibits about the state's history,

SWAMP TOURS

People might try to sell you on a swamp tour and if you don't know a local who can steer you through the bayou, this might be your best bet. You'll be comfortable and dry as you drift along the waterways—but swamp tours are far from restricted experiences. Early settlers survived by hunting and fishing on the bayou and local wetlands experts like to mock the cultural differences between the bayou and New Orleans. Your guide might feed the alligators marshmallows, or he'll chat with them in French (apparently gators are devoted Francophiles). As well as gators, you'll get up close and personal with birds, snakes and turtles. Keep in mind that there's more chance of seeing alligators in the warmer months of the year, as they hide away in the cold.

economy and culture. Look for the Civil War-era submarine, or try your feet at dancing to zydeco or Cajun music; the museum owns several musical instruments that belonged to noteworthy Louisiana tunesmiths like Fats Domino and Aaron Neville.

Magnolia Mound Plantation★

◐ *Allow 90min. 2161 Nicholson Dr. ℘ 225-343-4955. www.friendsofmangoliamound.org. Open Mon–Sat 10am–4pm, Sun 1–4pm. $10.*

Visitors may view an open-hearth cooking demonstration in the fully functional detached kitchen before touring the gracious house (c.1791), considered one of the finest examples of Creole-style architecture in the area. The house is furnished mostly with furnishings and decorative arts made in Louisiana. You'll also find numerous restored outbuildings, including the overseer's house and the carriage house.

Rural Life Museum

◐ *Allow 90min. 4560 Essen Ln. ℘ 225-765-2437. http://rurallife.lsu.edu. Open daily 8:30am–5pm. $7.*

Sprawling on broad open fields in suburban Baton Rouge, this fine outdoor museum gathers interesting examples of regional vernacular architecture, collected here to demonstrate the way of life of past cultures in Louisiana. Artifacts of rural life before the 20C are displayed in a large barn; from here you can explore plantation buildings and several rustic homes including a shotgun house and a "dogtrot" house.

Cajun Country★

A broad landscape of sugarcane and rice fields, boggy swamps and sinuous bayous, the Cajun Country offers visitors an excellent opportunity to sample the rich cultural heritage of one of the nation's best-known and most colorful ethnic groups. Comprising 22 parishes (the Louisiana term for counties), the region, formally known as Acadiana, extends north of the ragged Gulf Coast and west of the Mississippi River, encompassing the boggy Atchafalaya Basin and relatively high prairies ranging west of Lafayette to the Texas border.

Location:
Lafayette is about 130 miles (about 2.5 hours) from New Orleans via I-10 west.
Directions: Take the Pontchartrain Expressway (I-10) west toward Baton Rouge, and continue over the Mississippi River Bridge. Lafayette is about 50 miles from Baton Rouge. To get to Breaux Bridge, St. Martinville and New Iberia, exit I-10 at Highway 328 and drive south. Highway 31 leads from Breaux Bridge to St. Martinville and New Iberia.

ACADIANA

Formally named "Acadiana," the Cajun Country is mostly inhabited by descendants of French colonists who were deported from Acadia (now Nova Scotia) in 1755 for refusing to swear allegiance to the British Crown. After suffering terrible hardships on the deportation journey, Acadian refugees began arriving in southern Louisiana, infusing the region with the distinctive culture that flourishes today. Tourist attractions are sparse outside the regional capital of Lafayette, but the charm of a visit to this area lies in its people and their lifestyle. Explore the small towns of St. Martinville, Breaux Bridge or New Iberia, where fun-loving, hardworking and fervently Catholic Cajuns (the word is derived from "Acadian") welcome visitors to join their enthusiastic pursuit of a good time.

Lafayette★

○ *Allow 1 day. 135mi west of New Orleans via I-10. Visitor center at 1400 NW Evangeline Thruway. ℘800-346-1958. www.lafayettetravel.com.*

Founded in 1836 as Vermilionville and renamed in 1884, Louisiana's fifth-largest city is known as the "Hub City of Acadiana." Sights related to Acadian history and culture are located here, along with good restaurants and hotels, making Lafayette a convenient headquarters for forays into Acadiana.

Acadian Cultural Center★

○ *Allow 1hr. 501 Fisher Rd. ℘337-232-0789. www.nps.gov/jela. Open daily 8am–5pm.*

This welcoming visitor center, one of the six sites operated by the Jean Lafitte National Historical Park and Preserve, is an excellent place to begin your acquaintance with the Cajun Country. Displays and artifacts give a good picture of various aspects of historic and contemporary Cajun life in Louisiana, highlighting the ways in which Acadian traditions and methods were adapted to conditions in Louisiana. Be sure to see the 40-minute video presentation dramatizing the Acadian expulsion from Nova Scotia. In spring and fall, the center operates guided boat tours on languid Bayou Vermilion, former home to trappers, farmers and fishermen; it's a great way to get a feel for the traditional Cajun lifestyle of yesteryear.

Acadian Village★

○ *Allow 90min. 200 Greenleaf Dr. ℘337-981-2364. www.acadianvillage.org. Open Tue–Sat 10am–4pm. $8.*

Set around a placid "bayou," this rustic recreated village offers a glimpse of life in Acadiana around the mid-19C. Most of the structures were moved here from other locations in the region, donated by families whose ancestors once lived in them; others were constructed on-site with period materials. Helpful plaques provide insights into architectural practices of the time, while displays in each building focus on Acadian culture and traditions.

CAJUN LIFE
...LIKE A LOCAL

Not everyone who lives in Cajun country is of French descent but the influence can still be found in the language and food of the area, which is something you have to experience for yourself. Fiddles and accordions set feet flying in rural dance halls; headily spiced gumbos, seafood stews and boudin (rice and pork sausage) appear on local tables; and Cajun French is as prevalent as English on sidewalks and in shops and restaurants.

The heart of Acadiana is the city of Lafayette, about 2 hours west of New Orleans. Here, you can sample the most authentic Cajun and Creole cuisine to the sounds of zydeco. Use Lafayette or the nearby town of Breaux Bridge (aka the Crawfish Capital of the World) as a jumping-off point for the region's famous tours. These are the iconic images of swamps and bayous where alligators abound, along with some of the most abundant wading bird population in the country. Tour the scenic Cypress Island Preserve and Lake Martin on commercial fishing boats or high-speed airboats.

For the real Cajun food experience, ask the locals to steer you towards finding a crawfish boil or an old fashioned *boucherie*. A crawfish boil is pretty self-explanatory but the *boucherie* is a special occasion. Family and friends get together to cook a whole pig. The pig is divided into sections and everyone helps prepare and cook it with the main goal being to use every bit of the animal, snout to tail.

If you really want to get a taste of the Cajun lifestyle, join in the action at a dance hall or a local Sunday afternoon fais-do-do (the local term for a country dance). To find one, look on community bulletin boards, check at visitor centers, or navigate to the websites of the following places, all traditional Cajun dance halls with live music and foot-stomping fun.

La Poussiere
1301 Grand Point Ave.,
Breaux Bridge.
504-332-1721.
http://lapoussiere.com.

**Randol's Restaurant
and Dance Hall**
2320 Kaliste Saloom Rd.,
Lafayette.
337-981-7080.
www.randols.com.

Whiskey River Landing
1365 Henderson Levee Rd.,
Breaux Bridge.
337-228-2277.
http://whiskeyriverlanding.net.

Liberty Theater
Corner of South 2nd St.
and Park Ave., Eunice.
337-457-7389.
www.eunice-la.com.

ASK PETER...

Q: Is French still spoken in New Orleans?

A: Aside from its influence on menus throughout the city, little or no traditional French is spoken by people in New Orleans today—but Cajun French can still be heard, particularly (and not surprisingly) in the Cajun country.

Travel Tip:
You might not think it but New Orleans is actually one of the busiest port cities in the country. Everything from commercial tankers to luxury cruise ships pass through the area every day because of its central location and its direct access to the Mississippi river. All of the big name cruise lines operate out of the port including Carnival and Norwegian.

Vermilionville★

◐ *Allow 2hrs. 300 Fisher Rd.* ✆ *337-233-4077. www.bayouvermilion.org. Open Tue–Sun 10am–4pm. $8.*
Nineteen reproduced and restored buildings, including a 1790 farmstead, range along tranquil Bayou Vermilion at this living-history museum devoted to commemorating the Acadian way of life (c.1765-1890).

Costumed artisans demonstrate traditional crafts such as weaving, boatbuilding and blacksmithing, while Cajun bands perform regularly in a large dance hall. Don't miss a browse through the gift store for handcrafted items produced locally.

Breaux Bridge

◐ *Allow 2hrs. 12mi from Lafayette by I-10 and Hwy. 328. Visitor Center at 214 Bridge St.* ✆ *337-332-8500. www.breauxbridgelive.com.*
For a taste of life in contemporary Acadiana, spend some time in charming little Breaux Bridge, which dubs itself the "Crawfish Capital of the World." At the visitor center you can pick up a brochure detailing a short, pleasant walking tour of the historic downtown. Most weekend nights and Sunday afternoons, locals gather to eat, drink and dance to traditional live Cajun music.

St. Martinville

◐ *Allow 3hrs.15mi from Lafayette via Hwy. 90 and Rte. 96.* ✆ *337-394-2233. www.stmartinville.org.*
Pretty St. Martinville on the bank of the Bayou Teche was incorporated in 1817, but founded much earlier as Poste des Attakapas, a Native American trading post where first French then Spanish settlers established administrative centers for colonizing the region.

St. Martinville is probably best known as the site of the Evangeline legend of an Acadian woman separated from her fiancée during the deportation of Acadian setters from Nova Scotia in the 1750s; the stately old **Evangeline Oak**, located behind St. Martin Park, commemorates the story. Near the tree you can stroll a pleasant boardwalk along the banks of the slow-moving bayou.

Longfellow-Evangeline State Historic Site★

◐ *Allow 1hr. 1200 N. Main St.* ✆ *337-394-3754. http://crt.state.la.us/parks/longfell.aspx. Open Tue–Sat 9am–4pm. $4.*
A visitor center with a film and displays, and nicely preserved historic structures (a raised Creole cottage and an

Acadian farmstead) illustrate how the distinctive French culture of southern Louisiana was established and thrived, and why it survives today. The site is named for American poet Henry Wadsworth Longfellow, whose epic poem "Evangeline," published in 1847, dramatized the Evangeline legend and generated national interest in the story of the Acadians and their culture.

New Iberia
○ *Allow 3hrs. 20mi from Lafayette via Hwy. 90 and Rte. 182.*
www.cityofnewiberia.com.
Settled by Spanish colonists from Málaga who named it for the Iberian peninsula, New Iberia typifies a contemporary Cajun Country city, celebrating and preserving its Acadian culture amid the bustle of modern industry and commerce.

The historic downtown is charming; East Main Street, dotted with cafes and stores, abuts the Bayou Teche and makes for a pleasant stroll.

A visit to the small **Bayou Teche Museum** *(131 E. Main St.; ℘ 337-606-5977; www.bayoutechemuseum.org; $4)* is well worth your time; displays and artifacts within focus on the scenic bayou and its commercial and cultural role in the development of Acadiana.

Shadows-on-the-Teche★★
○ *Allow 1hr. 317 E. Main St. ℘ 337-369-6446. www.shadowsontheteche.word press.com. Visit by guided tour only Mon–Sat 9am–4:30pm. $10.*
Moss-draped live oak trees create a play of light and shadow over this elegant brick Greek Revival mansion, built by sugarcane planter David Weeks in 1834. The house is in a remarkable state of preservation, largely because it remained in the same family for four generations before being left to the National Trust for Historic Preservation.

Nearly every item in the house is original, including fine Federal and Empire-style furniture from New York and Philadelphia, Staffordshire china and family portraits. Family members lie interred in a tranquil corner of the beautiful, formally landscaped grounds fringing the slow-moving Bayou Teche.

ZYDECO
While in Cajun country you might encounter some music you have never heard before. Taking its roots out of jazz, blues, West African and Cajun music, zydeco is a style of music created by the black Creole people that inhabited the rural southwest plains of Louisiana in the 1920s. It's a unique style that was originally sung in Creole French and is characterized by the use of a *frottoir* or, scrub board, that hangs on the players chest and is scrubbed like a rhythm instrument. A zydeco band might also incorporate an accordian, fiddle, triangle and drums and modern zydeco music can be infused with Rhythm and Blues, funk and Hip Hop.

YOUR STAY IN NEW ORLEANS

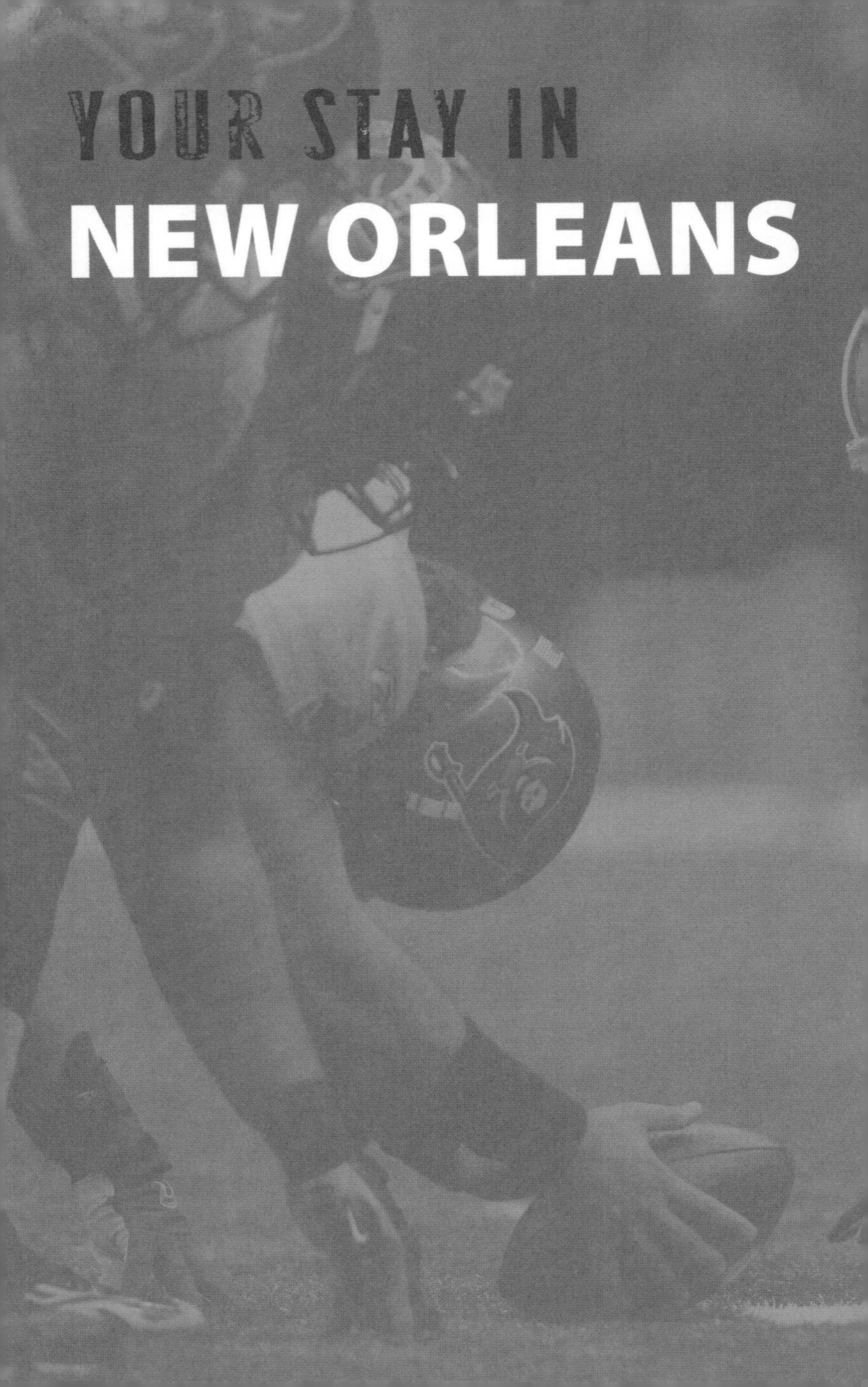

The New Orleans Saints against the Tampa Bay
Buccaneers at Louisiana Superdome in New Orleans
Photo: © Icon SMI/Photoshot

Travel Tip:
Prices here reflect
the "high season,"
which in New Orleans
means spring and
fall. Summer can be
oppressively hot, but
if you can handle the
heat, some hotels
offer a discount at this
time. It's always best
to book in advance
(at least six months
for Mardi Gras) but if
you need last minute
accommodation
the French Quarter
Welcome Center can
point you in the right
direction *(see p70).*

Where to Stay

Big Easy accommodations run the gamut from French Quarter historic properties to Garden District bed-and-breakfasts in Greek Revival mansions to funky Faubourg Marigny inns to reliable chain hotels around the CBD. Be aware that the party never stops in the French Quarter, particularly around Bourbon Street, so if all-night noise bothers you, be sure to ask for a room facing away from the street or stay in another neighborhood altogether.

Please note that while many hotels, particularly those in the French Quarter, the CBD and the Warehouse District, do offer on-site or valet parking, most charge additional rates of $25–$35 per night for this service and in/out privileges may be limited; it's best to ask when reserving. All hotels listed here accept credit card payments.

For price ranges, see the Legend on the cover flap.

French Quarter

$$ Prince Conti – *831 Conti St.;* ✕ 🅿; ✆ *800-366-3743; www.www.princecontihotel.com; 71 rooms.* This budget gem right off Bourbon Street has comfortable, sizeable rooms with smallish bathrooms and a friendly, helpful staff. Modern amenities are sparse but the location is wonderful, the price is right, and the place has the feel of a European *pension.*

$$ Place d'Armes – *624 St. Ann St.;* ☕ 🅿; ✆ *800-366-3743; www.placedarmes.com; 84 rooms.* This charming value find offers a perfect location just steps from Jackson Square. Rooms are petite but well kept and charming, and the front-desk staff provide an accommodating welcome. The courtyard pool is the perfect spot to cool off from your French Quarter wanderings.

$$$ Bourbon Orleans Hotel – *717 Orleans St.;* ✕ 🅿; ✆ *504-523-2222; www.bourbonorleans.com; 212 rooms.* The glittering Orleans Ballroom, once the site of 19C quadroon balls where Creole gentlemen and mixed-race women met and mingled, forms the centerpiece of this stately hotel. The lovely lobby sets the stage for luxurious guest rooms sporting marble baths and modern amenities, all excellent value. Ask for a room facing away from Bourbon Street.

$$$ Omni Royal Orleans – *621 St. Louis St.;* ✗ 🅿; *☎504-529-5333; www.omnihotels.com; 346 rooms.* Moderately priced in a prime location, the historic Omni Royal offers extras like a rooftop pool and the acclaimed Rib Room restaurant. Rooms are small but clean and nicely appointed in 19C style.

$$$$ Soniat House – *1133 Chartres St.;* 🅿; *☎504-522-0570; www.soniathouse.com; 30 rooms.* This classic Creole-style townhouse, now transformed as a lovely boutique hotel, occupies a convenient Chartres Street location, away from most French Quarter noise. Spiral staircases lead to rooms decorated with antiques, luxury fabrics and fine linens on the beds. Breakfast *($12.50 extra)* is served around the lily pod in the courtyard.

$$$$ Royal Sonesta Hotel – *300 Bourbon St.;* ✗ 🅿; *☎504-586-0300; www.sonesta.com; 500 rooms.* This busy hotel lies right smack in the heart of the Quarter; expect some noise if your room overlooks Bourbon Street. Rooms are furnished with antique reproductions; many offer French doors and semiprivate wrought-iron balconies. You'll find plenty of amenities here, including several bars, a fitness center and a heated pool.

$$$$$ The Monteleone – *214 Royal St.;* ✗ 🅿; *☎504-523-3341; www.hotel monteleone.com; 570 rooms and suites.* This landmark 16-story hotel sports a European vibe to match its dignified Baroque façade and lobby frescos. Service is top-notch and the rooms are sizeable and quiet. You'll find the rooftop pool a welcome retreat on a hot day, and the revolving Carousel Bar a fun spot for an aperitif.

CBD and the Warehouse Arts District

$ Baronne Plaza – *201 Baronne St.;* ✗ 🅿; *☎504-522-0083 or 888-756-0083; www.baronneplaza.com; 170 rooms.* This recently renovated Wyndham property occupies a beautiful Art Deco building just blocks from Canal Street and the French Quarter. Rooms are good-sized, with basic amenities including free Wi-Fi and a fitness center. Valet parking is available for an extra fee.

$$ Le Pavillon – *833 Poydras St.;* ✗ 🅿; *☎504-581-3111 or 800-535-9095; www.lepavillon.com; 226 rooms.* This historic property has been a CBD landmark since 1907; antiques grace its sumptuous gilt and marble lobby. Some of the guest rooms are small, but you'll enjoy the beautiful rooftop swimming pool at the end of a sultry day. Peanut butter and jelly sandwiches and cold milk are offered as a late-night snack buffet.

$$$ Renaissance New Orleans Arts Hotel – *700 Tchoupitoulas St.;* ✗ 🅿; *☎504-613-2330 or 888-431-8634; www.marriott.com; 217 rooms.* Just the right amount of modern artistic flair makes this former warehouse-turned-hotel in a quiet neighborhood near the museums an ideal spot for a sojourn. Admire the works in the lobby before checking into sizeable, well-appointed guest rooms with large windows. Take time for a soak in the rooftop pool or hot tub during your stay.

$$$ International House Hotel – *221 Camp St.;* ✕ 🅿; ☎*504-553-9550; www.ihhotel.com; 117 rooms and suites.* Renovated in 2007 by Los-Angeles-based designer L.M. Pagano, this boutique hotel just steps from the Quarter boasts large, simply designed rooms with every modern amenity, including complimentary Wi-Fi and large, flat-screen televisions. The "Apple" rooms offer glass showers, Apple TV and 12ft ceilings, while the "Rockstar" rooms are windowless for an extra-quiet night.

$$$$ Loft 523 – *523 Gravier St.;* 🅿; ☎*504-200-6523; www.loft523.com; 18 rooms.* This urbanely hip hotel, housed in a 19C warehouse, offers Soho-style lofts with massive wooden beams, stark spotlighting, Italian marble baths with dual showerheads and exquisite Frette linens. The two penthouses feature garden terraces.

$$$$ The Roosevelt – *123 Baronne St.;* ✕ 🅿; ☎*504-648-1200; www.therooseveltneworleans.com; 504 rooms.* A landmark since the 1900s *(see p109)* and now part of the Waldorf-Astoria chain, the Roosevelt is renowned for its storied past, lovely décor, amenities and especially attentive service. Luxury linens, flat-screen TVs, bathrobes and a rooftop pool make for memorable stays; make an appointment at the on-site Guerlain Spa to pamper yourself after a hectic day.

Garden District and Uptown

$$ Maison St. Charles – *1319 St. Charles Ave.;* ⌨ 🅿; ☎*504-522-0187; www.choicehotels.com; 128 rooms.* A property of Quality Inns & Suites, the Maison St. Charles offers good value in an excellent location on St. Charles Avenue. The modern rooms are unremarkable but comfortable, clean and recently renovated, with free Internet access, flat-screen TVs and in room mini-fridges and microwaves.

$$ Chimes Bed & Breakfast – *1146 Constantinople St.;* ⌨ 🅿; ☎*504-899-2621; www.chimesneworleans.com; 5 rooms.* The owner and her family live here at this charmingly renovated 1876 cottage in the Garden District. Individually decorated guest quarters may feature four-poster beds, claw-foot tubs and handmade lace curtains; each room has a private bath, Wi-Fi access and an entrance off the shady courtyard. And it's ideally located just a short walk from St. Charles Avenue and Magazine Street.

$$ Park View Guest House – *7004 St. Charles Ave.;* ⌨; ☎*504-861-7564; www.parkviewguesthouse.com; 21 rooms.* Personalized service and homey, yet elegant accommodations describe this very comfortable mansion at the corner of Audubon Park overlooking the St. Charles Avenue streetcar line. Snacks like popcorn and chocolate chip cookies are available all day, the breakfasts draw rave reviews, and the staff are devoted to guests' comfort. Many of the spacious guest rooms have balconies overlooking the park.

$$ Hubbard Mansion – *3535 St. Charles Ave.;* 🛏 **P** ; *504-897-3535; www.hubbardmansion.com; 5 suites, 2 apartments.* This elegant Greek Revival mansion is full of period antiques, yet offers modern amenities. A tasty continental breakfast is served each morning. It's the perfect spot to stay during Mardi Gras, as parades roll right past the door.

$$$ Sully Mansion Bed & Breakfast – *2631 Prytania St.;* 🛏; *504-891-0457; www.sullymansion.com; 8 rooms.* A historic Greek Revival Garden District mansion designed by noted architect Thomas Sully, this charming inn lies within walking distance of Magazine Street, with easy access to the St. Charles Avenue streetcar. You'll love the wide plank floors and elegant furnishings in the sizeable guest rooms, each with private bath; the large wraparound porch is the perfect place to unwind. A full, multi-course breakfast is provided on weekends while a lavish continental board is available during the week.

Tremé and Faubourg Marigny

$$ Lion's Inn – *2517 Chartres St.;* 🛏; *504-945-2339; www.lionsinn.com; 10 rooms.* A budget find, this quirky old bed and breakfast provides decent lodgings in a good location just a few blocks from the French Quarter. The easygoing owner makes his guests feel at home, and even provides bicycles for tooling around New Orleans. Some rooms share bathrooms. Amenities include free Wi-Fi, a daily afternoon wine hour and a nice swimming pool.

$$$ The Frenchmen – *417 Frenchmen St.;* 🛏 **P** ; *800-831-1781; www.frenchmenhotel.com; 27 rooms.* This quaint, older hotel boasts an excellent location in the heart of the Marigny. Rooms are a bit small but offer good value; some open onto a brick courtyard with swimming pool and lush plantings.

$$$$ Claiborne Mansion – *2111 Dauphine St.;* 🛏 **P** ; *504-301-1027; www.claibornemansion.com; 9 rooms.* This enormous, nicely restored Greek Revival mansion fronting Washington Square is a great choice for a stay in the Marigny. The spacious, suite like guest rooms boast high ceilings, marble bathrooms and luxurious fabrics, and there's a pool in the lovely landscaped courtyard. Guests are free to use the nicely appointed kitchen.

ASK PETER...

Q: Is it possible to volunteer with the rebuilding effort if I only have a few days available?
A: Even if you are only in the area for a short period of time, there are many opportunities for you to help out. Get in touch with the Habitat for Humanity's New Orleans branch who have spaces available at Habitat Home Builds and ReStore Assistance. You must organize your own hotel and transport and pack your own lunch—and be at the build site by 7:45am to start your day of volunteering. *504-861-2077; www.habitat-nola.org.*

Mid-City

$$$ Rathbone Mansions – *1244 Esplanade Ave.;* 🛏 **P**; ✆*504-309-4479;* *www.rathbonemansions.com; 25 rooms.* Two restored antebellum mansions offer romantic, if somewhat down-at-heel accommodations in Mid-City. It's the height of convenience if you're attending Jazz Fest. The saltwater pool is a nice place to cool off.

$$$$ Degas House – *2306 Esplanade Ave.;* 🛏 **P**; ✆*504-821-5009;* *www.degashouse.com; 3 rooms, 3 suites.* This beautifully restored 1852 home *(see p146)* boats polished hardwood floors and 14ft ceilings, plus modern comforts like flatscreen TVs, iPod docking stations and free Wi-Fi. A delicious Creole breakfast is served downstairs in the room used as a studio by French painter Edgar Degas during his sojourn here in the 1870s.

Excursions

$$ T'Frere's House – *1905 Verot School Rd., Lafayette;* 🛏 **P**; ✆*337-984-9347;* *www.tfreres.com; 8 rooms.* You'll be plunged into Acadiana at this white villa *(1880)* on the outskirts of Lafayette. The breakfast alone is reason enough to stay here, featuring eggs, spicy smoked sausage and waffles topped with cane syrup.

$$ The Juliet Hotel – *800 Jefferson St., Lafayette;* **P**; ✆*337-261-2225;* *www.ascendcollection.com; 20 rooms.* A property of the upscale Ascend Collection, this full-service boutique hotel makes a convenient base for exploring the Cajun Country. Housed in an historic building, the hotel offers comfortable, nicely appointed rooms, free Wi-Fi and an outdoor pool with hot tub.

$$$$ Nottoway – *31025 Hwy. 1, White Castle;* ✖ **P**; ✆*225-545-2730;* *www.nottoway.com; 40 rooms and 2 suites.* A stay at this historic plantation home *(see p161)* will truly immerse you in River Road history. Choose from rooms in the main mansion, the overseer's house, the boys' wing or the guest cottages. Rooms feature antique four-poster or half-tester beds, marble baths and flatscreen TVs. Come evening, dine at The Mansion restaurant, featuring Creole-inspired specialties.

$$$$ Madewood Plantation House – *4250 Hwy. 308, Napoleonville;* 🛏✖ **P**; ✆*985-369-7151; www.madewood.com; 8 rooms.* This 1846 Greek Revival mansion designed by Henry Howard sits in the middle of an active sugarcane plantation. Period antiques add authenticity. Breakfast, evening wine and cheese and candlelit dinners around the huge dining table are part of the deal.

Where to Eat

Simply put, food is the reason many visitors make the trip to New Orleans. Vacations are planned, conventions are scheduled, wedding dates are set with a view to making the most of eating out in the Big Easy. Eating well has a long history here; several of the "old-line" restaurants (Antoine's, Galatoire's, Tujague's, Arnaud's and Commander's Palace, to name a few) have been around for generations, justifiably drawing devoted fans of their well-honed versions of Cajun and Creole specialties, and it's good to indulge yourself with a meal in at least one of these venerable spots during your stay. But don't overlook the celebrity chefs, the cutting-edge cuisine, the longstanding neighborhood lunch spot, or the seedy-looking po-boy joint.

New Orleans food doesn't have to be complicated or expensive to be memorable, and most folks who visit run out of meals before they make a dent in the city's culinary offerings. So many restaurants, so little time.

For price ranges, see the Legend on the cover flap.

French Quarter

$ Acme Oyster House – *724 Iberville St.; ☏504-522-5973; www.acmeoyster.com.* **Seafood**. Get to the bar and watch the oyster shells fly at this unpretentious seafood destination. Briny Gulf Coast oysters, fried oyster po-boys, rich oyster stew or the massive oyster loaf should appease the most powerful craving. Line too long? Do what everyone else does and cross the street to Felix's Oyster Bar at no. 739.

$ Felipe's – *301 N. Peters St.; ☏504-267-4406; www.felipestaqueria.com.* **Mexican**. Finding inexpensive eats can be a bit of a challenge in the Quarter, but if you're in need of a fast, fresh pick-me-up, Felipe's tacos, tostadas, nachos and burritos more than fit the bill. They serve a mean taco soup as well. Try the margaritas, made with freshly squeezed key lime juice.

$ Stanley – *547 St. Ann St.; ☏504-587-0093; www.stanleyrestaurant.com.* **Creole**. Crowds line up at Stanley (owned by the same folks who brought you Stella!), a neo-diner spot right on Jackson Square. Breakfast and lunch are served all day here; you can't go wrong with creamy bananas Foster french toast or eggs Stanley (a twist on eggs Benedict with crispy fried oysters and Creole hollandaise).

$$ NOLA – *534 St. Louis St.; ☏504-522-6652; www.emerils.com.* **New American**. The casual French Quarter digs of celebrity chef Emeril Lagasse, NOLA ups the flavor quotient on Southern American favorites spiked with Louisiana twists, like sautéed Gulf shrimp with chili-Abita Beer sauce and double-cut pork chops with pecan-glazed sweet potatoes.

$$ Palace Café – *605 Canal St.;* ℘*504-523-1661; www.palacecafe.com.* **Creole**. Visitors and regulars rave about the crabmeat cheesecake and the Gulf fish specials *à la meunière* at this noisy Canal Street fixture. The white chocolate bread pudding is delicious enough to rank as a New Orleans experience. If you've a mind, opt for the daily Temp Lunch special, priced according to yesterday's high temperature.

$$ Bayona – *430 Dauphine St.;* ℘*504-525-4455; www.bayona.com.* **International**. Chef/owner Susan Spicer mines the global table—and the results are delicious, with specialties that look beyond Louisiana borders while somehow nodding to local traditions. You'll find excellent renditions of duck, sweetbreads, lamb and seafood on the menu, which changes seasonally.

$$ Mr. B's – *201 Royal St.;* ℘*504-523-2078; www.mrbsbistro.com.* **Creole**. This casual supper club, popular with the business crowd, is known for its contemporary spin on local favorites, like the fiery barbecued shrimp, fried soft-shell crab amandine and delicious Gumbo Ya-Ya. Go with rich bread pudding for dessert.

$$$ K-Paul's Louisiana Kitchen – *416 Chartres St.;* ℘*504-596-2530; www.chefpaul.com.* **Cajun**. Paul Prudhomme, Cajun cooking's voluble father of blackened everything, serves forth definitive gumbos, *étouffées* and crawfish dishes at the restaurant that established Cajun cooking at the forefront of American cuisine. For dessert, order the unforgettable sweet potato-pecan pie.

$$$ Arnaud's – *813 Bienville St.;* ℘*504-523-5433; www.arnaudsrestaurant.com.* **Creole**. Fine Creole cuisine in an elegant atmosphere (there's often live jazz) draws locals to this French Quarter classic. Start with tangy shrimp remoulade before moving on to beautifully turned-out renditions of Creole favorites like trout amandine, chicken Pontalba, and duck breast napped in blueberry sauce. Before you leave, take a pass through the Germaine Wells Mardi Gras Museum to admire the lavish costumes and memorabilia of a longstanding member of New Orleans Carnival royalty.

$$$ Brennan's – *417 Royal St.;* ℘*504-525-9711; www.brennansneworleans.com.* **Creole**. Breakfast at Brennan's figures on most lists of unmissable New Orleans experiences. You'll understand why when your crabmeat omelet arrives, airy and piled high with lumps of the sweet crustacean in a pool of hollandaise sauce. Or try the signature Eggs Hussarde, poached with Canadian bacon and *marchand de vin* sauce.

$$$ Galatoire's – *209 Bourbon St.;* ℘*504-525-2021; www.galatoires.com.* **Creole**. This old-line landmark, where local society eats to be seen, is set in its ways both good and bad and that's part of its charm. Dress up and tuck into delicious buttery Gulf fish, crabmeat maison or oysters Rockefeller and try not to gape at the antics of the regulars.

$$$ Tujague's – *823 Decatur St.; ☏ 504-525-8676; www.tujaguesrestaurant.com.*
Creole. One of New Orleans' beloved old-line stalwarts, Tujague's opened its doors in 1856, serving breakfast and lunch to waterfront laborers and seamen. The restaurant's culinary reputation leans heavily on just a couple of reliable favorites; the beef brisket, slow-cooked and doused with a piquant horseradish sauce, and the definitive shrimp remoulade. Take a peek at the wonderful old wooden bar, backed by an ornately framed French mirror.

$$$$ Stella! – *1032 Chartres St.; ☏ 504-587-0091; www.restaurantstella.com.*
Modern. Culinary virtuosity reigns supreme at this cutting-edge French Quarter spot with its elegant, comfortable dining rooms. Chef-owner Scott Boswell's dexterity in the kitchen is evident in his seasonal menus, where Creole-accented international dishes are conceived, executed and presented with precision. When in doubt, order the chef's tasting menu.

$$$$ Antoine's – *713 St. Louis St.; ☏ 504-581-4422; www.antoines.com.* **Creole**. The oldest of New Orleans' "old-line" Creole institutions, Antoine's has been expertly turning out fine steaks, Gulf seafood and Creole specialties like *pompano en papillote* and alligator bisque since 1840. This is the place for your initiation to oysters Rockefeller; the dish was invented here. Service is formal and absolutely top-notch; ask for a tour of the fourteen historic dining rooms (especially the Rex room) and the wine cellar.

CBD and the Warehouse Arts District

$$ A Mano – *870 Tchoupitoulas St.; ☏ 504-208-9280; www.amanonola.com.*
Italian. Chef Josh Smith turns out rustic, regional Italian cuisine at this relative newcomer to the Warehouse District. You can't miss with robust dishes like cavatelli made with squid ink, slow-cooked rabbit with olives and thyme, or any of the excellent bruschetta starters.

$$ RioMar – *800 S. Peters St.; ☏ 504-525-3474; www.riomarseafood.com.* **Latin**. Ready for a change from Creole seafood classics? Chef Adolfo Garcia's Spanish and Latin American fish dishes sparkle at this modern-style gem. Fans of ceviche will have a field day with the kitchen's regional renditions, while local drum arrives topped with a cumin-honey glaze. Finish with a hefty portion of *tres leches* cake.

$$ Cochon – *930 Tchoupitoulas St.; ☏ 504-588-2123; www.cochonrestaurant.com.*
Cajun. Put your cardiologist's number on speed-dial before stepping into to this irresistible, brick-walled neighborhood grill. The Cajun/Southern menu leans heavily on the pig in treats like the fried oyster and bacon sandwich, homemade sausage and the Louisiana *cochon* (roast pork) with cabbage and cracklings.

Travel Tip:
When making dinner reservations for any restaurant in town, make sure you ask what the dress code is—even if it's a casual restaurant. Some restaurants, including Emeril's New Orleans, have a dress policy that is casual but does prohibit sleeveless shirts for men.

$$ Mother's – *401 Poydras St.;* ☎ *504-523-9656; www.mothersrestaurant.net*. **Creole**. This down-home and extremely popular restaurant appears on everybody's list of the best places to eat a po-boy. Baked ham is the specialty, but don't overlook the seafood varieties or the roast-beef po-boy, covered in debris (bits of meat) and served "dressed" with lettuce, tomato, mayo and pickles.

$$$ Bon Ton Café – *401 Magazine St.;* ☎ *504-524-3386; www.thebontoncafe.com*. **Cajun**. The historic Bon Ton was among the first New Orleans restaurants to challenge the primacy of Creole cuisine by introducing Cajun dishes as a fine-dining alternative. The crawfish dishes, stemming from family recipes created in Acadiana, include delectable *étouffée* and an unforgettable crawfish bisque (pricey but oh so worth it). Finish with secret-recipe bread pudding and whiskey sauce.

$$$ Emeril's – *800 Tchoupitoulas St.;* ☎ *504-528-9393; www.emerils.com*. **American**. It's been a while since celebrity chef Emeril Lagasse established himself and his trademark cuisine at this namesake restaurant in a renovated warehouse space. Reserve one of the seats at the "kitchen counter" to watch culinary magic happening in novel takes on New Orleans dishes like *andouille*-crusted drum and sorghum-smoked duck. Can't get a reservation? Try one of Emeril's other Big Easy spots: Emeril's Delmonico in Uptown *(1300 St. Charles Ave.;* ☎ *504-525-4937)* and NOLA in the French Quarter *(see p175)*.

$$$ Herbsaint – *701 St. Charles Ave.;* ☎ *504-524-4114; www.herbsaint.com*. **French**. Chef Donald Link's gutsy Franco-American menu is rooted in down-home sensibility but infused with contemporary innovations. Try the Muscovy duck leg confit with dirty rice, the melting slow-cooked lamb neck atop a cake of borlotti beans or the spaghetti with *guanciale*, a new take on spaghetti carbonara.

$$$ Restaurant August – *301 Tchoupitoulas St.;* ☎ *504-299-9777; www.rest-august.com*. **French**. Precision cuisine holds sway at chef John Besh's New Orleans flagship. Reasons to head here include the outstanding redfish courtbouillon, the pork cheek ravioli, roasted-to-perfection short ribs and the flavorful breast of veal with Creole cream cheese dumplings.

$$$ Grill Room – *300 Gravier St. in the Windsor Court Hotel;* ☎ *504-523-6000; www.grillroomneworleans.com*. **American**. One of New Orleans' most elegant dining rooms is a fitting

spot to indulge in intriguingly conceived yet solidly grounded cuisine by chef Drew Dzejak. Try the grouper with a whimsical sauce of pickled ginger beurre blanc, or the seared diver scallops alongside corn *maque choux* kissed with pork belly. The cold-smoked ribeye ranks among the finest steaks available in New Orleans.

Garden District and Uptown

$ St. James Cheese Company – *5004 Prytania St.;* ℘*504-899-4737; www.stjamescheese.com.* **Deli**. Stop in for lunch at this friendly Uptown fromagerie, where the staff's knowledge of the huge cheese selection knows no bounds. A breathtaking selection of cheeses, meats and condiments will fill your choice of fresh-baked breads.

$ Casamento's – *4330 Magazine St.;* ℘*504-895-09761; www.casamentos restaurant.com.* **Seafood**. Down-home seafood done right is the watchword at this white-tiled Uptown institution. Tell veteran shucker Mike your raw order; he'll whip up some of his special oyster sauce for dipping. Move on to a cup of oyster stew, a fried oyster or shrimp loaf, or a big plate of crab claws, all simple, fresh and expertly prepared.

$ Domilise's – *5240 Annunciation St.;* ℘*504-899-9126.* **Po-boys**. Never mind Domilise's working-class aura; this place makes the definitive New Orleans po-boy. Take a number and watch the kitchen action while you decide on perfectly fried catfish, shellfish or roast beef, piled on airy French bread and dressed with lettuce, mayo and assertive Creole mustard.

$$ Jacques-Imo's – *8324 Oak St.;* ℘*504-861-0886; www.jacquesimoscafe.com.* **Cajun/Creole**. With its wildly painted walls, effusive owner and staff, and a dedicated crowd of regulars bent on whooping it up, this rambunctious Oak Street hangout wins points for its funky ambiance and delicious local fare like blackened redfish and alligator *sauce piquante*.

$$ Pascal's Manale – *1838 Napoleon Ave.;* ℘*504-895-4877.* **Italian**. You could dine in more exciting spots in New Orleans, but not if you want to sample barbecued shrimp from the folks who invented the dish in 1954. Buttery, spicy and dripping with seafood essence, the crustaceans arrive with shells and heads on; it's messy but heavenly.

$$ Dick and Jenny's – *4501 Tchoupitoulas St.;* ℘*504-894-9880; www.dickandjennys.com.* **Southern**. This charming little mid-19C clapboard cottage offers down-home fare gone uptown. Smoked duck breast arrives with alligator sausage and corn bread, while Gulf fish gets a snappy crawfish topping. The appetizer sampler is a winner, sporting fried oysters, eggplant fritters, alligator cheesecake and crawfish.

$$ Clancy's – *6100 Annunication St.;* ℘*504-895-1111; www.clancysneworleans. com.* **American**. A longtime local favorite, Clancy's is a great neighborhood lunch spot occupying a cute house. They serve dinner too, though the

ASK PETER...

Q: How can I bring back a little Southern cuisine to my home and cook for family and friends?

A: Take a cooking class at the New Orleans School of Cooking in the French Quarter *(524 St. Louis St.)*. Classes on Cajun and Creole cuisine are taught by local chefs. From two-hour lunch classes to food demonstrations to private events, the school has many options. Inside the building is the Louisiana General Store that sells some of Louisiana's best cooking products. ☎ 1-800-237-4841. www.neworleans schoolofcooking.com.

popular bar area makes for a louder, nightlife atmosphere. Go for the crabmeat salad, the smoked duck, or the tasty Veal Annunciation; top it all off with Lemon Icebox Pie.

$$$ Lillette – *3637 Magazine St.;* ☎ *504-895-1636; www.lilletterestaurant.com.* **French**. This upscale but welcoming neighborhood bistro plates thoughtfully prepared traditional French dishes graced with the occasional Italian fillip. Duck confit arrives atop arugula, steamed mussels with bruschetta, and Muscovy duck breast with Tuscan kale. The *braciola* ham dish is a house specialty.

$$$ Patois – *6078 Laurel St.;* ☎ *504-895-9441; www.patoisnola.com.* **French**. Southern classics with French flair describes the cuisine served up at this easygoing neighborhood bistro. Chef Aaron Burgaus makes delicious creations like salad with crispy duck confit, panéed rabbit with fennel, and sautéed sweetbreads with lentils and ham.

$$$ Brigtsen's – *723 Dante St.;* ☎ *504-861-7610; www.brigtsens.com.* **Cajun/Creole**. A student of Paul Prudhomme, chef Frank Brigtsen excels at fusing Louisiana's bounty of native ingredients with its deep-rooted culinary traditions. You're in the hands of an expert here; dive into *andouille* gumbo, cornmeal catfish with cheese grits and Creole sauce, T-bone steak bordelaise, or a seafood platter unlike any other.

$$$ Upperline – *1413 Upperline St.;* ☎ *504-891-9822; www.upperline.com.* **Creole**. Touted by its owner, die-hard New Orleans booster JoAnn Clevenger, as "not just a restaurant but a way of life," Upperline nonetheless wears its restaurant hat with aplomb. You'll know it in dishes like veal grillades with cheddar grits, roast duck with garlic port, salmon with crawfish bouillabaisse and aioli, and the excellent trio of soups (duck gumbo, turtle soup and oyster stew).

$$$ Commander's Palace – *1403 Washington Ave.;* ☎ *504-899-8221; www.commanderspalace.com.* **Creole**. The striped signature awning beckons at this must-eat old-line restaurant in the Garden District. The menu doesn't change much, but chef Tory McPhail inserts inventions such as Foie Gras du Monde in among the traditional treats like turtle soup laced with sherry, Gulf fish with pecans, and shrimp remoulade.

Tremé and Faubourg Marigny

$ The Joint – *801 Poland Ave.;* ✆ *504-949-3232; www.alwayssmokin.com.*
BBQ. Though a bit out of the Marigny, this barbecue joint in the neighboring Bywater district is well worth the hike. Fans of smoked meat rave about the ribs, pulled pork and beef brisket accompanied by sides of coleslaw and baked beans. Pull up a wood bench, douse your dinner with sauce, and revel in a southern barbecue.

$ Sukho Thai – *1913 Royal St.;* ✆ *504-48-9309; www.sukhothai-nola.com.*
Thai. Authentic Thai flavors rule at this contemporary Marigny spot, and the price is right. Try their *pad thai*, the excellent Panang curry with chicken, and the Thai coconut soup, perfectly spiced.

$$ Three Muses – *536 Frenchmen St.;* ✆ *504-298-8746; www.thethreemuses.com.*
American. Part restaurant, part nightspot, this fun Marigny hang out pops with good music, a lively crowd and a menu of tasty small plates including hanger steak with crab cake (a new twist on surf 'n' turf), lamb sliders, Gulf fish tacos, and innovative salads and sweets.

$$ Dooky Chase – *2301 Orleans Ave.;* ✆ *504-821-0535.* **Creole**. Helmed by beloved chef Leah Chase, this stalwart was the first fine-dining restaurant to cater to African-Americans. Order Creole from the menu or head to the buffet for a can't-miss spread of authentic soul food including some of the best fried chicken in the city. Hours are limited; it's best to call ahead.

Mid-City

$ Theo's Neighborhood Pizza – *4024 Canal St.;* ✆ *504-302-1133;*
www.theospizza.com. **Italian**. If pizza is your thing, this budget Mid-City hangout will more than satisfy. It's a favorite with locals. Order up at the bar, then sip an enormous soda while waiting for your fragrant pie (there are loads of meat and non-meat options) to emerge from the roaring pizza ovens.

$$ Mandina's – *3800 Canal St.;* ✆ *504-482-9179; www.mandinasrestaurant. com.* **Creole/Italian**. A definitive neighborhood joint in Mid-City, Mandina's has been drawing New Orleans regulars for more than a century. The menu is a hodgepodge of Creole and Italian specialties. Crab cakes, trout amandine, turtle soup and fried chicken all shine, as do the meatballs with red sauce. Try the bread pudding for dessert.

$$$ Café Degas – *3127 Esplanade Ave.;* ✆ *504-945-5635; www.cafedegas.com.*
French. This casual, yet unabashedly romantic, spot on Esplanade Avenue has a pecan tree growing right through the floor and on up through the roof. Look for classic French specialties like tender mussels steamed with Herbsaint, onion soup, pâté and Dijon-crusted rack of lamb.

$$$$ Ralph's on the Park – *900 City Park Ave.;* ☏ *504-488-1000; www.ralphsonthepark.com.* **American**. A Brennan family outpost in Mid-City, Ralph's welcomes (well-dressed) diners to its upscale dining rooms overlooking live-oak-draped City Park. The view can be enjoyed over appetizers like the peanut-butter and jelly foie gras or a plate of barbecued shrimp in a mushroom and beer broth.

Excursions

$$ Café des Amis – *140 Bridge St., Breaux Bridge;* ☏ *337-332-5273; www.cafedesamis.com.* **Cajun**. There's almost no better way to experience Cajun life than by coming to the Saturday morning Zydeco Breakfast at this friendly spot in downtown Breaux Bridge. Miraculous combinations of eggs, biscuits, tasso, crawfish and *boudin* emerge from the kitchen to the swing of live music. Local bands play here Wednesday nights.

$$ Blue Dog Café – *1211 W. Pinhook Rd., Lafayette.;* ☏ *337-237-0005; www.bluedogcafe.com.* **Cajun**. As much a gallery as a restaurant, this cozy cafe covers its walls with works by local son George Rodrigue, whose Blue Dog motif is a Louisiana icon. Try to hit the Sunday brunch for a broad menu of Cajun specialties expertly prepared, all accompanied by lively local bands playing Cajun, zydeco and swamp pop.

$$ Prejean's – *3480 N. Evangeline Thwy. (I-49), Lafayette;* ☏ *337-896-3247; www.prejeans.com.* **Cajun**. Nightly Cajun bands and award-winning cuisine make Prejean's popular with residents and visitors alike. Sautéed snapper topped with crawfish, crab and artichoke cream sauce, excellent *étouffée* and some of the best gumbo around are the best sellers at the north Lafayette eatery.

$$$ Café Vermilionville – *1304 W. Pinhook Rd., Lafayette;* ☏ *337-237-0100; www.cafev.com.* **Creole**. A comfortable old inn from the early 1800s is reborn as one of Lafayette's finest restaurants. Raveworthy specialties include jumbo shrimp in spicy herb sauce, crawfish *beignets* and Steak Louis XIII, stuffed with crawfish.

Performing Arts

The very idea of seeking out the performing arts in New Orleans seems redundant—after all, the whole town is a stage, and some of the best performances you'll see anywhere take place on the streets of the French Quarter and in bars all over town. But if your aim is higher on the cultural scale, here are some theatrical venues where the entertainment is more, shall we say, traditional.

Mahalia Jackson Theater for the Performing Arts
1419 Basin St. ℘504-287-0351. www.mahaliajacksontheater.com.
Presenting a broad slate of performances year-round, this 2,100-seat theater opened in 1973 as the city's preeminent performing arts venue. The Louisiana Philharmonic Orchestra makes its home here, as does the New Orleans Ballet Association, and the New Orleans Opera. The theater hosts Broadway touring shows, gospel concerts, touring solo performers and occasionally local talent; it was a favorite performance venue for beloved Big Easy trumpeter Louis Armstrong.

New Orleans Arena
1501 Girod St. ℘504-527-6826. www.neworleansarena.com.
Rising next to the Mercedez-Benz Superdome in downtown New Orleans, the ultramodern New Orleans Arena hosts rock concerts and large-format traveling shows and spectacles such as Cirque du Soleil and Sesame Street Live. A long list of musical performers has passed through the arena, and it is also home to the New Orleans Hornets professional basketball team.

Le Petit Théâtre du Vieux Carré
616 St. Peter St. ℘504-522-2081; www.lepetittheatre.com.
Touted as one of the oldest community theaters in the country, Le Petit was founded in the French Quarter in the 1920s by a cadre of art-loving New Orleaneans who called themselves the Drawing Room Players. The theater is currently under renovation, with plans to reopen in late 2012.

Saenger Theatre
143 N. Rampart St. www.saengertheatre.com.
Long a fixture on the New Orleans cultural scene hosting Broadway traveling shows, rock concerts and a classic film series, the historic Saenger Theatre began its life as a movie theater before being reconfigured as a live-performance theater in the 1970s. Today it's listed on the National Register of Historic Places. The building suffered severe water damage during the flooding after Hurricane Katrina, and is now being renovated by the city, with plans to reopen in 2012.

Southern Repertory Theatre

333 Canal St. at The Shops at Canal Place (3rd floor); ☏ 504-522-6545; www.southernrep.com. Founded in 1986 to provide an outlet for Southern playwrights, Southern Rep staged productions in several venues around town before finding a home in the French Quarter's Shops at Canal Place in 1991. Tennessee Williams, Carson McCullers and Barrett O'Brien are just a few of the playwrights whose work has been performed here. A typical season may present new works like Yasmina Reza's Tony-winning *God of Carnage*, plus Tennessee Williams' classic *A Streetcar Named Desire*. Tickets range from $25 to $35, and seating isn't assigned.

Stage Door Canteen

945 Magazine St.; ☏ 504-528-1943; www.nationalww2museum.org.
The 1940s come back to life via the Victory Belles (an Andrews Sisters tribute group), and other acts presenting pitch-perfect versions of Swing-era hits. The venue is designed to recreate the era of USO shows and canteens where big-name acts entertained troops heading off to the battlefront. The lively step-back-in-time is a treat for young and old alike.

Nightlife

New Orleans boasts some of the best nightlife of any city in America. Just name that tune—blues, jazz, folk-rock, funk, zydeco—and you'll find it here. If you have the energy, you can see two or three great musical acts a night, on any night of the week—even Monday. Take your pick from the rather predictable offerings along Bourbon Street, or strike out for Frenchmen Street in the Marigny, where a new crop of bars and nightclubs has sprung up, fostering a cornucopia of live music by groundbreaking new groups and tried-and-true artists. Wherever you go, be sure to wear comfy shoes; the proximity of some of these places makes it fun and easy to barhop the night away, and you'll definitely have trouble keeping still once the joint gets shaking.

French Quarter

Preservation Hall – *726 St. Peter St. ☏ 504-522-2841. www.preservationhall.com.* From the outside it may look a little down-at-heel but inside, Preservation Hall is a mecca for traditional New Orleans jazz. The club mounts three 45-minute sets a night; your ticket buys you one set, then the room is cleared for the next bunch of ticketholders. It's bare bones and family-friendly; no refreshments are sold and you may end up sitting on the floor. This place is all about the music.

Balcony Music Club – *1331 Decatur St.* ☏ *504-599-7770.*
This rocking bar and music club, on the edge of the Quarter,
books great local talent (think brass bands, jazz, blues and
rock), doesn't charge a cover during the week, and draws
a lively, get-up-and-dance crowd looking for (and finding)
something different from the usual Bourbon Street scene.
Blues band the Royal Rounders hang here most Tuesday
nights, and local trumpeter Kermit Ruffins has been known
to drop by for a few sets.

Buffa's Bar – *1001 Esplanade Ave.* ☏ *504-949-0038.*
www.buffasbar.com. "On the border of the Quarter," Buffa's
combines neighborhood friendliness with great piano
jazz and combos in the (smoke-free) Back Room. Walter
"Wolfman" Washington gigs here, as do the Royal Rounders
and pianist Tom McDermott. Try coming for the Sunday jazz
brunch.

Davenport Lounge – *921 Canal St. in the Ritz Carlton Hotel.*
☏ *504-524-1331. www.ritzcarlton.com.* Tucked inside the
Ritz-Carlton hotel, the Davenport Lounge is a hot spot for
grown-ups. The draw is house bandleader Jeremy Davenport,
a protégé of Harry Connick Jr., with a Sinatra-esque set of
pipes and a mean set of chops on the trumpet. Davenport
performs regularly on Thursday, Friday and Saturday nights; a
revolving guestlist of local musicians stop by regularly to sit in
with the band.

Funky Pirate – *727 Bourbon St.* ☏ *504-523-1960.* One of the
best of the Bourbon Street clubs, this cozy blues venue
features a dynamite house band—Big Al Carson and the
Blues Masters—and a lethal house drink, the Hand Grenade,
a potent mix of rum and vodka served in neon-green plastic.
Like most clubs on Bourbon Street, expect high drink prices
to offset the lack of a cover charge.

Fritzel's European Jazz Pub – *733 Bourbon St.* ☏ *503-586-
4803. www.fritzelsjazz.net.* If you need a break from Bourbon
Street noise and chaos step into the calmer surrounds of
Fritzel's, one of the older jazz bars in the Quarter. Excellent
traditional jazz bands get booked here; look for locals Tom
Fischer, Mike Fulton and the Jumbo Shrimp Jazz Band.

Travel Tip:
Preservation Hall
opened for business
in 1961 in the heart
of the French Quarter.
Every night you can
hear the finest New
Orleans jazz played by
veteran musicians—
some in their 70s
and 80s. The hall
opens at 8pm, but its
recommended you
arrive early, the room
almost always fills to
capacity with locals
and tourists.

House of Blues – *225 Decatur St.* 📞 *504-310-4999. www.houseofblues.com/ neworleans.* There's no getting around the corporate-franchise feel to this national entertainment chain, which takes up a half-block on Decatur. The gospel brunch is fun (if overpriced), but the headliners are the reason to come; bands benefit from a music room with good sight lines and great acoustics. The chain's buying power delivers big names like out-of-towners Béla Fleck and Colbie Caillat along with local faves the Neville Brothers and Irma Thomas.

Irvin Mayfield's Jazz Playhouse – *300 Bourbon St., in the Royal Sonesta Hotel.* 📞 *504-553-2229. www.sonesta.com.* For a truly memorable night out, book a table at local trumpeter Irvin Mayfield's namesake lounge off the lobby of the Royal Sonesta. It's cool and classy here; order some appetizers to tide you over and take in the sweet jazz sounds. Brass bands take the stage on Saturday; Friday nights are devoted to burlesque shows.

One-Eyed Jack's – *615 Toulouse St.* 📞 *504-569-8361. www.oneeyedjacks.net.* This French Quarter theater and nightclub is the place for let's-not-kid-ourselves burlesque shows (complementing the red wallpaper and beat-up couches). Thursday nights are "Fast Times" nights, devoted to 80s music.

Oz – *800 Bourbon St.* 📞 *504-593-9491. www.ozneworleans.com.* This two-level disco is the place to see and be seen for the (mostly) young gay crowd, with featured calendar-boy revues, underwear contests and female impersonators geared to whip the crowd into a frenzy. The music features house and dance mixes, with a great laser-light show, and the occasional go-go boy atop the bar.

Palm Court Jazz Café – *1204 Decatur St.* 📞 *504-525-0200. www.palmcourtjazzcafe.com.* An elegant venue for traditional jazz, the Palm Court is a more refined place to catch some of the same acts that frequent Preservation Hall. Music is featured Wednesday though Sunday, with the emphasis on classic jazz. Take note of the collection of jazz records for sale in a back alcove. Make reservations for dinner—the Creole food is excellent—and stay for the duration.

CBD and the Warehouse Arts District

Circle Bar – *1032 St. Charles St.* 📞 *504-588-2616.* Calling all lounge lizards: this tiny spot will soon become your home away from home. With its neon K&B drugstore sign on the ceiling, slightly shabby decor and excellent jukebox, Circle Bar is a hipster's paradise. It attracts an eclectic array of live artists, from surf duos to local singer-songwriters and jazz trios, who squeeze into an impossibly small bandstand and proceed to rock out.

Howlin' Wolf – *907 S. Peters St.* 📞 *504-522-9653. wwwthehowlinwolf.com.* This locally owned and operated club is one of the best in town, host to such high-quality indie rock acts as The Airborne Toxic Event. The music isn't limited to rock—you're just as likely to see a burlesque show or a brass band (local heroes Rebirth Brass Band play regularly). On Silent Disco night, your cover buys you a pair of wireless headphones; tune in to your choice of DJ and rock the night away.

Mulate's – *201 Julia St. ✆ 504-522-1492. www.mulates.com.* Although under different ownership from the original Cajun Country location, Mulate's in the trendy Warehouse Arts District is your best bet for Cajun music and dancing. Bands like Lee Benoit, La Touche and Jay Cormier burn it up with swamp boogie music. If you work up an appetite, you can order a decent gumbo or *étoufée* from the kitchen.

Garden District and Uptown

Dos Jefes Uptown Cigar Bar – *5535 Tchoupitoulas St. ✆ 504-891-8500. www.dosjefescigarbar.com.* Blue smoke hangs and live piano jazz sings at this neighborhood hangout. The calendar features good local artists; try a stiff premium whiskey on the rocks in the dimly lit atmosphere and feel your blood pressure go down.

Maple Leaf Bar – *8316 Oak St. ✆ 504-866-9359. http://mapleleafbar.com.* A tin roof, a small dance floor and a lineup of great funk, Cajun, R&B and blues music describes one of the city's best music experiences. Walter "Wolfman" Washington is a Sunday-night regular, and if Beausoleil or the Rebirth Brass Band is playing, you won't have a better time anywhere in town.

Tipitina's – *501 Napoleon Ave. ✆ 504-895-8477. www.tipitinas.com.* Named for a song by the legendary Professor Longhair, Tip's is the quintessential New Orleans club, even though its luster has dulled over the years, due to increased competition in the marketplace. While it may not have the booking muscle of years gone by (Taj Mahal, Dr. John and Bonnie Raitt all played here), it's still a reliable spot for local acts, brass bands, and touring alt-rock and roots acts. Sunday afternoons bring music workshops where students are invited to sit in with established musicians to learn the craft; Sunday nights Tip's hosts a traditional Cajun fais-do-do with Bruce Daigrepont.

Rock 'N' Bowl – *3000 S. Carrollton Ave. ✆ 504-861-1700. www.rocknbowl.com.* Perhaps it isn't the only nightclub located in a bowling alley, but Rock 'n' Bowl has to be the only place where you can eat a fried bread pudding po-boy and listen to zydeco music while toppling the pins. Accordion-meister Geno Delafosse and the French Rockin' Boogie show up regularly here, as do Guitar Shorty, Beth McKee and Nathan and the Zydeco Cha-Chas.

Tremé and Faubourg Marigny

Apple Barrel – *609 Frenchmen St.* 504-949-9399. This tiny neighborhood hole-in-the-wall is known for its strong drinks, friendly crowd, awesome acoustics and smoking blues and jazz. It's the kind of place where talented locals just wander up on the stage and start playing with the regulars for epic, once-in-a-lifetime musical moments.

Blue Nile – *534 Frenchmen St.* 504-948-2583. Local bands take the stage at this rather eclectic club in the Marigny. The get-up-off-your-chair music attracts a mostly younger crowd, but it's a great place to head for jazz, blues and alternative music.

d.b.a. – *618 Frenchmen St.* 504-942-3731. *www.drinkgoodstuff.com/dbano*. The New Orleans outpost of this chic New York club isn't as gritty as most great bars in town, but it does offer an array of good live music, featuring local acts like Walter "Wolfman" Washington, the New Orleans Nightcrawlers Brass Band and Cyril Neville. The beer list tops 160 labels—the best variety in town. Cypress wood walls and low lighting make for an intimate vibe.

Maison – *508 Frenchmen St.* 5371-5543. *www.maisonfrenchmen.com*. Live acts at this hopping spot run the gamut from funk, jazz, hip-hop and blues to rock and electronic (via DJ). Check the website's calendar, especially if you want to try Swing Night or a real Cajun fais-do-do. There's a full-service restaurant here and rarely a cover, so make a night of it.

R Bar – *1431 Royal St., in the Royal Street Inn.* 504-948-7499. *www.royalstreetinn.com*. This funky local hangout attracts an offbeat mix of artists, wannabe artists, inebriated intellectuals and musicians who stop by after their set. There's a great alt-rock jukebox, a large selection of imported beers, friendly bartenders, and on Mondays you can get a haircut (in the antique barber chair) and a shot for $10.

Snug Harbor – *626 Frenchmen St.* 504-949-0696. *www.snugjazz.com*. Snug Harbor is a must for both food and music. The menu is American and the upstairs jazz venue, while cramped, is the place to see Ellis Marsalis (patriarch of the Marsalis clan) on a Friday night. Contemporary jazz, blues and R&B combos are the usual fare, with Charmaine Neville a Monday-night regular you won't want to miss.

Spotted Cat – *623 Frenchmen St.* 504-943-3887. A tiny little club in the Marigny, the Spotted Cat never charges a cover, yet it delivers some of the best local music, from brassy jazz combos to acoustic strummers. Traditional jazz is featured regularly, mostly by talented local bands. It's a great place to escape the Frenchmen Street madness.

Sweet Lorraine's – *1931 St. Claude Ave.* 504-945-9654. *www.sweetlorraines jazzclub.com*. This down-home venue lies on the edge of tourist New Orleans, and draws a very local crowd of devoted regulars who come for the good traditional jazz. Angela Ball and Deacon John have both played here. Weekend sets start at 10pm and midnight so grab a cab and pull up a chair to hear local music done right.

Three Muses – *536 Frenchmen St. ☏ 504-252-4801. www.thethreemuses.com.* Great music (small-band and soloist jazz and blues), great food and great atmosphere win praise at this hip Frenchmen Street spot. You can easily make a dinner of the terrific small plates turned out by the kitchen; it's a new and fun way to do nighttime in New Orleans.

Vaughan's Lounge – *4229 Dauphine St., Bywater. ☏ 504-947-5562.* Thursday night is the time to take a short cab ride from the Quarter to this homey Bywater bar, where Kermit Ruffins, the local trumpet player often likened to a young Louis Armstrong, holds court. His band is called the Barbecue Swingers, a reference to both their swinging groove, and the barbecue Kermit usually cooks up before the show. The bartender will call you a cab when you're ready to leave.

Spectator Sports

New Orleaneans are fervently proud of their professional sports teams. As is typical in the land of *"Laissez les bons temps rouler,"* **home games are a reason to have a party, both in the stadium (dancing in the seats is not uncommon) and at parking lot tailgates. Attending a game and cheering for the team is a surefire way to make yourself an honorary New Orleanean.**

Football

The **New Orleans Saints** football team plays its home games in the Mercedes-Benz Superdome in downtown New Orleans during the National Football League regular season, which extends over 17 weeks from early September through January 1. Tickets to home games sell out to season-ticket subscribers, but that doesn't mean you can't catch a game while you're here. Check with Ticketmaster's **NFL Ticket Exchange** *(☏ 800-745-3000; www.ticketmaster.com or www.ticketexchangebyticketmaster.com).* and reputable ticket resellers like **StubHub** *(www.stubhub.com)* or **GreatSeats** *(www.greatseats.com)* for options.

New Orleans Saints – *www.neworleanssaints.com.*
Mercedes-Benz Superdome – *Sugar Bowl Dr. ☏ 504-587-3663, ☏ 800-756-7074. www.superdome.com.*

Travel Tip:
If you're looking for
some excitement
and team spirit
spend your Saturday
afternoon tailgating
at Louisiana State
University supporting
the Tigers at their
Baton Rouge stadium
an hour and a half
north-west of the
city. Tickets to Sunday
afternoon games at
the Mercedes-Benz
Superdome are
usually sold out, but
downtown sports
bars have a great
atmosphere if you
want to support the
New Orleans Saints.

Basketball

The **New Orleans Hornets** professional basketball team, a member of the National Basketball Association (NBA) plays its home games at the New Orleans Arena, which stands next to the Superdome in downtown New Orleans. The NBA season begins in late October and lasts through the middle of April (teams play a total of 82 regular-season games, of which half are played at home). The New Orleans Hornets and the New Orleans Arena limit sales to season-ticket subscribers only; for single-game tickets, contact Ticketmaster, StubHub or GreatSeats *(see above)*. Prices range from $20 for an upper balcony corner seat to $200 for a mid-court seat on the lower level.

New Orleans Hornets – *www.hornets.com.*
New Orleans Arena – *1501 Girod St.* ℰ *504-587-3822,* ℰ *800-756-7074. www.neworleansarena.com.*

Baseball

The **New Orleans Zephyrs** minor-league baseball team plays its home games at 10,000-seat Zephyr Field in Metairie. The Zephyrs are currently a triple-A affiliate of the Florida Marlins major-league team, and the season runs from April through early September (the team is likely to play about half its games at home). You can buy single-game tickets for a seat in the grandstand, or choose a ticket for the Levee, a green hill located behind center field (a great option for kids). Ticket prices range from $6 for the Levee to $12 for a grandstand seat.

New Orleans Zephyrs – *http://neworleans.zephyrs. milb.com.* **Zephyr Field** – *6000 Airline Dr., Metairie.* ℰ *504-734-5155. www.zephyrsbaseball.com.*

Soccer

The **New Orleans Jesters** professional soccer team is a member of the Player Development League of United Soccer Leagues. Players from Brazil, Great Britain, Chile, Finland and Europe have appeared on the team's roster, honing their skills for a move to the top levels of professional soccer in the US and abroad. Games are played at Pan-American Stadium in City Park during the regular league season which runs from late May to mid-July. Tickets prices are $10 for adults, $5 for children.

New Orleans Jesters – *www.nolajesters.com.*
Pan-American Stadium – *corner of Wisner Blvd. and Zachary Taylor Dr. in City Park.*

WHO DAT NATION

New Orleans was granted the 16th National Football League franchise in 1966, and the team itself was formed in 1967.

The Saints got off to a rocky start, however; the team didn't have a winning season until 1987, earning itself the depressing nickname "the Ain'ts." The long dry spell didn't dampen local residents' devotion however, and fan loyalty has been rewarded in recent years as the Saints, currently helmed by head coach Sean Payton and quarterback Drew Brees, posted winning seasons from 2008-10. The team's heartstopping triumph over the Indianapolis Colts in the 2009 Superbowl made heroes of its players and staff; for weeks New Orleanans wore their black and gold team colors, while Payton, Brees and other Saints rode in Mardi Gras parades, and were generally treated as heroes wherever they went. During your stay you'll probably see and hear the words **Who Dat** here and there. It's the short version of the fans' raucous, local-accent cheer "Who dat say dey gonna beat dem Saints?" and becomes something of a regional mantra during football season.

Horseracing

The New Orleans thoroughbred racing season at the New Orleans Fair Grounds Race Course traditionally begins on Thanksgiving Day and runs through late March. Races are held Wednesday through Sunday in December and January, and Thursday through Sunday from February through March. Race-day post times begin at 12.40pm and admission to the grandstand is free *(clubhouse seats cost $5)*; exceptions include days when major stakes races are held. The Fair Grounds also hosts Quarter horse racing in September.

Fair Grounds Race Course – *1751 Gentilly Blvd.* ✆ *504-944-5515. www.fairgroundsracecourse.com.*

Travel Tip:
It is not customary
to haggle, but many
stores will give a
reduction if you pay
cash. It is sometimes
possible to get a
refund on the IVA
(21 percent), the
equivalent of VAT.
The shops must be
licensed and carry
the sign "Tax Free."
Keep your receipts
for a refund at the
airport before your
departure.

Shopping

From kitschy souvenirs to world-class art and antiques, New Orleans offers shopping for every taste and budget. Whether you're browsing the galleries and antique shops of Royal Street, getting funky on Magazine Street, gallery-hopping in the Warehouse Arts District or sampling the gourmet goodies in the French Market, you're guaranteed to find something you didn't know you needed.

French Quarter

Free of chain stores and fiercely proud of its owner-operated retail sector, this neighborhood boasts fine art galleries, eclectic boutiques and quirky ateliers for everything from handmade perfume to hammered-silver jewelry.

Royal Street occupies the stratosphere of high-end antique and art galleries; everyone is welcome to browse but your wallet better be fat to buy. Most of the Royal Street action is concentrated in the ten blocks between Iberville Street and Ursulines Avenue. A few French Quarter highlights:

Ida Manheim Antiques – *409 Royal St.* ℘ *888-627-5969. www.idamanheimantiques.com.* In business at this location since 1919, the Manheim family brings long experience to its selection of European art and furnishings from the 17C–19C.

Vintage 329 – *329 Royal St.* ℘ *504-525-2262. www.vintage329.com.* Autographed memorabilia from celebrities in the worlds of entertainment, sports and history make for fun browsing.

Bourbon French Parfums – *815 Royal St.* ℘ *504-522-4480. www.neworleansperfume.com.* This ooh-la-la French perfumery, housed in an authentic Creole cottage, specializes in custom-blended fragrances, along with imported soaps, lotions and other body delights.

M.S. Rau Inc. – *630 Royal St.* ℘ *504-523-5660. www.rauantiques.com.* Shop for French, American and English furniture and art at this century-old, third-generation family business.

Rodrigue Studio – *730 Royal St.* ✆ *504-581-4244. www.georgerodrigue.com.* Named for the Cajun artist who became world-famous for his portraits of the woebegone Blue Dog, the gallery features paintings and serigraphs. The artist took his inspiration from the *loup-garou*, or Cajun ghost dog.

Valobra Jewelry and Antiques – *333 Royal St.* ✆ *504-525-6363. www.valobra.net.* Fine watches, jewelry, art and antiques are the primary focus of this family-owned shop.

Waldhorn & Adler – *343 Royal St.* ✆ *504-581-6379. www.waldhornadlers.com.* Max out your credit card at the oldest antique shop in town, where you'll find a wide selection of antique furniture and estate jewelry.

Faulkner House Books – *624 Pirates Alley.* ✆ *504-524-2940. www.faulkner house.net.* New, used and first editions line the shelves at this charming independent bookshop, as much a French Quarter community as a store.

Papier Plume – *824 Royal St.* ✆ *504-988-7265. http://papierplume.com.* Billing itself as the definitive supplier of "fine supplies for the discerning writer," this lovely spot stocks an amazing collection of exquisite pens, inks, paper, journals and stationary, all utilitarian artworks appealing to those who prefer the old-fashioned way when it comes to written communication.

French Market – *N. Peters St. between Dumaine St. and Esplanade Ave.* ✆ *504-522-2621. www.frenchmarket.org. Open year-round daily.* Originally a Choctaw trading post, the French Market dates back to 1791, the oldest documented farmer's market in America. The market extends from Café du Monde through seven buildings to the Farmers' Market and Flea Market buildings on the far end nearest Esplanade Avenue. Gift shops, clothing stores and a restaurant or two occupy most of the space in the structures nearest Jackson Square. In the Farmers' Market you'll find heaping stands of fresh produce, snack stands and purveyors of culinary souvenirs such as Cajun spices, pralines and boxes of mix for local favorites like dirty rice and *beignets* (the latter never tastes like the real thing, so save your money). Organized like a giant swap meet, the Flea Market gathers individual vendors selling innumerable hats, T-shirts, jewelry, sunglasses and all kinds of questionable items made from alligator hide. This is the place to try your hand at bargaining—depending on the owner's mood, the time of day and how much you're planning to buy, you might get a good deal.

Dutch Alley Artists' Co-Op – *912 N. Peters St.* ✆ *504-412-9220. www.dutchalleyartistsco-op.com.* Tucked in among the French Market shops, this gallery of works by diverse local artists is managed by the artists themselves. Here you'll find pottery, fine wood bowls, whimsical hats, quilts and fabric art, glass and metal art, tile works, prints and more; it's a great place to find a true made-in-New-Orleans souvenir.

Artist's Market – *1228 Decatur St.* 📞 *504-561-0046. Open year-round daily 10am–5pm. www.artistsmarketnola.com.* Steps away from the French Market, this artist's cooperative is run by a talented crew of local artists who make ceramics, art-to-wear, garden ornaments, Mardi Gras masks and hammered copper and silver jewelry. There's also a huge selection of beads for budding jewelrymakers.

Shoe Be Do – *324 Chartres St.* 📞 *504-523-7463.* Fun and funky footwear walks out the door of this fashionable-yet-easygoing boutique. The friendly sales staff make expert recommendations; everyone will wonder where you got those shoes.

Hove Parfumeur – *504 Chartres St.* 📞 *504-525-7827. www.hoveparfumeur.com.* Fragrances created here and only here come in cologne, perfume, oil, powder, lotion and soap form at this dainty, genteel shop on Chartres Street. Don't walk by without stepping in; it smells like heaven and feels like another day and age.

Lucullus – *610 Chartres St.* 📞 *504-528-9620. www.lucullusantiques.com.* This fascinating shop specializes in culinary antiques, from antique china and silver settings to rustic farmhouse implements and accoutrements for the ritualistic serving of absinthe (which was banned in 1912).

A Gallery for Fine Photography – *241 Chartres St.* 📞 *504-568-1313. www.agallery.com.* The list of noteworthy photographers represented here is eye-opening; you can purchase prints by Ansel Adams, Diane Arbus, Henri Cartier-Bresson, Annie Leibovitz, Helmut Newton and Alfred Steiglitz, to name a few.

Aunt Sally's Praline Shop – *504 Chartres St.* 📞 *504-642-7457. www.auntsallys.com.* You pretty much have no choice; you have to take home a box of New Orleans pralines. Brown sugar, butter and pecans are the holy trinity that make Louisiana pralines so darn good. This shop makes the treats fresh daily in their open kitchen.

Louisiana Music Factory – *210 Decatur St.* 📞 *504-586-1094. www.louisianamusicfactory.com.* This is the place to come for the local music you can't get at home, including an outstanding selection of zydeco, blues and traditional brass bands. Stop by on Saturday, when as many as three local music acts stage an in-store performance. The Factory is the unofficial music headquarters of the New Orleans Jazz and Heritage Festival.

Jax Brewery – *600 Decatur St.* 📞 *504-566-7245. http://jacksonbrewery.com.* This 1891 brew-house is now a riverfront mall with a good assortment of shops and a small food court with a deck overlooking the river. Cajun Clothing Company is a great place to pick up Mardi Gras polo shirts with that unmistakable crawfish logo.

The Shops at Canal Place – *333 Canal St.* 📞 *504-522-9200. www.theshopsatcanalplace.com.* Anchored by Saks Fifth Avenue, this upscale shopping mall includes Anthropologie, Banana Republic and Brooks Brothers, to name a few. Non-chain stores are included in the mix, most notably Saint Germain Shoes and the RHINO Gallery—for Right Here In New Orleans, which is where its unique mix of crafts and art jewelry is made *(504-523-7945; www.rhinocrafts.com)*.

CBD and the Warehouse Arts District

The heart of big corporate business in New Orleans, the CBD's retail offerings are nonetheless pretty limited. Art galleries abound in the Warehouse District, a burgeoning area for both visual and performing arts. Saturday afternoon is an excellent time to gallery-hop *(see Gallery Row p120)*, and the district hosts several annual art-related events like White Linen Night and Art for Art's Sake *(see Calendar of Events p64–67)*.

Riverwalk Marketplace – *500 Port of New Orleans Pl.* 504-522-1555. *www.riverwalkmarketplace.com.* The same developers who brought you South Street Seaport in New York City and Harborplace in Baltimore designed this festival marketplace stretching right along the riverfront both above ground and belowdecks. There are more than a 100 stores here, many of them locally-owned; Brookstone and Gap top the list of major national chains.

Tremé and Faubourg Marigny

American Aquatic Gardens – *621 Elysian Fields Ave.* 504-944-0410. This wonderful haven for indoor and outdoor home décor stocks an amazing selection of garden art, unusual sculptures, fountains, trees, rare lilies and other aquatic plants. Browse awhile to the soothing sounds of trickling water and pick out a treat for your garden.

Magazine Street

Magazine Street Merchant Association. 504-342-4435. *www.magazinestreet.com.*

Stretching six miles parallel to the Mississippi River from Canal Street through the Warehouse District and Uptown all the way to Audubon Park, Magazine Street occupies a category all its own when it comes to shopping in New Orleans. Originally named for a warehouse that Spanish Governor Miro built to house Kentucky tobacco and other exports, funky Magazine Street is an antidote to the typical mall experience.

Clusters of shops are interspersed with residential properties, a down-to-earth mix of renovated 19C warehouses, shops and galleries selling homewares, pottery, period furniture, clothing, books, glassware, toys, china, soaps and jewelry. It's an ideal spot for a leisurely walkabout, with plenty of coffee shops, cafes and restaurants to provide refreshment for the tired shopper. From the French Quarter or the CBD, take a cab or hop aboard the 11 Magazine Street bus.

Crescent City Farmers' Market – *700 Magazine St.* ☎ *504-861-5898.* *www.crescentcityfarmersmarket.org. Sat 8am–noon.* More than 50 vendors proffer farm-fresh produce, seafood and flowers at this friendly little market every Saturday (there's also a Tuesday market at 200 Broadway in Uptown and a Thursday market at 3700 Orleans Avenue in Mid-City). The same local purveyors supply some of the city's best restaurants, including Bayona, and Commander's Palace *(see Where to Eat p180).*

Scriptura – *5423 Magazine St.* ☎ *504-897-1555. www.scriptura.com.* Fine writing instruments and "essential papers for living" stock the shelves at this charming, family-owned Uptown shop. They also do a land-office business in engraved invitations, journals and stationary products.

Blue Frog Chocolates – *5707 Magazine St.* ☎ *504-269-5707.* Delectable chocolates stock the trays, baskets and boxes of a very happy clientele at this fun sweetery. They also sell a nice assortment of confections from around the world, such as French truffles from Lille and too-beautiful-to-eat candy flowers from Italy.

Derby Pottery and Tile – *2029 Magazine St.* ☎ *504-586-9003. www.derby pottery.com.* Victorian-inspired handmade tiles, New Orleans street-sign tiles and gift objects made from cast versions of the city's whimsical water meter covers stock the shelves at this very popular shop.

Fleur d'Orleans – *3701 Magazine Street.* ☎ *504-899-5585. www.fleurdorleans. com/catalog/.* This pleasant shop is the place to come for anything and everything in fleur-de-lis jewelry, beautifully wrought in fine silver. Stop in and pick out the ultimate packable gift or souvenir.

Mignon Faget – *3801 Magazine St.* ☎ *504-891-2005. www.mignonfaget.com.* Named for an award-winning local artist, this shop specializes in jewelry inspired by symbols synonymous with New Orleans, from a gumbo necklace dripping with shrimp, crab and okra charms to king cake pendant earrings and French fleur-de-lis designs.